To Hugh

all Best Wishes.

Gone a'Soldiering
Jonas Green of the 24th Foot
(1787-1845)

by
Neville A Davis

Published by

Neville A Davis, 56 Cambridge Road, North Harrow, Middlesex, HA2 7LE

ISBN 978 0 9564386 1 4

British Library Cataloguing in Publication Data. A catalogue record for this book is available from the British Library.

Cover by StewArt, Hove, East Sussex.
Typeset in Times New Roman

Printed and Bound in the U.K by the
MPG Book Group, Bodmin and King's Lynn

Other Works by the Same Author

"Jumping for Joy: 50 Years of Kodak Rugby", 200pp, 297x200mm.,
100 photographic illustrations, cloth-covered hardback covers, Initiated and
Published by the Kodak Rugby Football Club in 1986. *All 500 copies sold and
'Out of Print' since 1987.*

"Commissioned Gunner RN: Alfred William DAVIS (1895-1941)",
A deeply-researched biography of the author's late father, who served in the Royal Navy
from 1911-1941, losing his life in WW2 in a gallant attempt to save his ship from
catastrophic explosion. 742pp, 290x210mm., 230 photographic illustrations, printed
hardback covers, with printed dust-jacket. **Published by Heritage Books, an Imprint of
Bernard Durnford Publishing, in 2006, ISBN 1 904470 068.**
*As at March 2012, some copies are still available at a modest price via the author, or
from CPI Antony Rowe, Bumper's Farm, Chippenham, Wiltshire, SN14 6LH,
Email: sales@antonyrowe.co.uk Website: www.antonyrowe.co.uk*

"Trees & Tales of Fifty Families", A deeply researched work on the history of the
author's family and wider family, 482pp, 297x210mm, 200 illustrations, printed hardback
covers. **Self-published by the author, in 2010. ISBN 978 0 9564386 0 7.** *As at
March 2012, some copies are still available at a modest price via the author.*

-oOo-

The Cover of this Book: *The original image for the soldier was produced by the
author, after having examined various prints of the appropriate period, which all differed
slightly in the details of the uniform and equipment. It shows a British infantryman with
light green facings on the collar and cuffs of his uniform jacket, as worn by the 24th Foot.
[The regiment later became The South Wales Borderers, and, later still a part of the
Royal Regiment of Wales (24th/41st FOOT).] The author is deeply obliged to 'StewArt'
for having so well transformed the bare picture into the elegant and fully finished cover.*

FOREWORD by the Author

This book is solidly based upon historical fact. I am greatly obliged to the Brecon-based Museum of the South Wales Borderers and the Monmouthshire Regiment of the Royal Regiment of Wales (24th/41st FOOT) for supplying some of the key data for it. Amongst various other sources, including the India Records Office of the British Library, I am also indebted to the National Archives, whose 'WO' series of military documents has been truly invaluable for the research (See Appendix.).

Jonas Green, the central figure in the book, really did exist and his adventures as a common soldier did indeed take him to the distant places and the principal events portrayed. These events included a dramatic sea-battle on 3rd July 1810, in the Indian Ocean. Jonas was definitely present in a land war fought by his battalion high up amidst the Himalayan Mountains in 1817 and he really did become an Out-Pensioner of Chelsea Hospital in 1823. The large number of casualties suffered by his regiment through combat, accident and disease during the sixteen years of his service, especially when in the East Indies, is distressingly accurate. He was very fortunate to come through it all, if not totally unscathed, at least still 'in one piece'.

The actions taken by the senior officers are closely based on still-surviving accounts, and biographical notes on some of these gentlemen still exist in the public domain. However, although regimental muster books survive to this day, and show the location, the pay awarded and the basic state of health of each man, month by month, until the day the man was discharged, precious little detail was ever recorded about the ***personal lives*** led by the ordinary soldiers, such as Jonas. Also, whilst we know the bare facts of our soldier's marriage and the children born to him – we have none of the surrounding details of his courtship, nor of his previous love life, if any. Hence, to add 'colour' to the whole story, ***some*** of the personal incidents, and ***some*** of the characters who most closely interact with Jonas have been invented. This has been done in sympathy with the known facts, and on a closely 'authentic' basis.

<u>A Dedication:</u> This book is dedicated to the many persons, but above all Liz and Rosie, who have kept me in this life during and after three major operations, dealing with bowel cancer and a heart-valve replacement.

5

CONTENTS

Page

Chapter One

The Year 1804:
JONAS JOINS THE MILITIA
(The On-Going War with France.)

"Ouch! Humbugger it!" The young farm labourer Jonas Green was fast becoming tired by his long day's labour, and he swore almost involuntarily as a half-broken branch of hawthorn sprang back viciously from the hedgerow, the spiteful thorns slashing open his cheek and only narrowly missing his right eye. A few drops of bright red blood spattered over the leaves.

Jonas hoped that the blood-letting was not an unfortunate omen, for this was a very frightening time, with the seemingly all-conquering French Army gathered in enormous force at Boulogne and at other ports just on the other side of the English Channel. The nearest port was only twenty sea-miles away from the English coastline. The 'Johnny Crapauds' were alleged to be just waiting for the right weather-conditions to invade England. They had already defeated the armies of virtually every nation throughout mainland Europe.

By making clever feints with their own main fleet the French had already made skilful attempts to draw away the major men o' war of the British Navy, distracting them from their essential role of protecting our island fortress. Should these French tactics ever succeed, their assault troops would be able to cross the Channel more or less unmolested.

The English popular press carried a lot of jingoistic derision of the French, but this clamour was actually under-laid by considerable fear and ever-increasing nervous tension in the population all around the south-east of England – in Essex and Suffolk as much as in Sussex and in Kent.

The drastic anti-invasion measures being taken by the government, specifically designed to prevent an invading army from being able to 'live off the land', had added considerably to those fears. The measures had included the recent *Levée en Masse* which involved the recruitment of older men and youngsters, and a possible 'scorched earth' policy of burning all the invasion-threatened towns and farmsteads if the defenders were ever forced to fall back from the coast. The situation could rapidly become very frightening and ominous indeed for all the resident population.

Just this morning, when setting up Jonas for his day's work, his boss Mr Prentice had been bursting with the latest information about the war. Seemingly, Mr Prentice had been at the market in Ipswich the previous day, and he was agog to talk about Lord St Vincent, who was one of the most famous British admirals, and who had said in public, *"I do not say that the French can not come: I only say they can not come by sea!"*

Ever since that statement had been made, the good people of Ipswich had been arguing amongst themselves as to what, exactly, the great man had intended by his words. Some said that he was being completely reassuring by saying that the French could not come at all – because they would have to use a sea-route, and the British Navy was simply too strong for them. Others, perhaps wiser, said that the admiral was simply 'hedging his bets' by implying that, whilst the French might not risk sending their initial assault by sea, they might still be sufficiently clever and cunning to arrive *by other means*

– say by digging a great tunnel under the Channel, or maybe by crossing the Channel in massive balloons floating in the sky. Maybe they did indeed have secret weapons, of which we British were still ignorant. After all, the news pamphlets which were printed in London were full of imaginative drawings of such weird 'flying machines' and even of a huge tunnel being secretly dug. Having been deeply impressed by the arguments he had heard about balloons carrying soldiers and cannon, Mr Prentice had told Jonas that he was now keeping a spyglass by his side at all times, and that he proposed to stay constantly on the lookout for any such fiendish devices!

The wound on the cheek of Jonas continued to bleed quite freely, and, not for the first time, Jonas wondered whether labouring on the land was really the life he wanted. All down through the march of time, the wages of farm labourers had been derisory. Men were worked until they became too infirm to carry on, or until they literally dropped dead at their labour. They never earned enough money to have savings to put by, and so, once they were no longer able to earn a living, they immediately became paupers, and were thereafter totally dependent upon the stingy parish relief until the day they died.

Despite all this distressing background, Jonas recognised that his forebears had always been involved in farming in one way or another, as far back as anybody could remember, and he knew that they had pretty well always managed to survive as a family group. They might not always be well shod, so to speak, but there was almost always *something* to eat, even if a little discreet poaching sometimes had to be undertaken. There was also the aspect that there were few other jobs which gave a man so much freedom on a day-by-day basis, and where one lived so healthily and so close to nature and worked happily with various kinds of domestic animals under the clear blue sky. Almost every day was different, and one was always learning new skills. To work in a factory environment, under direct and probably oppressive supervision, and at a drearily repetitive task, would be the nearest thing to Hell on earth which Jonas could imagine. Yet, to 'break the mould', and to find an alternative and reasonably attractive means of reliably earning a living was clearly going to be very difficult. There was also the aspect that he might encounter much 'family opposition' to the very idea of breaking away from their ancient traditions.

Today's work wasn't one which was normal in the experience of Young Jonas, for slashing and 'laying' the branches of hedges was a task at which he was comparatively new, and at which he was bound to make a few mistakes. Despite being under the teaching and close supervision of his boss, Mr Prentice, Jonas was still finding that the branches of the hedgerows seemed to have a mind and a wilful resilience of their own, and the toil-worn hands and wrists of Jonas were already a mass of new grazes and cuts. He also had a couple of new tears in the patched trousers which he wore, and yet another rip in his ancient smock. Both had been 'hand-me-downs' to him, after Samuel, his older brother, had grown out of them. His step-mother would sigh heavily when Jonas handed the toil-worn garments to her for further patching.

The old bill-hook which Jonas was using was by now seriously blunted, and it would need a thoroughly good honing, before he could use it efficiently again. He was ham-fisted at such tasks, and he'd have to call on his father's highly competent skills to put a really sharp edge on it again.

Jonas had been busily repairing hedges all day, to fill in the gaps which had been created by the livestock as they sought better pasture in the adjacent fields. The trouble arising from their pillaging was that the farmer was doing his level best to preserve the root crops in those nearby fields for winter feed. He could not afford to let the farm animals get in amongst them.

Although still aged only seventeen, Jonas was inured to hard work. Nevertheless, his cheek had become increasingly sore and his hands, arms and shoulders ached considerably by the time that he was released from this day's hard and demanding physical labour. Dusk was falling fast as Jonas Green made his weary way home along the quiet lanes that led to the village of Great Bricett, in Suffolk.

Indeed, by the time that Jonas approached the hovel that his parents called home it was it was nearly full-dark, though the warm glow of candlelight from a small window made of horn bade him a sort of welcome as he came nearer. As he entered the cottage he saw that his step-mother, who was rapidly becoming old before her time, was busy at the glow of the hearth, turning a spit on which a plump rabbit carcase was roasting, and which she was basting the while. She was also watching over a small cauldron in which vegetables were being boiled. His step-mother was a good cook, using her judgement when adding a few herbs to make the most of whatever 'vittles' she could get her hands on, limited though the meals usually were in both quantity and variety. The aromas wafting from these particular items tonight smelt delicious, and Jonas suddenly realised how hungry he felt. His step-mother looked up, and exclaimed, *"Oh, Jonas! Whatever ha' you done to your poor dear face! Best yew do bathe that there cut right away with water and vinegar, bor, even tho' it'll sting a bit, an' then put some o' my soothing goose grease and herb mixture on it. There's some fresh-drawn water in the sink, and a clean rag on top of my sewin'-box on the table. Dew yew use them, my boy."*

She went on, *"This tender young rabbit be nearly done an' the wegetables are nigh ready. Yew're the last one home, Jonas, and we can all sit down and eat, just as soon as yew've cleaned yerself up."*

Her words made Jonas realise that his elder brother Samuel and their father Joseph, who was the undisputed head of the family, were both already back from their work. Not only was Joseph the head of the family, he was also their strong mentor and advisor. Despite having had very little 'book-larning' as a child, he had the gift of being a calm and natural teacher. Doubtless aided by his experiences as an elder of the local Non-Conformist Chapel, he was of a very independent mind, often argued strongly against those who simply followed convention and he liked to think all matters through very carefully before committing himself one way or another. The vicar of the local parish church was a highly opinionated and bigoted man, who had managed to retain most of his parishioners by scaring them stiff of 'divine retribution', should they ever consider joining the massive trend throughout Suffolk towards 'Non-Conformity'. Joseph and the vicar had often 'crossed swords' about the vicar's rigid attitude in such matters.

Joseph had always done his utmost to make his elder boys use logic and common sense to resolve all and any problems, and quite a lot of this mental attitude had already 'rubbed off' on to them – so, whilst they 'knew their place in society' well enough, neither was afraid of trying to answer questions for themselves – nor of asking reasonable questions of 'authoritarian figures' if they needed more facts. Now Joseph was starting to do the same teaching with little Joshua, by far the youngest of his three sons.

Joseph and his eldest son, Samuel, were, in fact, seated in their chairs, in the dark shadows on the far side of the room, well away from the fire. Jonas hadn't noticed them before, partly due to the inability of the light from the oil-lamp to pierce the gloom there, but also because they were in exceptionally quiet conversation, their fair heads (so different to his own dark mop) very close together. Joshua, also fair-haired, was quietly playing with a wooden spinning top on the hardened mud floor, close by the two older men. Their father was given to saying that their fair hair was a direct result of their Saxon and Viking ancestry, but that Jonas had been given his dark hair from his late mother's line – which was rumoured to contain Romany Gypsy blood just a few generations back That could go some way to explain why she had reckoned she was 'fey', as well as demonstrating a remarkably fine knowledge of herbs, and also of 'country medicine'.

Very sadly, she had departed this life in 1799, and Jonas, for one, deeply mourned her loss. He was still adjusting to his new step-mother, whom he had heartily rebelled against at first. That had been back in 1801, when his father (left 'stranded' with young Joshua, then aged only seven, as well as the two older boys), had suddenly decided to re-marry – this time to an old childhood flame. Ever since the marriage, Mary, the step-mother, had been doing her level best to form a good relationship with every member of the family, and it could be said that Jonas was the only one of the three sons who was still keeping her at arm's length. Sam, the eldest son, always more prosaic and practical than Jonas, had certainly adapted to her well – and was already calling her 'Mother', which greatly pleased her, though it still did not go down at all well with Jonas, who saw it as a betrayal of their late birth-mother.

By the time Jonas had tidied up his cuts and taken his place at the table, his father had said a brief but fervent grace, and the hungry family were already beginning to tuck into a good meal – the best they had enjoyed for some days. *"Samuel managed to knock this rabbit on the head today when it suddenly jumped up from almost under his feet as he was a'piling up the hay rakings in the Rectory Field."*, said Mary, the step-mother. *"Yes, he's got quick God-given reactions, has our Samuel,"* said Joseph, the father, with a strange and slightly quizzical smile on his face.

"Yes! It didn't half make me jump! interjected Samuel, *"And, well, in a way, Mother, my quick reactions are a small but important part of what Father an' I ha' been a'talking about e'er since I got home!"*

"Why, whatever are yew mitherin' about, my boy?" said his step-mother, *"What 'xactly ha' you an' your father been chatterin' about altogether this last half-hour an' more?"*

"Well," her husband chimed in, *"It wus just 'man's talk', and we didn't want yew to start upsettin' yerself – that's why we was 'mithering', as yew puts it, so that yew wouldn't take on and start to fret, perhaps all unnecessary loike".* And, hearing her indignant intake of breath, he hurried on before she could speak, *"Any road, not to put the wagon before the hoss, it's thisaway. Old Smithers, my boss, was in a right ol' state this morning. Yew see, he do owe his landlord, Mr Johnson, a mighty great lot o' rent. Happen that Mr Johnson ha' suddenly offered him somethin' of a way out from his difficulties wi' money – but Old Smithers doan't see how he can possibly oblige Mr Johnson in what he is seekin'– not nohow. He's arsked all around, but none of his men are in the least interested in helpin' him out - so Old Smithers is naow really angry with hisself and wi' everything and everyone around him!"*

The step-mother broke in, *"How is that then? Why can't he oblige Mr Johnson? Why is he is such a state about it all? Why doan't Old Smithers just pay off what he owes and be done with it?"*

"Well, quite apart from the fact that he is a mean man by nature, as yew do well know, woman, that there corn crop last year was not a good 'un, and it means that Old Smithers can ill-afford to pay all that outstanding rent that he's built up. The reason why this here tied cottage and the others hereabouts are all more or less a'fallin' down, is partly because Smithers always hates spending ev'n a penny for repairs, due to his mean nature, and partly 'cos he has to pay so high a rent to Mr Johnson – so there ain't much to spare in his pot anyways. Any road, it seems that Mr Johnson has said that he will let old Smithers off from paying half of what he owes as back-rent, if he can just find him two likely-looking men or even lads."

"Whatever do yew mean by 'Two likely men', Joseph?"

"Why, wife, two men who are young enough an' willin' enough to join the Militia as volunteers! In other words, two fellers who are stupid and silly enough to risk having their heads blown off!"

"I still doan't fully understand yew. Let's get down to brass tacks. Why were you and Sam as thick as thieves in talking about it? We surely doant know of any men who'd volunteer, do we?! Arta all, we be peaceable, God-fearin' an' good chapel folk! We doan't want nuthin' to do with killin' people, be they enemies of this country or not."

"Well, afore I gets on to that, I must say that it all comes down from the fact that Old Smithers' landlord, that there Mr Johnson, who is a Member of Parliament, has had a really bad ol' piece of luck. That is to say, with the outcome of the latest ballot for the militia – yew know, those ballots that were started up in Suffolk and every other county a couple o' year ago, so that all the militia regiments could be kept up to strength, especially wi' the French getting themselves all set to invade us with their massive army."

"But how on earth can that M.P be in any difficulty, husband? From what I've heard tell, the ballots only apply to the ordinary menfolk, and the names of M.Ps, doctors and gentry such as them never gets to be entered in the ballot at all."

"Aye! – That's as true as 'Bob kissed Betty under the apple tree'! And I b'aint too sure at all about the matter o' gentry such as 'em a'bein' kept out of the ballot, altogether. Strikes me that they could at least be called upon to be h'officers. Howsumever, yes, sure enough, Mr Johnson and his kind are what they call 'exempt' - but the names of any <u>sons</u> they may have <u>do</u> hav'to go into the ballot, just as soon as their 18th birthdays come around and then, o' course, arter that whenever the ballots are held. Now, d'ye see, the Honourable Mr Johnson M.P. has had the almost unbelievable bad luck that the names of not just the one, but that the names of <u>both</u> of his two sons have been drawn! A lot of names go into the ballot, and 'tis generally said that there's only about one chance in ten of being drawn. I mean, so far as I know, nobody from our village of Bricett has ever become a 'Drawn Man', as it is called. The odds against having the names of <u>two</u> members of the same family being drawn in one ballot must be uncommon high!"

Joseph reflected a moment, and then he added, *"To have that happen to anyone would be hard luck, even in times of peace, when the Militiamen are required to serve only at weekends, and to go along to a Summer Camp for manoeuvres on just a couple o'* *weeks in the year. But now, o'course, with the French Army threatening to invade our country at any moment, the Militia are obliged to serve <u>full-time</u> – and perhaps to serve continuous-loike for as many as five year if the war do go on for that long! There is the compensation that they'll never have to serve overseas like the Regulars may be called upon to do – but that's just about the only good bit of it at all!"*

Joseph paused only momentarily, then continued, *"Last year, o' course, they brought in the so-called 'Levée en Masse', which would drag the younger teenagers and the older men, up to age 60 into it <u>as well</u>, if Old Boney do happen to send his tens of thousands o' men agin' us, an' should matters then become really desp'rate-loike. Practically all the able-bodied working men in the whole of the south-east would then be directly involved. Larst year, towards that end, I had to give Jonas's name, as well as my own, to Constable Perkins, who wrote them down in a long list in a record book he wor puttin' together."*

Turning a little in his chair to look at his eldest son, he went on, *"O' course, being 18 now, your name, Sam, is already in the ballot list for the Militia – and I reckon that just about <u>all</u> the men in that list might be liable to be called upon in an emergency, to join the Militia in the fighting."*

He went on, *"Howsumever that might pan out, Sam, should the French Army force their way ashore and start to move inland, the likes of me and Jonas may be called upon by the parish constables to strip the country roundabout of all foodstuffs, so as to leave nuthin' for the French to eat. The great Napoleon himself is said to have uttered the famous conundrum, 'An Army marches on its stomach' – really meanin' o' course that soldiers <u>must</u> have food if they're to keep goin'!' So <u>anything</u> that we can do to starve the French must be a good thing! Anyroad, working with the other old men and other local young lads and, under the directions of Constable Perkins and his loike, we'll have to strip the farms bare and evacuate the civil population, using what they call 'commandeered' hosses and wagons, taken from the farming stock in the vicinity. What they call a sort of 'martial law' will prevail, with all the terrible and more or less instant judgements which might then hav' to be made. Nearly every man-jack in the country will be involved, if things really do become serious! We may even ha' to <u>burn down to the ground</u> the farmsteads that we strip! Any civilians who try to stop us, or wot doan't do 'zactly what they're told, may have to be shot dead out of hand – because there simply won't be any time to hold debates about anythin' at all! I dread to think what will happen to all the helpless women and children in such an emergency, but I 'spose each man will try to look to his own, the best he can. I ha' jus been a'praying hard to the Good Lord every day and night that it will never come about. And the Lord help us if it do!"*

Turning back to face his wife, he went on after a moment, *"Going back to talk of the Militia, as always, for those who have sufficient money, there is, o' course, a way in which service can be avoided, without breaking the law. That is, if any 'Drawn Man' can find what is called an "eligible man" who is willing to serve in his place. That means a man who is <u>not</u> already a soldier or a militiaman, and who has at least two arms and two legs – so that he'll pass muster wi' the doctors at his medical examination. For such 'standing in', it's the custom for the 'Substitute', as he be called, to be very well rewarded in money by the person he is replacing. Arter all, it could well be his life he is sacrificing for the sake of some total stranger!"*

After a moment, he went on, *"From what I have heard, Mr Johnson already has his elder son working in his business in London, an' he is shaping him up for high office. He has the same sort of plans for his younger son. Moreover, he's already got a young heiress betrothed to marry the elder son, and its hardly surprising that Mr Johnson's hopping mad about the whole issue of both his youngsters having been 'Drawn'. That cuts right across all his plans, that do. The joke is, of course, that, to preserve his image as a 'patriotic Member of Parliament' he carn't let news of his rage spread around the City o' Lunnon. So everything has to be handled as discreetly as possible. I am told that Mr Johnson is prepared to be very generous in 'greasing palms', so long as no word at all gets out that he is seeking two Substitutes for his sons!"*

"Yes, Mother", chimed in Samuel, *"An' that's what Pa and I ha' been talking about, because we sure could do with some real money! Pa had set his mind 'gainst me joining the Militia, but just look at the state of this place – it's fallin' down about our ears, and Old Smithers always claims that he aint got two ha'pennies to spare for doing any repairs to it. To tell the truth and shame the Devil, the draughts and dampness in winter are fully dreadful, and your rheumatism is getting worse an' worse. Just look at the girt swelling of your poor ol' finger-joints – you can barely hold that there spoon even as we be a'talking here an' now! How on earth you manage to do any needlework at all wi' yer poor ol' fingers is totally beyond me – and – looking at the state our Jonas ha' come home in this evenin' - he is sure going to need some clever needlework and new patching doing on them clothes wot he's a'wearing – an' maybe e'en some o' yer very best stitching on that girt ol' cut on his cheek! That's a'goin' to test yer skills – an' yer poor old rheumaticy fingers!"*

He paused for a moment, and then went on, *"Pa says that he doan't want me to join the Militia, because, as a Christian, he doa'nt like the idea of me havin' to harden my heart and maybe kill other men. He also do say that he has heard that the training of the Militia is usually half-baked, and the officers are all too often just wealthy and pompous half-wits who have no idea at all as to how to fight a battle. Pa says that the men are never really shown how to fight proper-loike. Pa also says that matters are pre-ordained so that the Militia will be used as 'cannon-fodder', fighting the French on the beaches and holding them as long as possible, to provide time for the military authorities to make up their minds where best to position the regular soldiers to make their stand. So our main Army'll be held a bit further inland at first – leaving just the Militia to get on wiv it - because some landings will probably just be feints, rather than main attacks – and they doan't want the regulars to be chasing shadders, going off everywhere all at once an' at half-cock, so to speak."*

Samuel, well-trained by his father, and who had always been a bit of a one for 'larnin' about things and to try to speak his mind as best he could, continued what was probably the longest passage of speech he had ever made, *"To my eyes, every soldier, be he a regular or a militiaman, has to take his chance. Pa has already said that, if matters become really critical, I may be conscripted into the Militia willy-nilly. So, why doan't I just join them anyway, and right away, too? My reactions are quick, I know how to handle myself, and it is to be hoped that I will get at least some training before being flung into action. Besides, the French may not come at all. Or, if they do, they may try to land at a place which is well distant from wherever I will end up by being based. There again, the Navy may well destroy most of the French ships long before the soldiers they are carrying can get ashore. So I may well end up by never havin' to kill anybody at all by my own hand!"*

He went on, *"There's talk in Ipswich that the French are a'building battleships and invasion barges all along their coastline, just as fast as they can go! I know there are cartoons in the news pamphlets of the French also coming by big balloons floating in the sky, or by a massive girt tunnel dug under the sea – but I don't think that's how t'will be. I think that Pa is worrying too much – and just think how useful some good money would be to us as a family. Besides that, I want to marry my Sarah ere long, and the two of us will not be able to live on air. I certainly want a better house than this here one to raise our little'uns in!"*

Stopping just long enough to take a deep breath, he went on, *"So, I say, let's go for it! Let's strive for just as much money as Dad can wring out of Mr Johnson. Why doan't Pa go along to see Mr Johnson personally, to try to get the best possible deal out o' him, because Old Smithers will never press the point, and he'll also take a big cut for hisself if he possibly can. It is clear that Mr Johnson wants to keep matters real quiet at the Lunnon end of things, and, if we stress that we'll forever keep our mouths shut tight, he'll probably be willin' to arrive at a fair ol' sum o'money!"*

Jonas had been listening to all this with rapt attention, thinking how nearly he had lost an eye earlier during the day, and gazing at the day's damage to his sore and roughened hands. This might at least be the start of a pathway to somehow escape to another world altogether. He always had to be careful how he expressed himself, because he knew he could be impulsive and hot-headed – almost incoherent, so that his words sometimes simply tumbled out, and always in danger of turning to invective. Both his parents were staunch Baptists and regular attendants at Wattisham Strict Baptist Chapel. They did not like any blasphemous reference to the Almighty, no matter how vague the reference in the swear words might be.

Now, unable to restrain himself any longer, he suddenly blurted out, *"Yes, by George! We risk our lives and limbs working the land every day! Old Mr Gorringe was gored by his bull last twelvemonth an' died of it, and then his son wor mortally injured when that cart-hoss bolted, and a wheel of the careering wagon crushed him against a gate-post! I darn nearly lost an eye today when that broken branch of hawthorn flicked back at me! Life is always a risk. The French may not come. If they do, we will defeat them in one way or another. I'd like to join the Militia too, and stand side by side with our Sam. 'Sides, we will then be able to guard each other's backs!"*

He ruminated for a moment, and went on, *"Yes, we will double the money if I volunteer, too. Nay, we should do better than that, because we'll totally resolve Mr Johnson's problem in one fell swoop, and he ought to be a very relieved and happy man."*

He glanced at his step-mother, and was suddenly very embarrassed to see that she was quietly weeping. *"Oh, Jonas, No!"* she said brokenly. *"You're only seventeen, and too young to even have your name entered in the ballot until next year. Stay here, son. I can't abide the thought of losing both my two lovely elder boys! To lose one would be bad enough – to lose two would be the end of my world! Stay, son, stay!"*

But Jonas was fired up and determined. *"Let Dad go and see this M.P."*, he said, *to find out just how much money we might receive.* Suddenly inspired, he added, *"If Dad can make a good bargain, we might be able to have enough money to buy a good-sized plot of freehold land, and maybe even have enough to build a decent house on it for Dad and you to live in, with the prospects of later adding extensions, or maybe even a couple of other houses – so that Sam and I could each later bring a wife into them and start our own families. What we currently pay as rent could go towards building the house."*

Further inspired, he added, *"Step-Mother, I know that you have a great affection and admiration for Sam's lovely girl Sarah, and I know for a fact that you have been worrying a lot about where she and Sam are going to live. Just think how changed the fortunes and comfort <u>for all of us</u> could be. We haven't lived in a house of our own since way back in Grandpa Isaac Green's time, and we lost that long ago to Dad's eldest brother, Uncle William, and his line – because, unfair tho' it may sometimes be, it's always the eldest brother who inherits all the family land and the house when his father passes away. We cain't go on living forever in this tumbledown rented shack! We simply must dew somethin' to make our lives better! As I just said, when you move, the rent we currently pay to old Smithers can all go towards completing the new house and then to buying extra bits and pieces for it as time goes on. You and Dad could end up with a lovely dry and warm house in which to see through the winters!"*

And so, despite more heart-searching, and against all the chapel-going beliefs, especially of the step-mother, that the taking of human life was a sin, the decision was made. A good deal was indeed struck between the Honourable Mr Johnson M.P. and Joseph, the father of Sam and Jonas, who acted as 'bag-holder'. The deal was well-honoured by Mr Johnson. A good-sized patch of land was then purchased in the adjacent village of Upper Somersham, in a part of the parish which was known to have never flooded, regardless of the time of year. The land had rights to a well and a pond, the latter fed by the stream which wound its way through the village, sometimes being in spate and flooding, but with the flooding always affecting only Lower Somersham.

After buying the land at Upper Somersham there was indeed sufficient money left over for a small house to be started, which had the traditional A-Frame structure, and would have wattle and daub walls, and a good thatched roof. To reduce the building costs, the father, Joseph, would provide his own labour, especially in rendering the wooden lathes of the walls with a mixture of mud and cow-dung, and then in lime-washing them externally in the traditional 'Suffolk pink' after they had dried out. He would fix windows in the house, using the spun 'plate-glass' that was now becoming generally available. He would paint the inside walls in white lime-wash, to make the house as light and airy as possible. There would be an earth-closet built in the garden, a good distance away from the existing well, which he would have re-dug and brick-walled, with a stout rope-winding mechanism for the bucket placed above it. Joseph and his wife, Mary, would move into the house with their meagre possessions as soon as it was sufficiently finished to begin to provide shelter. Piece by piece, they would be able to improve on it steadily down the years, by their own efforts. It would be a far healthier, drier and warmer home than the rented shack they had been living in up to that time.

Hopefully, they would have a small-holding beside the house, on which they could grow their own vegetables and run poultry and perhaps even keep a few larger animals. Their lives would be transformed forever, especially, as was profoundly to be hoped, after the boys had got through their period of service in the Militia and returned home. The family would be reunited in five years or less, and there would then be more hands to cope with the labour of building a further house or two on the plot. Truly, this was going to be an epic time in the history of the little family called Green.

There was, however, something of 'a sting in the tail' so far as the two brothers were concerned, for the ballot had been for the Westminster Militia, and not for their local one, which was the Suffolk Militia. So, having bade farewell to their parents – causing more tears to flow from their step-mother's eyes in what she greatly dreaded might be her last-ever embrace of her elder sons - Sam and Jonas had to make their way from Suffolk to Colchester to enrol – for it was at Colchester that the headquarters of the Westminster's was located at that time. Happily for them, Mr Johnson instructed his bailiff to put them on the stage-coach at nearby Ipswich, and to pay their fares for the twenty-mile trip to Colchester. Coaching was a totally new experience for them, for it was normally only the wealthier members of society who could afford to travel by 'stage'. The weather was fine and, on the bailiff's advice, they travelled 'on the outside', sitting high up on the roof of the coach, so that they could see the unfolding views on the way to Colchester.

Once the passengers had all been hurried aboard, the coachman cracked his long whip causing the well-trained horses, which had been champing at their bits, to immediately set off at a near gallop. The fast take-off made the coach sway back and forth violently on its springs, jolting all the passengers about, and nearly flinging the totally inexperienced Jonas and his brother right off the coach, to the scarcely-hidden amusement of the coachman and the well-armed guard. *"Due yew hold on tight, bors!"* called out the coachman, whose unusually large hands and fingers had an expert grip on the multiple black leather reins. And, thereafter, the brothers kept at least one hand on or near the guard-rails, and very quickly learnt to be prepared for the often violent back and forth swaying at any sudden stops and starts the coach had to make, and also to look out *en route* for the side-sway caused by the more pronounced of the bends and the more uneven of the ruts along the route, presenting the lads with further balancing problem with which to cope. The swaying they experienced was aggravated by the rather primitive springing of the coach and magnified by the considerable height of their seats above ground-level.

On their arrival at the garrison town of Colchester, they were directed to the Militia Headquarters. There, after reporting to the rather frightening figure of the sergeant of the guard, with his bristling 'walrus' moustache, his fierce bark of a voice and his magnificent and immaculate uniform, the brothers were swiftly handed over to a corporal, who put them in with a couple of other young recruits, and saw that all four were given a meal, before being medically checked. This checking seemed fairly basic – *"Just to see that we've got two good arms and two sound legs, and that we're still breathing!"* as Sam expressed things rather bitterly to Jonas – but it did include a quite critical examination of the soundness of their teeth. This was for very good reasons, as the brothers were soon to find out. Sam and Jonas were officially enrolled on the next day, 24th March 1804, swearing an oath of allegiance to King George III, before a magistrate.

Chapter Two

The Year 1804:
WITH THE MILITIA ON THE EAST COAST
(On Guard against French Invasion.)

Jonas and Sam had listened with some bewilderment to the frightening terms of the main points of the 'King's Regulations', a summary of which had been read out to them at a rapid rate on the day they were accepted as Militiamen, with Death as the penalty for nearly every infringement of the 'KRs', as the regulations were called – *'Death for everything from pickin' yer nose to scratching yer arse',* as Sam rather bitterly expressed it to Jonas. By that time there was a handful of other new recruits with them, including a couple of young but 'hard-bitten' Londoners from the 'Seven Dials' district, who had been in prison for what they averred to have been only minor offences. The voices of most of the men were hard for Sam and Jonas to understand, for they were in the rapid-fire nasal whine of London, and they often used Cockney rhyming-slang, which was like a closed book to the squarely-built and slow-speaking Suffolk-raised brothers. Jonas and Sam also soon found they were going to be constantly teased about the slow way they responded to any situations or questions, about the soft country burr in their accents, and over their natural reluctance to quickly commit themselves to one side or another in any conversations or arguments.

Settling in was a novel experience for the brothers. The fact that they could support each other in any argument was a real benefit in grabbing two of the better-positioned bunks in their barrack-room – also in keeping half an eye on each other's scanty possessions – for they did not feel they could trust some of the other recruits not to pilfer them, were they to be given even half a chance. But the night actually passed off reasonably enough, and they were again given a fair breakfast..

On that second day, with further new recruits added to their group, they were marched to the barber's shop, where their heads were cropped bare and washed, to combat the risks of head-lice. The Green brothers had never seen or heard of lice, but the ugly red patches to be seen on the newly-cropped heads of the 'gaol-bait' youngsters from London clearly showed that they were victims of just that sort of infection. The whole group was then taken into the depot, told to strip off their civilian clothes (when the brothers were astonished to see the old, smelly and tattered pieces of paper used as 'thermal body-insulation' by some of the poorest-clad recruits) and then washed under a stream of cold water surging from a pump in the yard which was worked by Militiamen on fatigue duty. The new recruits were then told to dry off with towels that were handed to them, and they were then kitted out with their shirts, bright red uniform jackets, white breeches, shoes, side-buttoned gaiters and the horridly uncomfortable leather stocks. These stocks were intended to go around their necks, and had the aim of keeping their heads held high. The leather stocks, which buttoned-up at the back of the neck, were going to take a lot of time to adjust to.

The new recruits were told that they would have to let their hair grow one-foot long, as it came back, and to turn it up into a roll (called a 'club') which had to be greased, powdered and held in position by a leather strap, because that was the fashion in their regiment at that time. For the time being, however, they were issued only with soft caps to wear. Their tall, stiff and high-crowned bicorne hats would be issued once their hair had grown back.

The recruits now learned how to march. The first need here was to teach the recruits how to distinguish between their left and right feet. For those who could not remember, a short length of straw was stuck in the outside edge of the sole of the shoe worn on the left foot. Sam and Jonas quickly came to the conclusion that the sergeants and corporals considered that any man needing such a 'marker' was a 'simpleton' who would deserve much loud haranguing – and that they would do well to avoid any such 'branding'! All the men then had to learn (half by repetition and half as a sort of reflex) 'which orders came on which foot', and in understanding how to march well, chests out and swinging their arms proudly. Sam and Jonas swiftly began to enjoy the feel of swinging along in column, like an almost solid and impregnable-feeling mass of men, with the adjacent files somehow 'lifting one along' – in the mind, at least. The better that the squad marched, and the more they were in exact time, the more enjoyable it became.

They practised at marching for almost three weeks, spending about four hours each day at 'footslogging', as they came to call it.

Eventually, however, the exciting day came when they were marched to the armoury, where they were issued with India-pattern 'Brown Bess' muskets, and also with long bayonets in steel scabbards, and the white cross-belts and webbing equipment which would support the bayonets and ammunition boxes around their bodies. They were also given haversack packs to wear across their shoulders. These packs had uncomfortably stiff and horsehair-covered backboards incorporated in their structure. Only half-jokingly, the Corporals who were going to train them said they would each do well to swap these haversacks for the far more comfortable goatskin-covered haversack of the first French soldier that they each managed to kill.

The muskets were heavily daubed in hardened grease, and most of the rest of that day was spent in the filthy task of cleaning the weapons with boiling water, rags and brickdust. So-called 'prickers','augers' and 'worms' were available, to ensure that the short distance from the touch-hole within the firing–pan through to the charge within the musket was clear, and that the inside of the barrel itself was free from rust or other obstruction – though, at that time of their training, the lads hardly knew what they were doing. The armourer sergeant was on hand, however, and, although caustic-tempered and sardonic, he was prepared to advise them to some degree – though, as he himself put it, he was certainly not prepared *'to boil his dumplings twice'*, and *'gawd 'elp any dozy soldier who expected him to repeat anything he had already told 'em abart!'*

Their basic training on the weapon began the very next day, when they were paraded on the barrack-square under the baleful eye of Sergeant Smith, a man with a nut-brown complexion who, as they soon learnt, was a veteran soldier newly returned from active service in the East Indies. He held a musket in his powerful hands.

"This here", he said in a loud voice, whilst he brandished the weapon aloft, *"Is yer best friend – otherwise known as yer 'bundook'! Wiv its aid, you can kill a h'oncoming enemy whilst 'e is still 100 paces orf from closing wiv yer! Should yer happen to miss the enemy wiv yer ball, yer can quickly fix yer bayonet to the weapon, making its reach damn nearly six foot long, and you can rip out yer enemy's guts afore he*

can get anywhere near enough to touch you wiv 'is 'tulwar' – that's wot you'd call a sword, Jenkins, you dozy soldier! What's a 'tulwar' again, Jenkins'?!"

"Um, a sword, Sir", said Jenkins, wondering why he had been picked on yet again. (Jonas was just relieved that it was Jenkins being picked-on – and not him!)

"Yus, a sword – but call me sergeant, not sir!" yelled Sergeant Smith, *"You only use 'Sir' if there is an officer on parade wiv' us!"*

"Yes, Sergeant!"

"Nah then" went on Sergeant Smith, *"I'm a'goin' to teach you dozy sods how to use this musket to best advantage. When I've finished wiv yer, you'll be the best bleedin' Militia in h'England at slaughtering the enemies of His Majesty the King! What are you lot going to be, Jenkins?!"*

"The best bleedin' Militia in England, sergeant!"

"And what is your duty?"

"To slaughter the enemies of the King, sergeant!"

"Yus! Kill, boys, kill! – an' doan't you forget it!"

"Nah then, I'll show you how to load an' fire yer weapons later – but fust we've got to learn how to set it up to fire reliably."

And the sergeant then began to instruct the men how to ensure that their muskets were free from burnt powder, the touchhole clear and also that the flint was a well-selected one and accurately and tightly held by the setting-screw, so that it would create a good *'flash'* when sharply struck by the steel hammer of the musket. In many ways he was repeating and endorsing what the armourer sergeant had covered the previous day, driving home the key messages.

It was not until the next day that the new recruits began to be taught how to fire their weapons. The procedure was quite complex, and Sergeant Smith literally 'taught them by numbers', initially taking the pace of instruction at the speed of what appeared to be the slowest members of the squad. Since the *slowest spoken* were Sam and Jonas, it was naturally on them (Soldiers 'Green One' and 'Green Two') that the Sergeant's weight initially descended. They started off in 'open order', and with their muskets in the 'rest' position, standing upright with their butts on the ground, muzzle upwards, beside each man.

"Nah then, Green Two, you dozy soldier! What is this thing wot I am 'olding 'ere?"

"Er – a 'Musket', Sergeant, otherwise known as a 'bundook'".

"Very good, Green! Yer doant 'appen to be one of them bleeding 'ship's lawyers' by any chance, does yer?

Jonas had never heard the term, and didn't have an inkling as to what the Sergeant meant – though he guessed that the Sergeant didn't have a very high opinion of such people – whoever they might be, so he replied, *"Er, no, Sergeant – not so far as I know."*

"Good! I hate buggers such as 'ship's lawyers'! And, casting a truly terrifying look to left and right over the whole squad, *"Do any of you other lads aspire to that black art!?"*

"No, Sergeant!" replied the squad, equally ignorant, and as one man.

"Right!" Nah then, when you 'ear me giv' the order "Prime and Load!" you will make a quarter-turn to the right, and, at the same time yer will bring the musket to the

priming position, wiv yer left hand at its point of balance and yer right 'and placed in front of the 'ammer wiv its fingers clenched, like this. This means that yer will 'ave the weapon diagonally across yer chest, wiv its muzzle pointing slightly upwards."

"Right, we'll all try that now. What's the command to do so, Green Two?"

"Er, is it "'Prime and Load', Sergeant?".

"Yus, it bleedin' well is. Well done, Green – you ain't quite as stupid as you looks! Right, then – (and opening his huge lungs) – "SQUAD, PRIME AND LOAD!"

"Oh my God! Said Sergeant Smith a few moments later, *"What a bleedin' rabble! We'll do it again. This time I want you lot calling out numbers – On 'One' transfer the weapon entirely to yer left hand, on 'Two' bring it up across yer body – and hold it there, awaitin' the next order. You will only move when I shout the next number!"*

"RIGHT! SQUAD, PRIME AND LOAD! ONE – TWO!"

"Right! Now, as you dozy sods may have noticed, yer right hands is free at present – but not fer long, for yer now have to open the hammer wiv yer right hand and move the cock to the half-cock position. This 'as the effect of opening up the pan. We'll do this on numbers 3 and 4.

"SQUAD, THREE! – FOUR!

"Nah then, 'ere's where you each 'as one of them 'life-changing moments'! You takes one of these paper cartridges from yer cartridge box, using yer right 'and, and yer bites off the top of it wiv' yer teeth, sah yer reveal the powder in the cartridge! We'll do that on commands 'Five...six'." Yer should end up wiv the opened cartridge in yer right 'and.

"SQUAD, HANDLE CARTRIDGE!...FIVE...SIX!"

There then ensued an absolute shambles. Half the squad failed to tear the top off their cartridges, and those that did manage to do so, coughed and spluttered, spitting out the horrid taste of the gunpowder.

"Nah then, NAH THEN!", shouted Sergeant Smith, *"BEHAVE LIKE SOLDIERS, NOT BABIES! Grip hard wiv' yer teeth! Yank the package hard acrost yer face. Yeah, I know that the taste of the powder ain't nice, but it's yer life-saver if a Johnny Crapaud is trying to close wiv yer and wanting to stick his baynet up yer jacksie. Learn to love the taste of the gunpowder! In any case, yer face will be black wiv' burnt powder arter a bit o' volley-firin' and the taste o' the powder will be wiv' yer for days afterwards. One thing is fer sure – you'll welcome a drink later – even just o' water – as never afore in yer whole lives! Yer water-bottles will become very precious to yer – believe me!"*

"Nah then, we'll try again. READY – SQUAD, HANDLE CARTRIDGE! FIVE...SIX!", and this time the result was somewhat better.

"Right! We'll take it that you've all got the cartridges open – though I well know that some on you ain't. Just for the moment, those of you who haven't yet managed to rip their cartridges open can mime what the rest now do. Do you know what 'mime' means, Jenkins?

"Er, 'imitate', Sergeant?"

"Yus, imitate – well done Jenkins!"

"Right, now pay attention all ov you! On 'Seven', you now tip up the cartridge (like this) and shake a little of the powder from it into the pan. Not too much, mind – just a little! On 'Eight', yer now snaps the frizzon forward wiv' yer bottom fingers, to cover

the powder in the pan, but still keepin' yer cartridge upright in yer right 'and, so yer doan't spill any of the remainin' powder.

"Right, we'll now do that. SQUAD – PRIME!...SEVEN!...EIGHT!"

"All right. We'll now use our <u>left</u> hand which has still been holding the musket at its point of balance. On 'Nine', using our left hand, we'll now bring the musket down, so that the butt is in contact wiv the ground at our feet, close by our left calf, and the weapon is standing vertically in front of us, muzzle upwards. All got that? Right, do it now, "ABOUT! NINE!" Now just follow me as I do the rest. On 'Ten', we'll then pour the rest of the powder from the cartridge down the barrel through the muzzle. TEN!... Good!

On 'Eleven' we'll reverse the empty cartridge and push it dahn the muzzle a little way with the forefinger of our right 'and. ELEVEN!... On 'Twelve' we'll take a ball from our ammo box wiv our right hand, an' put the ball in the muzzle. TWELVE!... On 'Thirteen' we'll take the ramrod out from the stock of the musket, spin it rahnd from end to end, to reverse it, and then use it to push the ball dahn an inch of two....DRAW RAMRODS!...THIRTEEN! On 'Fourteen' we'll drive the ball right down the barrel, using the cartridge as a wadding for it, and briskly ramrodding until everything feels well dahn the barrel and sorta 'solid'. RAM DOWN CARTRIDGE!...FOURTEEN! – Ram – RAM – ALL RIGHT – THAT'S ENOUGH!

The wadded ball is now sitting on the powder-charge at the bottom of the barrel. On 'Fifteen' we'll replace the ramrod in its position under the stock of the musket. REMEMBER THAT! The last thing that we want to do is ter leave the ramrod sitting in the barrel! And remember ter spin it rahnd back agin' before replacin' it! Right! REVERSE and RETURN RAMMERS!...FIFTEEN!...Yer ramrod is back in place in the stock of yer musket and we are now ready to fire the musket, BUT FOR ONE THING! What's that, Green Two?"

"Er – something to do with the hammer, perhaps Sergeant?"

"H'm, could be. What about you, Green One – are you wiser than yer brother?"

"Isn't there an expression about not going off at 'half-cock', Sergeant. Could that have something to do with it?"

"Well (grudgingly), *yer both near, as yer might say. The hammer has to be pulled right back to 'full cock' before the musket will fire. This is a safety precaution. The last thing we wants is to hav' a musket firing prematurely and maybe accidentally killing one of our own mates – or maybe even shooting ourselves, perhaps right smack under the chin! We always need to remember that these are lethal weapons, and we must be constantly on watch for potential misfires of every sort. Wiv the weapon at 'full cock', pulling the trigger will release the hammer which will immediately spring forward pushing the 'frizzon' forward as it does so, and, as the hammer continues to descend it will almost immediately hit against the flint and create sparks. These sparks will immediately ignite the priming charge and, through the touch-hole, as near as makes no difference, the explosion of the priming charge will immediately ignite the main charge too."*

"SQUAD! In a moment I'll give yer the order 'MAKE READY'. Thereupon, you will raise the weapon and, at the same time, using yer right thumb, you'll pull back the hammer all the way back – just as far as it will go, when it will give out a click. That is a noise which you will find to be a surprisingly satisfying one – because it means that yer

musket is ready to fire. You will see that yer action has the effect of raising the muzzle slightly...SQUAD...MAKE READY"...SIXTEEN! Good...That's the last number I shall use. Just follow my direct orders nah, which will be 'Present' and then 'Fire'.

Right, I'll nah giv' you the order, 'PRESENT', whereupon you will set the butt of the musket into yer right shoulder at the same time lowering the muzzle end of the weapon to the firing position, parallel to the ground. The firelock should be close agin' yer right cheek. Then adjust both yer hands until you are holding 'Bess' comfortably and securely – and then, wiv yer left eye closed, I want yer to look along the barrel wiv yer right eye, pointing the musket at yer target. Yus, that wide target of white linen abart fifty yards ahead of us. Yer will want to line up the musket wiv the middle of the target, near as yer can judge it."

"SQUAD – PRESENT! THAT'S IT! Get 'em up an' pointing steady. You can all do it. Yer musket weighs less than ten pahnd – get used to it – love it! THIS IS FOR REAL! GET THAT MUSKET STEADY – STOP IT WAVERING ABAHT! Aim at the white sheet. Nah, when yer fires, doan't just use yer trigger-finger, but squeeze wiv all yer fingers togevver, just like we've showed yer earlier. Nah, steady men...SQUAD – FIRE!!"

There then followed a ragged and quite deafening volley from all the muskets which had been fully loaded. Smoke billowed all around the squad. The bruising recoil on the shoulders of the recruits who had successfully fired their weapons had surprised them. Some recruits had also felt slight powder-burns on the sides of their faces. Two of the recruits had experienced misfires. Fragments of the paper wads, most still burning, littered the ground just in front of the squad. The squad began to chatter amongst themselves, sharing their experiences.

"SILENCE IN THE RANKS!" screamed Sergeant Smith. *"You are soldiers, not women! Right, first fing ter do is to wait one second after firing... then lower yer musket to the loading position, wiv its butt agin ter right hip and the muzzle slightly off to the left and the musket raised to the 'port' position – that is, about half-vertical. Yer should nah look dahn to check in the open pan that yer powder has been burnt away. Do that nah – SIXTEEN!*

Nah then, SQUAD – Shoulder...ARMS! SQUAD will advance and inspect the target. Forward MARCH!"

And they moved forward some fifty paces, noting the many holes ripped in the cloth by their lead balls, which each weighed about one ounce, and had diameters of nearly ¾". *"Yus – Them balls can do serious damage!"* Said Sergeant Smith, *"Nearly all on 'em holes could have been a nasty wound in a Johnny Crapaud if they'd ha' been the target and coming on us in close-packed ranks. A lot of 'em would nah be dead or dying!"*

"Mind you," went on Sergeant Smith, *"I reckon that about one-third of you lot fired too high, so that yer shots buzzed orf into space, doin' no 'arm to man or beast. But, all things considered, not a bad first attempt! Nah, termorrow, we'll do it all over agin', and agin' and agin. In fact, well before we finish training you, we'll long have stopped using numbers, and we'll be doing the exercise with the bare minimum of orders. In fact, you'll be able to fire yer muskets in yer sleep. Well-trained infantrymen can get orf four rahnds per minute. We'll be trying to get orf five! Now, though, you can all dismiss – As YOU WERE! STAND STILL! ONLY WHEN I gives the command! And*

Corporal Rogers here will see that you each cleans yer weapon of burnt powder afore yer gets off to the wet canteen for that drink that I talked about – and the Armourer Sergeant here will tend to the two muskets which had misfires. I doant want any accidents from half-trained men trying to clear misfires. Is that clearly understood?"

As one man, *"Yes, Sergeant!"*

"Good! SQUAD! Come to attention properly! – Stick yer belly in, Green Two! Get them muskets close in by yer sides. Remember, everybody, yer does a smart right turn on my command. SQUAD, DIS-MISS!"

Their practice at marching was not neglected at this time. They usually marched at least two or three miles at a time – but often considerably more. Sometimes they marched without their arms, but more often than not they carried their full set of kit, including their muskets. At nearly ten pounds weight, the muskets became quite heavy on a prolonged carry, and the recruits swiftly came to appreciate the order *"Change Arms!"*, by which the weight of the weapon was smoothly changed from the right to the left arm (or vice versa) at appropriate intervals of time as they marched along – *"Hup – cross – down!"*

They also practised at bayonet-training. Combat with bayonets fixed was hand-to-hand and bloody. The wielder of a musket armed with a bayonet needed to be utterly resolute, resolved and ruthless, striking hard with the bayonet or hitting with the heavy butt of the weapon as most appropriate to any given moment in the hectic battle. The feet and/or knees of the soldier also sometimes needed to do their part, kicking the enemy hard where it hurt most, especially if the musket could not be brought to bear at that precise second – and bearing in mind that the soldier might be fighting two or even three opponents at any given moment. A useful drill was practised on the 'stab and instantly recover' principle, but it was always obvious that, to survive, each soldier needed to develop his own expertise and skill to the maximum he could – and also his own mental toughness. To train, they either 'fought' against straw-filled dummies slung on ropes from beams, stabbing them with their bayonets, and clubbing them with the butts of their muskets – or they fought each other with long staves, using reasonably 'ritualised' moves. Fingers and hands sometimes became bruised in such encounters – and the corporals and sergeants in charge of the training had to keep a close watch on their men to ensure that the bouts did not become 'over-keen', since a soldier made angry could do serious damage to his opponent. As a balance to this, the soldiers were also taught to fight in working pairs, with the second man covering the stabbing action of the first man, (which could leave his abdomen exposed to a quick thrust by the bayonet of an enemy who was closely supporting the targeted man). The main factor which was taught was that a resolute and well-practised group, continuously shouting very loudly a hearty battle cry, and moving forward at a fast rate with their bayonets to the fore, was a fearsome spectacle for an enemy to face – and that panic might well be engendered in the enemy ranks, so that they would turn and run. Bayoneting a fleeing enemy in the back was a lot easier than facing a resolute foe.

As Private Soldiers in the Militia Jonas and Sam received regular pay, some of which they managed to send home, despite the relatively heavy payments which they had to make for various elements of their kit. Happily, although entering as Substitutes, they were each awarded a bonus as Volunteers, and this provided further money of which they were able to send a proportion home to aid in the on-going 'building project' back at Somersham.

Because Militia units might be ordered to fire on civilians and their homes at times of civil insurrection, it was official policy that no Militia unit would ever be posted to the area in which it had been raised. This meant that the Westminster Militia would almost certainly never have to serve in Central London. Instead (and most ironically where Sam and Jonas were concerned), it was to invasion-threatened Suffolk that the Westminsters were posted. It was thus in their own home-county that Sam and Jonas might have to impose martial law – albeit against one of the cardinal principles of the Militia!

As it was, within a short month, travelling mainly on foot, but with much of their kit and supplies of ammunition and provisions being carried in the horse-drawn general service wagons which accompanied them, Sam and Jonas found themselves back in their home county – though a little to the east of their actual birthplace. In fact, they were based in Ipswich, as support for the Regular soldiers who were guarding the general area around Felixstowe and Harwich. This was considered to be one of the most likely targets for the still actively-threatened French invasion! As Militiamen on the coast there, they might indeed stand a high chance of becoming embroiled as 'front-line cannon-fodder'. Twice during weekend leaves they actually managed to walk the distance to their home, where their parents were overjoyed to see them, and their step-mother fussed around them exclaiming how burly and fit they were becoming under the healthy exercise and solid rations they were constantly receiving as soldiers. Almost against himself, Jonas was beginning to love the life, though his brother Sam was rather more reserved about it. Sam was certainly missing his beloved Sarah, and made the most of his short time at her side.

Initially the recruits were kept in barracks at the garrison town of Ipswich. The main problem whilst they were stationed there was that there were occasional 'alarms and excursions' when the authorities took it into their heads to believe that the French had begun their invasion attempt, and so started to rush units of the Militia hither and thither, but always in vain – so that high expectation, nervous tension and excitement all-too-often ended in an exhausted and somehow rather disappointing anti-climax when their unit was officially 'stood-down' and returned to barracks, with no sign of the French having really made any invasion attempt at all. As Militia they also had other duties to perform, and they were called out to stand guard against possible civil insurrection at the time of the local elections to Parliament. Happily, all passed off well – though it did give the brothers something of an insight into the corrupt world of bribery and applied pressure which generally bedevilled politics at that time – albeit that the likes of common soldiers and 'ordinary men' did not qualify to vote at that time in our history – so that it was only gentlemen and 'men of property' who were caught up in the racket!

Then, come late April, Jonas and Sam found themselves to be members of a platoon of thirty men of the Westminsters on the march from Ipswich to Felixstowe. They soon learned that they were actually bound as reinforcements for Landguard Fort, at

Felixstowe. Landguard Fort turned out to be an imposing place, well-built in brick, and with sloped earthen ramparts to provide additional protection against enemy cannon-fire. The Fort had a considerable battery of heavy guns, manned by men of the Royal Artillery. It was sited on a spit of land jutting out into the sea and very well-placed to defend the joint estuary of the Stour and Orwell rivers, and, to an extent, also the sea-approaches to Felixstowe and Harwich. The previous 'base' of Jonas and his comrades, at Ipswich, lay only a few miles up-river. Ipswich was not only a sizeable garrison town but also an inland port which an enemy would doubtless perceive as a valuable target to capture early-on.

In the event of an invasion threatening Landguard Fort, the initial duty of the Militia would be to provide covering volley-fire against any *Voltigeurs* of the French Army who might manage to get ashore in advance of their main columns of infantry – in an attempt to 'take out' the British artillery which would be firing on the invasion shipping and the landing-beaches. The special expertise of the *Voltigeurs* would consist of sniping at the British gunners, and the first objective of the Militia would be to counteract any such sniping. Thereafter, as the main enemy force landed, the battle would become more general. The Militia trained for both phases, though it was clear that their main need for both aspects was to be able to fire volleys at short intervals of time, and that was the constant preoccupation of their sergeants and corporals in training the new men. (The Militia also had to learn how to manoeuvre quickly, as from column into line, or vice versa. This, too, they constantly practised.)

Both lads managed to avoid the classic error of new troops firing repeated volleys – that is, of accidentally leaving their ram-rod in the weapon, during one of the multiple rapid firings, so that the ram-rod flew out like a bullet, but far more erratically, and thereafter leaving the soldier with no means of tamping his bullet and charge down the barrel (apart from banging the butt of the weapon hard on the ground, which was very dangerous and officially frowned-upon). By managing to avoid this classic error the two brothers avoided the heaviest censure of their instructors.

About a month after they had joined, the brothers found themselves in a section of nine men under Corporal Fothergill, ordered to patrol the two-mile stretch of beach running northwards from the small coastal town of Felixstowe towards the even smaller port of Felixstowe Ferry, at the mouth of the River Deben. Until officially relieved, they were to make this patrol every morning and evening for the next week, co-ordinating with other patrols which functioned in the afternoon and at night. It was the intention that a constant twenty-four hour watch should thus be maintained against any hostile incursions, including possible small-scale landings of spies. Smuggling was rife along the East Coast, and could become linked with the landing of enemy agents. A watch – especially by night – was therefore also to be maintained for smugglers attempting to land brandy or other valuable goods illegally purchased by British fishermen when out at sea, from ships of French, Belgian or other European nationalities. Such contacts were usually made at a secret *rendezvous*, and by prior arrangement.

The local population tended to profit illicitly from any such goods which were smuggled ashore (once the smugglers had successfully by-passed the ever-watchful customs officials and their patrol vessels). Hence, the Militia could expect only nominal assistance from the local fishermen and various other citizens should the Militia encounter a group of armed smugglers at their nefarious work The customs officials were well-used to this ambivalent behaviour by the locals, and long-inured to it – but the Militia found difficulty in adjusting to its two-faced nature.

Each section was due to be stood-down after a week, and to come back on duty eight days later. They were to use their normal quarters at Landguard Fort, Felixstowe as their main base, and the 'Old Ferry Boat Inn' at Felixstowe Ferry as a stop-over at the 'other end' of their patrol, seeking sustenance, and resting up for a few hours, at each place, as necessary. The rankers thought this was amusing, since the 'Old Ferry Boat Inn' was popularly believed to be one of the primary haunts of the local smugglers at that time.

The coastline hereabouts consisted of low cliffs of clay. The shore was mainly of shingle, though interspersed with short stretches of sand. There were various large shoals of sand and shingle offshore, so that shipping emerging from the joint estuaries of the Rivers Stour and Orwell had to head northwards up the coast before it could gain the open sea. In fact, it had to proceed to an area almost opposite the mouth of the River Deben, where there was a natural channel heading eastwards between great shoals of shingle and sand, and thence out into the North Sea. Ships approaching from the North Sea had to navigate the reciprocal of this course to head into Harwich, or to gain the Orwell Estuary (and thus to be able to head upriver to Ipswich), or even to take the more southern route up the River Stour and head for Sudbury.

Mariners needed good and constantly up-dated charts or, even better, good up-to-date local knowledge, to navigate safely in these waters. Despite these potential hazards, Jonas could see that this coast was a distinct possibility for the French to make an assault landing, and he and his brother Sam were agreed that there was plenty of point in maintaining regular patrols, such as theirs, along the shore both by day and by night. Indeed, it was surprising that there were not fortifications there, to supplement their usual base at Landguard Fort, on the north coast of the Orwell estuary and just to the south of Felixstowe. It was clear that their patrols were only to maintain a watch rather than to combat any landings. Indeed, it was almost incomprehensible to the two brothers that the inexperienced Militiamen, even when assembled in battalion strength, might ultimately be expected to actually oppose any landing in force by the veteran French troops in such an open landscape. *[Jonas was not to know that (to improve the defences) eight very substantial 'Martello Towers', each to be occupied by a small force of regular troops and each armed with a cannon on a swivel, would be built along this very stretch of coast during the next few years (as an extension to the towers already being built along the more southerly coastline), and that, in later times, a substantial battery of coastal artillery would be installed at Brackenberry Fort, in the dead-centre of this very area.]*

This particular day of 1804 was, however, a bright and sunny one, and there there was a brisk on-shore breeze causing the sea to have got up a bit, with fair-sized waves rolling in to the beach and 'white' horses appearing here and there in the open sea beyond. It was the sort of sparkling day to drive dismal thoughts far away from anybody's mind, and Jonas, made even more fit by his active life in the Militia, was just enjoying the feeling of crunching along in the shingle as the section marched from Felixstowe northwards, past Cobbold's Point, on their way to Felixstowe Ferry. At Cobbold's Point, the tide had just receded enough from the cliff-face to let them pass dry-shod along the beach, rather than having to mount the cliff for a short distance. As they rounded the point, Corporal Fothergill suddenly exclaimed,

"Aye, aye, Lads! There's a strange small boat out there! It doan't look like one of our normal fishermen's craft!"

And, looking seawards, Jonas saw that an unfamiliar boat was indeed heading for the beach, now being only about 200 paces off-shore, though still some distance ahead of them up the coast. It seemed miraculous that it had already managed to fight its way through the immediate offshore shoals, where the surf was breaking heavily on the shallower places. The boat had no oars out, and was evidently being driven only by a tattered lugsail at its stump of a foremast. Indeed, it looked to be in a bad way, with little freeboard. Maybe it had just received a further battering as it had part-coasted and part-dragged over the half-submerged shingle of the shoals a little way offshore.

Corporal Fothergill led his men forward at the double northwards along the beach towards where the boat seemed to be heading. Suddenly, struck by a passing thought, he stopped them in their tracks, *"HALT! FIX BAYNITS, MEN! There may be Froggies aboard, and we don't want any of their nonsense! Best to be on the 'qui vive'!"* Chests heaving, the section stopped momentarily, whilst the men withdrew the wicked seventeen-inch long bayonets from their belts, placing their ring-like hafts around the muzzle-ends of their muskets and giving them a little twist to fix them firmly in place in the locking-pin. The strong steel bayonets, which were of triangular cross-section, glittered wickedly in the sun.

And, thus prepared and armed the section rapidly closed with the incoming boat, arriving just as its prow grazed the shingle-packed sand where the waves were breaking. Immediately it did so, a man part-stumbled and part-fell out of it into the shallows. He staggered a couple of paces up to Corporal Fothergill, and his horribly bloodshot eyes stared as if into Fothergill's very soul. The man looked dreadful, for his lips were swollen and cracked, and his face blistered and peeling from exposure to the elements. There were several days growth of beard on his thin cheeks and chin, and his clothes were ragged and sun-bleached, as well as just having been part-saturated from his stumbling in the waves. His feet were bare and white, with gaping sores, and the bones were very prominent.

"W'ter – w'ter!" He croaked, clawing desperately at the chest of Corporal Fothergill, who was still carrying his musket at the high port position.

The latter understood the position immediately. *"Poor sod is desperate for water, Lads!"*, he said, and. quick as a flash, he transferred his musket to his left hand, whilst, with his right hand he whipped out his water-bottle from his belt, immediately handing it to the man from the boat. At once the man inverted the water-bottle high to his mouth and began to avidly gurgle the water down his throat.

"NO!" yelled Jonas, and, in the twinkling of an eyelid he closed with the man and, with a swift blow of his fist, he smashed the water-bottle clean away, so that it fell to the sand. He then immediately put his foot on it, as the remaining water flowed away into the sand, and as the man fell to his knees and began to scrabble desperately for the bottle and the precious water, sobbing bitterly, *"No, no – W'ter, w'ter, ahh!"*.

"WHAT THE HELL DO YOU THINK YOU'RE DOING, GREEN?!" yelled Corporal Fothergill, *"CAN'T YOU SEE THE DESPERATE CASE THIS POOR MAN IS IN? WHAT ARE YOU – A DAMNED VICIOUS PERVERT!?"*

"Permission to explain please Corp!"

"GO ON THEN! This had better be bloody good!"

"Yes, Corp. Well, my Dad always said that a man who has been starved of water should never be allowed to 'drink his fill', so to speak!"

"OH, YES! WELL – TELL US MORE!"

"Yes, Corp. Er, that is to say, in his desperation, any such man will naturally want to glug and glug and glug. Trouble is, he will then burst his stomach or dilute his thickened blood so quickly that he will surely die. The only possible way to save him is to give him water in little sips and at fairly long intervals of time, to gradually restore his body back to normal. The same applies with feeding him, though his first drive will always be to try to drown himself in drink. He will be literally mad for it."

"My God, Jonas Green! Old Sergeant Smith wondered if you was a bleedin 'ship's lawyer' just a day or two arter you joined. I reckon you've now shown yerself to be a bleedin' 'ship's <u>surgeon</u>' an' all! Any of you other blokes heard the like o' wot Jonas ha' said?"

And, after looking at the blank faces of his men for a moment, Corporal Fothergill went on, *"Huh, only you, Sam Green, nodding yer head, and agreeing wiv him, eh? Just backing up yer brother, are yer? I'd have expected nothing less! Well, the M.O. had better confirm your story when we gets back to base, Jonas Green! Otherwise, it'll be 'jankers' for you – or somethin' a lot worser!"*

"Right, you lot, RECOVER BAYNITS! Put 'em in their scabbards, MOVE. Then STACK YER ARMS – RIGHT THERE!" (pointing to a spot a little above the line where the sea-foam currently reached) *– Private Stevens, you stand guard over them muskets until I tells yer otherwise! Private Jenkins, you attend to this poor bugger from the boat – and, no matter wot his craving may be, just giv' 'im small sips of water taken from yer bottle – but ONLY to suck from a finger every ten minutes or so. I want you four, Sexton, Smithers, Wilson and Williams, to arrange yourselves on the far side of the boat, whilst myself, Jones and the Green brothers arrange ourselves on its near side. YES, that certainly DOES mean wading out into the sea, Private Smithers! Yup, we can kick orf our shoes and gaiters, and we can roll up the legs of our breeches a bit, but we'll all have risk getting the lower parts of our breeches wet…Too bad! Do it nah, MOVE!... Good!... Now, into the sea, MOVE!..."*

"Right, now we're all in the water, we'll haul the boat a few yards up the beach, to stop it broaching-to. Grab the sides, lads! ALL TOGETHER, TWO-SIX, HEAVE! AND AGIN, Two-SIX HEAVE! GOOD!... Nah she's a bit steadier, we'll climb into the boat to look for any signs of life in the other bodies!"

Sure enough, there *were* other bodies in the boat. They found that two of them were still alive – just. Two others were already quite lifeless, and had probably been dead for a day or two. The bilge of the boat contained several inches of water and it was obvious that its gunnels had not been far above the surface. Now that the bow of the boat was standing on the beach, her stern had dipped down a bit, and the waves were splashing heavily at her transom, sending much spray flying into the stern-sheets. Before her beaching the boat had still 'swum', but it would have only been a short while more before she sank.

Scattered in the wet bilges were a number of small silver herrings, with their mid-sections gnawed away, evidently where the men had sucked on them in desperate attempts to find 'drinkable' moisture to satisfy their cravings. Clearly, the men had also been trying the old sailors' trick of trapping rainwater in their spread-out shirts, then wringing them out and drinking the water thus obtained. Fishing rods and other gear and impedimenta lay in the wet bottom of the boat. And there was an anchor with a short hempen line. Corporal Fothergill, who had clearly learnt something about boats during his career, got one of his men to carry the anchor up the beach a little way, and to dig its spike into the sand, ensuring that the anchor-line was fixed in the boat, and thus avoiding the risk of the boat drifting away as the tide came in.

It was only with difficulty that the section managed to rouse the other two surviving men from the boat sufficiently to induce them to take sips of water. One of them gradually rallied as the day wore on, but the other simply faded away, despite all their efforts, and quickly died. The first man from the boat also survived, and he was later able to tell the story of their ordeal, which was as follows.

There were originally six men in the boat. They had set out from Scarborough for a day's fishing. Without any warning, a south-westerly gale had suddenly sprung up. Despite all their efforts to regain the shore, the adverse wind, coupled with a strong tide had swept them far out from the East Coast and then, as the gale worsened, they had drifted eastwards, right across the North Sea, almost to Norway – whose snow-capped mountains they could then see in the near distance. It was only by baling furiously that they had managed to stay afloat, for waves had kept breaking aboard. They had thought about continuing in the direction of Norway to seek aid, but the south-westerly wind had suddenly reverted right round to a strong north-easterly one, and they had begun to drift back towards England. Unfortunately, they had taken only a day's water-supply, and, though they had rationed it, the water had quickly run out. Somebody had the bright idea of sucking water from the few fish they had caught, which helped a bit. They had also spread out their shirts to catch the rain, but little rain had actually fallen. Great thirst kicked in to such an extent that one of the men, who had been covertly drinking sea-water, simply went mad, and threw himself overboard. None of the others had the strength to stop him. After five days they were all pretty well 'gone', and badly suffering from exposure to wind, sun and wave in the open boat.

They no longer had the strength to row, and soon little energy left even to bale the boat sufficiently to keep it from sinking. They had become almost totally reliant on the wind blowing on their scrap of a lugsail, and the tides, to bring them ashore <u>somewhere</u>. At the end, going through the waves breaking on the offshore shoals had been terrifying, with the boat bumping heavily on the shingle at times, and the waves crashing all around them, but, by that time, they were so far gone that they just had to steer the boat as best the exhausted steersman could manage, and to leave the rest to Providence.

Under Corporal Fothergill's directions, the section made improvised litters from their jackets, passing muskets through the sleeves, and later carried the two survivors to the Old Ferry Boat Inn at Felixstowe Ferry, which was about a mile distant. Before they left the scene, the boat, and the other three bodies, were brought well above the high-tide mark, and Jonas and Sam were appointed to guard them. Jonas thought it was with a slight measure of spite that Corporal Fothergill told them that they were entitled to use whatever little remained of the day's rations in their packs for the rest of the day and for their overnight sustenance.

However, Sam had previously spotted a small fisherman's hut part-hidden in the dunes behind the beach, and, once the section had left the scene, Sam who could readily exhibit an outward veneer of a sort of 'childish innocence', quietly wandered up to the hut and knocked politely on its rough wooden door. The primitive hut proved to be occupied by a poor but very kindly man and his homely wife, who, on hearing a bit of the story, spontaneously provided the brothers with a finely cooked meal of freshly-caught plaice and some potatoes. Sam partook of his first, so that the dead men from the boat could be respectfully watched over by at least one guard at all times.

The afternoon patrol 'passed through' them in the afternoon on their way back to base, agog to hear more about the morning's events, and their own section passed through them on their southward return that evening. As they did so, Corporal Fothergill told Jonas he would be reporting the incident when he got back to Landguard Fort, and that a detail would be sent out early the following morning to collect the bodies. A separate detail, probably accompanied by the M.O., would head for the Ferry Boat Inn, where the two survivors had been left *pro tem*. The section then went on their way.

Early that evening, again taking it in turns, the brothers were kindly invited back into the fisherman's hut where they were each given a comfortingly hot leek and potato potage accompanied by a thick slice of rough, crusty home-made bread.

They subsequently donned their greatcoats, wrapped their blankets around themselves, and, standing alternate two-hour watches, they each slept extremely well, despite some overnight rain. They were aided in this by having found a small, sandy hollow, out of the keen night wind. Moreover, Sam, somewhat irritated by the constant slapping noise of the wind-driven canvas lugsail against the mast of the boat, had been struck by a bright idea. That is to say, he had taken down the sail, and stretched it as a sort of roof over the small hollow where they were to sleep, stopping the sail from blowing clean away by holding down its edges and gaskets with a few large stones he had collected from the beach. The sail had a strange, salty smell all of its own, but it did a good job in keeping the worst of the rain off the two brothers.

Happily, the hollow was situated upwind of the bodies, for the two longest-dead had begun to smell rather foul by that time. (This was an odour of human decay with which Jonas was fated to become only too familiar during his subsequent career.)

The brothers were up early the following morning, splashing refreshingly cold water from their water-bottles over their faces, pulling their uniforms straight, and stuffing their folded blankets and greatcoats into their packs. Scarcely had they done so, and as predicted by Corporal Fothergill, Sam and Jonas were relieved of their mournful guard duty, when a small detail with a horse-drawn service wagon arrived. Having helped to load the three bodies aboard, Sam and Jonas hitched a ride with the detail for the sad return to camp. The men of the detail (who were also new recruits) had been quite shocked when the dead men 'belched' and 'farted' most foully when picked up, ready to be lifted into the back of the wagon. The skin of one of the bodies was also beginning to slough off as they handled the corpses, leading to one of the detail vomiting violently with a sudden nausea. Jonas felt a parallel sense of sickness, and was glad that he and Sam had enjoyed that morning what Sergeant Smith called *"A Soldier's Breakfast"* – so there was nothing at all in his stomach to be brought up! However, after the bodies had been transferred to the mortuary at Landguard Fort, the brothers were able to wash and clean themselves well (for they felt badly soiled), and they were then given some food which they managed to keep down. Later still, they were able to enjoy the luxury of a shave using their cut-throat razors – and so returned to the everyday world.

The gratitude of the two survivors to the Militiamen for slowly and carefully re-hydrating them and thus successfully maintaining them in life (and also for safeguarding their boat), was enormous, and Corporal Fothergill received a special commendation from the commanding officer at Landguard Fort. *"Such are the privileges of rank"*, murmured Sergeant Smith to Jonas, with a quite kindly wink at him. As his service life continued Jonas would become deeply inured to the old Army saying, *"If you can't take a joke, you shouldn't have joined!"*

It was quite clear that smuggling was rife all along the East Coast, and the Militia found various traces of it as time went on. There were even some joint operations mounted with the Customs Officials in attempts to catch the perpetrators, albeit more or less in vain. The smugglers were a very efficient lot, and it seemed likely that they were being tipped off by various wealthy people who were 'in the know' about each of the operations being conducted by the military. Jonas was aware of some of the specially organised patrols, but neither he nor Sam ever came to be directly involved. Generally, they just went about their standard duties, regardless of the weather, often on the same routine marches along the beach. As Autumn came, and then the Winter, the patrols became much harder on the men, despite being huddled in their greatcoats and wearing mittens and scarves, for the East Coast wind could be a bitter one indeed. *"Straight from the Ural Mountains in Russia, with nothing in the way!"* would say Corporal Fothergill, *"That's a lazy wind, is that! – Won't go rahnd you, but prefers to go straight on through!"*

"Yes, Corp! would say Private Smithers, *"It sure is bleedin' cold! Any chance of a hot toddy from you when we gets to the 'Old Ferry Boat Inn' – I ain't got no money left!"*

"You'd be lucky, my son!" would reply the Corporal, *"But try young Green here – he don't smoke like you an' me does…"*

"I might just get us three some toddies in, and perhaps one for my brother," would say Jonas, *"but* (looking at the way the shingle and sand had rubbed away at his shoes) *I've got these fine shoes which will need a really good polish when we gets back to base!"*

"Oh, all right!" would say Joe Smithers, *"But you ain't 'arf a mercenary bugger!"*

They had a few other 'adventures' – such as providing the guard for a wooden tower which was being built at the top of the tallest building just a little way up the hill from the top of Bent Hill, the main way up the cliffs at Felixstowe. This was just about the highest point in the immediate area. Military engineers and civilian carpenters were busy at the top of the tower, installing a strange arrangement of shutters, under the close direction of a Major in the Royal Engineers. Clearly an impatient and hot-tempered man, the Major was striving to bring the device to fruition, working from copies of quite elaborate printed plans which had been laid out on large sheets of canvas-backed paper. The plans were clearly not of his own making, and he was finding them very difficult to understand. The more he became frustrated, the worse became the invective flowing from his lips. *"Humbuggering things!"* he exclaimed, *"What a bloody shambles! I don't see how the semaphore arms can possibly work! The designer must be a blithering idiot!"*

Corporal Fothergill stood his men at ease, and he and his section listened respectfully to the invective pouring forth. Jonas wondered idly how the matter might be resolved. At the moment, things were just going from bad to worse. However, the Major easily outranked everybody else on the site, and any soldier who tried to intervene would certainly get his head bitten off – especially as the Major was already hopping mad!

One of the older civilian carpenters ambled gently up to the cursing figure. *"Beg pardon, yer Worship"*, says he, *"Might I have a bit of a peek at them plans – I might just be able to help."*

"I don't know about that!", says the Major, *"They're a military secret, you know – They may be useless, but, look, the drawings have 'SECRET' stamped all over 'em! – and in red, too! I reckon they've been written in blood!"*

"Yus, I can see that they're secret", says the old carpenter. *"But supposing I look at 'em with only one eye open, and wiv a very short memory. Arter all, me an' my mates are supposed to be putting the bleedin' fings togevver, an' we doan't want to be here all week. The government woan't want to pay us for too much time spent! There might be enquiries made, and, as the h'officer in charge, you might even be held responsible."*

"Oh, bugger it! Here, take the bleeding plans! Mind you don't lose them! I'm going into that inn to have a drink before I die of thirst." And off the Major went. He returned a couple of hours later, by which time the old carpenter had already begun to convert the plans into reality, and the system of shutters was swiftly taking shape under the skilled hands of himself and his mates.

Jonas and his squad watched and smiled, but very discreetly, well out of the sight of the choleric Major, who was already beginning to glow in the success of 'his' enterprise – the redness of his face doubtless aided by the strong spirits he had clearly been consuming in at the nearby inn.

Jonas later learned that the tower was intended for the transmission of messages to the Admiralty in London. This was done by a so-called 'semaphore' system, the shutters being varied in position to indicate different key words and phrases. The coded message they exhibited was in sight of a similar tower set on high ground a few miles inland, where the message was received and immediately copied and passed on to the next tower in a chain of towers running all the way inland to the Admiralty. In this way, a message could be sent to London in a matter of minutes, provided that the men posted in all the towers were constantly alert, and provided that the weather was clear. It was better for the messages to be passed in daylight, but some communication was also possible by night, using lanterns of different colour-combinations. Importantly, messages could also be passed in the reverse direction, from the Admiralty to the coast.

For some reason, the tower at Felixstowe was not put into regular operation, and the local memory of it faded away. However, the general system was used quite extensively for some years, especially in regard to a line of towers running from Kent to London. (In the latter part of the 19th Century it would be replaced by the electric telegraph.) There was also a successful line based in Essex.

Jonas and his brother Sam adapted quite well to life in the Militia, gradually picking up all the 'old soldier's tricks by which one could best survive, and learning just how far one could safely go when dealing with 'authority', the 'limits' being quite different for the well-experienced NCOs as compared with the (usually) haughty officers.

By 1805 the threat of French invasion had vanished. Napolean Bonaparte had decided to withdraw all his troops and to send them on other Continental duties, some to the Iberian Peninsula. A few years later, many of the others would be involved in the ill-fated invasion of Russia. This meant that a considerable host of them were doomed to die, mainly in the terrible cold and privations of the so-called 'Retreat from Moscow' – though (as we shall see) very large numbers also died in Portugal and Spain - where their wounded had a high chance of having their throats cut by *guerillas* who were out to avenge earlier atrocities by the French troops.

In 1806 the British Government decided that their best option would be to carry the war to France. A direct cross-Channel invasion was too dangerous to contemplate, but, for example, sending a force of troops to aid the Portugese and the Spanish in fighting the French on the Iberian Peninsular was a much more realistic venture.

Unfortunately, the first force sent was simply not large enough, and, after a series of well-fought defensive battles, the Army had to retreat to Corunna, from whence the Navy evacuated it brilliantly. Sadly, however, the British General, the celebrated Sir John Moore, was mortally wounded by cannon-fire in the related covering battle – a grievous loss to the future of the British Army. Clearly, a much larger Army needed to be put together, ready for a further landing on Portugese soil.

In order to expand the British Army, the law was changed in 1807, so that men in the Militia, formerly strictly forbidden to join the Regulars, were now entitled to volunteer for service with that arm. Moreover, if they volunteered to serve in the Army for 'unlimited service' (nominally twenty years), they would be entitled to a pension for life, assuming that they were discharged with 'a clean sheet'. The chances of completing twenty years and remaining free from death, injury or disease were not good, but the possibility of retiring with a pension was certainly a great attraction and numbers of Militiamen did indeed volunteer for 'unlimited service' with the Army. There was no equivalent pension at all in civilian life, where men worked until they literally dropped dead – or went on to the miserly parish relief. *(It would not be until 1906 that a civilian 'Old Age Pension' would be introduced – almost exactly a century later!)*

On the advice of Sergeant Smith, and after a lot of personal indecision, Jonas was one who decided to go for the option of 'unlimited service'. This was a big decision for a young man to make, committing himself from the age of 20 until he would be 40 or so. However, the other option, of going for only a seven-year period of service, did not hold the potential attraction of an 'old age pension', for there was no guarantee that one would be able to extend one's service later, towards gaining a pension. Also, one would be no better off on coming out at age 27 in regard to getting a job in civilian life – indeed, one might be in far worse case, if (say) one's health had been damaged by tropical service or by combat conditions. These were the sort of arguments which Sergeant Smith had deployed to Jonas.

So, after quite a lot of heart-searching, and also after much discussion with his brother Sam, and with various other men within the unit as a whole, Jonas decided that he would take the option of joining the regular Army for unlimited service. A good many of the Royal Westminster Militia joined the Regulars at the same time, although only about half of them went for the unlimited service option.

On the other hand, Sam, the elder brother of Jonas, decided to take completely the other route, by serving out his compulsory five years in the Militia, and then returning to civilian life. He was relatively well-set for doing so, for his father had been steadily improving the home-plot, and he was more than willing to aid Sam in building another house on the same large plot, ready for Sam to marry his girl and then for Sam and Sarah to move in and to start to raise a family.

This was exactly how things panned out. But at the time of Sam's marriage Jonas would be in the Army, totally out of touch with home and a great many thousands of miles away.

Chapter Three

The Year 1807:
Jonas Joins the Regular Army

On the 29th September 1807 Jonas was enlisted into the 24th Regiment of Foot. He was far from being alone in joining that regiment, for about 210 other young Militiamen from the Royal Westminster Militia had joined with him. There was also a very large influx from the Warwickshire Militia, another large contingent from the Royal Bucks Militia, and also quite large contingents from the Lincolnshire and the Northampton Militias. In fact, at least ten different militias from around the country were represented in the groups which enrolled in the 24th at about that time.

It was clear that, following the revision of rates of pay and the introduction of the pension for long-serving soldiers, considerable interest in joining the Army had been stimulated around the United Kingdom, and especially amongst the Militia. Immediately thereafter, Army recruiting sergeants and their small detachments of men had been very active indeed around the different parts of England – and they had been obtaining good results, especially amongst militiamen who were, in civilian life, ordinary tradesmen and labourers, and who were aged between twenty and thirty. Perhaps men of this age felt, from their experiences in the Militia, that they could handle military service comfortably enough. They probably also considered that the Army would reliably keep them 'clothed, fed and watered' in a way that civilian life could never match. Moreover, they were also still young enough to feel the need for some sort of excitement and colour in their lives. It also became clear to Jonas that some men were 'on the run' from their parish constables or other authorities from having committed some sort of crime, probably mostly to do with 'putting food in their empty bellies' – either by stealing food directly, or by stealing articles to pawn, with the same intent – and the Army offered these men a 'home' in which they would probably remain safe from any civilian prosecution.

One of the aforementioned recruiting groups had worked their way down the East Coast from Lincolnshire to Suffolk, sending forth advance parties, and with both precursors and the main party flying colourful flags, 'beating the drum' and putting large boastful posters in prominent positions all about various towns as they made their progress south. This particular group represented the 24th Regiment of Foot, whose uniform had distinctive so-called 'green facings', whereas most regiments had yellow or blue facings. The 1st Btn of the 24th was not long returned from fighting in Egypt, where it had distinguished itself at the Battle of Alexandria, and before that, from being in combat against the colonists in North America, who had been seeking independence from the British Empire.

It was the recruitment group from the 24th which Jonas and his fellow Westminsters had joined on its noisily proclaimed arrival in Suffolk, where they were based. They had then proceeded with the recruitment group as it marched to Malden in Essex, with each recruit having long coloured ribbons fluttering about his person, as a sort of exciting lure, intended to draw in yet further young men. It was at Maldon that they were officially enlisted, Jonas being incorrectly recorded as having a birthplace at

'Brickett, Suffolk' – perhaps because the recruiting sergeant had heard of 'Brickett Wood' (actually in Essex), but never of the little village of 'Great Bricett', which was actually in Suffolk. The civilian occupation of Jonas was correctly recorded as a 'Labourer', and his age as 20 years. He was shown as being 5 ft 6½ ins tall and as having dark hair and 'black' eyes – probably confirming that he did indeed have swarthy gypsy blood in his ancestry.

The whole group of new recruits had been deeply impressed on their arrival in Malden, for the fields on each side of the long road leading into the port of Malden were cram-full of hundreds of circular white tents arranged in neat lines. There were also latrines dug in the soil, and rather primitive washing facilities. Marquees housing the messes of the officers, and large tents for the cookhouses and the 'wet canteens' of the men were carefully interspersed amongst these circular tents. There were a great many troops from a wide range of regiments to be seen. Here and there were also the horse-lines of dragoons and light and heavy cavalry units, and the horses and light cannon of field artillery. Ammunition dumps and sutler's wagons could also be discerned here and there. The British Army was certainly burgeoning for the war against France. It was estimated that some 28,000 men had transferred from the Militia to the Army – and, by means of the ballot, Castlereagh, the Secretary for War, had raised 36,000 recruits to supplement the weakened ranks of the Militia. Virtually the whole of the enormous farming community country-wide was engaged in growing crops or raising livestock for the Army, or in producing equipment and weapons, with the daily needs of the country itself coming a poor second.

Once the new recruits reached the built-up area of the town itself, they found that the port below the town was armed with batteries of heavy cannon, some mounted on central pivots which enabled to guns to be readily rotated to fire in any required direction. There were one or two troop-ships to be seen at the quaysides, mixed together with the fishing vessels and trading barges which worked out of the port from day to day. The houses of the port had a prosperous look to them, and it was clear that some of the inhabitants were becoming very wealthy people indeed, by acting as middle-men in supplying the massive needs of the Army for victuals and various sorts of equipment.

On the day they arrived, the new recruits were each taken before a magistrate, and sworn in. Once again, Jonas was struck by the harshness of the principal terms of the King's Regulations, which were read out to them at that time, and whereby death by hanging was the punishment for nearly every offence 'against the Crown'. Clearly, he was going to have to be very circumspect in his behaviour in the years ahead. Indeed, he would have to maintain a 'clean sheet' for as long as the next 20 years or so, leading up to his eventual discharge from the army. It might be the case that his service in the militia, which had already labelled him as being a 'ship's lawyer', might have brought a sort of notoriety with it, and this might well count against him in the future. Although he was normally of a quiet and patient disposition, he knew that, if provoked beyond his level of endurance, his temper could sometimes burst forth most dramatically. This could lead him to over-react in a situation and to lash out in some way – even to become physically violent to an extent. In future he would have to watch his step very carefully indeed. It was all-too-easy to 'race up the ladder of military crime', and to end up in military prison. Jonas was also very conscious that he no longer had the support of his brother, and that he would have to stand very much on his own two feet. He would not even have the support of men from his own county, because the 24th had remarkably few men from Suffolk within its ranks.

The fact that the newly-joining men came from all the different corners of England meant that the variety of dialects and accents to be heard on all sides was truly amazing, and there was often considerable difficulty in the comprehension of one man with another. It was weeks before they all really began to come to any sort of mutual understanding, and, whilst Jonas could accommodate quite easily to the voices of men from Bucks, Middlesex and Norfolk, and even to those from Lincolnshire, he found that the twang of the Lancastrians and the Warwicks, and the dialect of the men from Durham and Yorkshire, was particularly hard to understand. There were also a few Irishmen, and their accents were often quite impossible to interpret! And the inverse was also the case, for many of the men had difficulty in understanding what Jonas was saying in his Suffolk dialect – especially in moments of stress and urgency!

One feature which Jonas had found rather unsettling was that only about one in five of the men had volunteered for 'unlimited service'. In fact, of the large contingent from the Warwickshire Militia, it seemed that *not one man* had gone for the 'unlimited service' option. Much seemed to have depended upon the advice which had been given to them by the senior non-coms in their previous militia units, and it seemed that the NCOs of the Warwick Militia had been exceptionally cynical. (Perhaps some of the loudest may have not long been returned from painfully hard service in the West Indies or some such place, where they'd had pals dying all around them from 'yellow jack' or 'black-water fever'.) One could almost hear them saying, *"What's the point? You're going to have to fight the French abroad, and if you fight 'em in the tropics, as seems likely, many of you will quickly die of yellow fever, malaria or whatever! You might just about survive seven years of exposure like that – but twenty years of such exposure – don't be daft! The government knows that most men will be too sensible to go for unlimited service – and that's exactly why they have suddenly come up with this new idea of a pension. Tell you what – very few soldiers will live long enough to ever draw it! You stick wiv only seven years of service my lads, and then get the hell out of it!"*

As things later turned out, such words were far from being alarmist.

On joining, the '7 years men' received a bounty of five guineas, whereas the 'Unlimited Men', like Jonas, received seven guineas. That was a lot of money in those days, when most items were priced at only a few pence or shillings. So, Jonas again sent most of his money home to his father, though he found that he was charged a number of 'expenses' for small (but important) items to supplement his kit, which did whittle down the sum he actually received. He also found that his fellow-recruits expected him to 'stand his round' (and more!) of beer, whenever they managed to get to the 'wet canteen'.

One satisfying feature was that he no longer had to grow his hair with a short pigtail, nor to powder it to make it white, as had been the practice in the Militia. Now his hair was expected to be simply kept clean and cut comparatively short. If he so wanted, he could also ask permission to grow a moustache and/or a beard – and that permission would not be unreasonably with-held. Unfortunately, the leather stock was still to be worn, to keep the soldier's head up – but he was becoming inured to it. He now wore trousers rather than breeches and gaiters, and his tall stiff cap had been replaced by an attractive black shako, with a decorative brass plaque showing the number of his regiment. This uniform was much more practical than the former version.

There had also been a significant change in the structure of all infantry battalions, in the matter that each battalion now had a so-called 'Light Company'. This was modelled somewhat on the French '*Voltigeurs*', who skirmished ahead of their main force, sniping at officers and other 'targets of opportunity', and generally trying to create mayhem in the ranks of their opponents. There was also the recent influence of the American backwoodsmen, whose accuracy with the rifle, and their skills in using natural cover, both for 'cover from view' and 'cover from fire', had caused the regular British troops considerable difficulties and many casualties in the American War of Independence. This 'American influence' had already led the British to convert the 60th Regiment into the 'King's Royal Rifle Corps', armed with rifles and marching at high speed, also being skilled at skirmishing and using natural cover, with which their green uniforms and non-reflective black buttons blended. Most of the newly-formed 'Light Companies' of the standard infantry had retained their red uniform jackets and muskets (rather than as yet converting to the rifle), but they were all now being trained in skirmishing and in rapid deployment – some now marching at 140 paces per minute as compared with the 120 paces per minute of a regular infantry unit, and all generally manoeuvring much faster than the regular companies of a standard infantry battalion. Jonas was serving in a regular company, but he had half an eye on the possibility of joining the light company of his regiment. The light companies had quickly come to be called "The Light Bobs" throughout the British Army. Currently, the 'Light Bobs' of the 24th were serving with the 1st Btn, of which more presently.

Initially, however, Jonas and his fellow-recruits found themselves in the 2nd Battalion of the 24th, which remained in England at that period, acting as a '*cadré*' for the 1st Btn. The 2nd Btn was constantly sending out recruiting parties around the country to enrol men to subsequently go out to the 1st Btn as reinforcements, in an attempt to keep it right up to its full strength.

Naturally, the 2nd Btn also acted as the training battalion for the 1st Btn. This training was basic, and was much as Jonas and his mates had received in their early days in the militia. However, a few of the new recruits had entered direct from civilian life (and not through the militia). These men tended to be as 'green as grass' and, in training them, the Army was working on the principle of 'the lowest denominator'. So the more experienced men, such as Jonas, just 'cruised' along quietly, overtly obeying orders to the letter and doing what they were told – though some were clever enough to find ways of 'dodging the column' and of avoiding the more physically demanding of the exercises. Several men, selected from those who had the ability to read and write, were picked out as 'chosen men', and were groomed to some degree by the instructors, ready to be promoted to the status of corporal as time went on. Jonas did not receive such attention – maybe because his writing ability was not very good and maybe also because, fairly or not, it did appear that he had been marked down as a possible 'Ship's Lawyer', and hence suspected of being 'potentially difficult' and only too ready to argue a case at the drop of a hat – thus risking being accused of 'insubordination'.

Regimental musters were held at intervals, normally on the 24th of each month, when each man was marked as 'present' (or, if not, had his whereabouts stated, e.g. 'in hospital'). Each man also had his pay calculated for the service he had completed since the previous muster, the pay being dependent on how many days of the month he had spent 'in quarters', and how many days 'on the march'. (A newly-joined man's basic pay was about 6d per day when based 'in quarters', though rather more when 'on the march'. A pint a day of beer was reckoned to be part of a man's pay, and absence of beer could also extend his wages over the number of days he was thus deprived.) After seven years of service all the privates would receive an increase of 1d per day, then another 1d per day after a further seven years, and so on – and those pennies made a real difference.

The 2nd Btn had a number of companies, each of about 100 men and commanded by captains. Jonas was initially in the company which was officered by Captain W STRAWBENZEE.[1] As NCOs for the company, there were three sergeants and two corporals.

Most men found life in the 2nd Btn, whether spent under canvas or in barracks, rather dull, though the fact that they were now doing route marches of 12 to 14 miles twice a week in full marching order kept the men physically fit and their 'energy' and 'adrenalin' levels more or less under control. In the meantime, rumours were sweeping through the 2nd Btn that the 1st Btn had been in action.[2] The word was that, prior to the joining of Jonas and his comrades, the 1st Btn had been going through a rather frustrating period of service. That is to say, in 1805 they had been embarked in East Indiamen for an assault on Rio de Janiero. However, that operation had been cancelled just after they left English shores, and they had then been held in a large bay called 'The Cove of Cork', in south-west Ireland. Here, the men had stultified on board, with vitually no shore leave, whilst the days had stretched into months, before fresh orders had at last arrived from

[1] Surnames rendered like this one, with capitals throughout, are actual names taken from the official records in the 19th Century War Office (WO) files still maintained in the National Archives (or from HEIC files kept in the British Library). In this book surnames which are capitalised throughout usually apply to actual figures of commissioned officer status – or sometimes to O.Rs who had become casualties. The roles played by the most 'senior' persons are closely based on surviving historical records.

Surnames given in minor case, with just an initial capital letter, have been invented. In this book they mainly apply to men having only non-commissioned rank, or their wives. The roles played by these persons are mainly 'relatively authentic' but a few are 'pure invention'. They are intended to lend colour to the story.

The 'background' deployments of the military units, and the battles fought by them, together with the related voyages by ship, have been made as close to historical record as possible.

Reported speech is a sort of amalgam, slightly tempered by 19th Century English and its dialects, but highly flavoured by early-20th Century Army jargon, to try to create a 'flavour of understanding' as Jonas might have experienced it in his day. He is shown as having a rather more enquiring mind than the average labourer of his day – though most of the men would have had a fair level of 'sturdy commonsense'.

It is hard for people living today to understand the overall English culture of the early 19th Century. At that time the public's general perception of ordinary soldiers (as opposed to officers) was that they were all-too-often drunkards and thieves who came from the lowest sweepings of society – though it was well recognised that there were sometimes idealistic volunteers amongst them – indeed all were hailed as heroes when danger threatened the country and the Army had to go into combat – too often heavily outnumbered, and as the famous 'Thin Red Line'.

[2] The main substance of the rumours shown here has been derived from the regimental histories as currently maintained in the Museum at Brecon. Some fragments of additional data have been acquired from sundry contemporaneous accounts.

Horseguards – the place in central London in which the senior command of the British Army was then based.

The new orders had led to the East Indiamen setting forth in convoy, in late August 1805, bound for South Africa. They were escorted by a small fleet of naval vessels under Sir Home POPHAM. By that time, they were part of an Army of 6,000 men, under the direct command of Sir David BAIRD, the impressive officer who, a few years earlier had attacked Seringapatam in India, and whose forces had killed the notorious and murderous Tippoo Sahib. Now, they were going to invade South Africa at the Cape of Good Hope, and to take over the trading station which had been successfully set up a century and more ago by the so-called 'Batavian' settlers from Holland. This trading station had been well-developed over the years *(and it had also been fortified to a degree, under a brief period of British rule. That rule had been ended in 1802, following the Treaty of Amiens).* The station contained various farms and commercial gardens. The Batavians were very religious but also very tough men, skilled at hunting wild animals for food. They had formed treaties with some of the tribes of dark-skinned native Africans, had totally suppressed such little active opposition as they had met, and nowadays used numbers of natives as virtual slaves.

The conventional course followed by the convoy had taken them westwards right across the Atlantic and back, as they followed the trade winds. This voyage had taken several months to accomplish, the troops badly needing to 'stretch their legs' and to eat some fresh produce of various kinds before their voyage was even half-complete. The enforced respite – which had lasted for three weeks – had taken place at San Salvador, in the Bahamas - a delightful place, where the troops had at last been landed for some exercise, and with a number of sick men being left there to recover as the fleet eventually sailed on.

Details of the actual invasion of the Cape were still coming in, but it was understood that the operation had gone well, and that the Batavians had surrendered to the British forces. However, there had been casualties on both sides. The combat losses to the 24th, which had started off well short of its full complement, and which was now coupled with a smallish number of men having fallen sick, and requiring repatriation, was why the 1st Battalion now needed some reinforcements.

Apparently this news had filtered back to Horseguards in England by March 1808…

One other piece of news was that General Sir D BAIRD had been appointed to the honorary role of Colonel of the 24th Regiment in 1807, and Lt-Colonel KELLY had now been promoted to take operational command of it.

Chapter Four

The Year 1809:
The Journey out to 'the Cape'

Like most of his new comrades, Jonas was simply aching to join the 1st Battalion. On 25th April 1808 his wish was granted, when he and most of his company were officially transferred. In fact, a large detachment of reinforcements had now been formed from the 2nd Btn. They were under the overall command of Lt-Col R MARRIOTT. The officers who accompanied the Colonel included Captain Daniel BABY and Lieutenants TT GRINDLEY, EG SMITH, C DOOLAN, J BLAKE, and J FERRIS. Three ensigns, D WHARBURTON, R WALTON and A N FINDLATER were promoted to Captain and also formed part of the group, and the young Ensigns who completed the officers being transferred were J C MEE, T MAXWELL, E JACKSON, R ADAMS, H C LLEWELLYN, F GRANT, J HARRIS and J BELL. So, as befitted professional soldiers, it seemed that the officers, too, craved action with the 1st Btn. – which, as we have seen, was by now known to its 2nd Btn to be involved in the campaign against the Batavians, out in South Africa.

Quartermaster Sergeant R BELCHER was also in the group being transferred, together with no less than seven Sergeants, about a dozen Corporals and some three hundred Privates. *(Only a skeleton of the 2nd Btn was being left behind, although these men would be recruiting very busily indeed in the near future. That is to say, a further change in military policy was about to mean that more regiments of the British Army – including the 24th – would be expected to have not only a 1st Battalion, but also an <u>operational</u> 2nd Battalion, both being available for active service overseas. So the rate of recruitment for the 24th would soon need to reach considerably higher levels of success than had so far been achieved.)*

The detachment of reinforcements for South Africa had been paraded at 6 am on the 27th April 1808, in full marching order, and with their heavy equipment (mainly tents, ammunition, spare clothing and cooking vessels) being carried in horse-drawn service wagons. They were formed up in three companies, each under the command of a captain. As it happened, Captain STRAWBENZEE was remaining in England, and the company in which Jonas was serving found that they were now under the command of the strangely-named Captain BABY. This unusual name had led to a certain amount of quietly derisive comment in the ranks – but with great diligence towards silence being shown whenever an officer was in hearing.

Colonel MARRIOTT, to the eyes of Jonas a handsome but rather fearsome-looking man with a heavy black moustache and large side-burns, was at the head of the detachment, riding a spirited black gelding. The reinforcements now faced a march of some 20 miles, to take them to Tilbury.

Most of the detachment had been well-used to walking quite large distances in their former lives, and the battalion had made regular shortish route marches during the previous month. On this occasion their marching had a spice of entertainment at times, because the detachment was preceded by a small fife and drum band playing lively airs for much of the time. The men knew some disgraceful words to sing as an accompaniment to some of the tunes. This led to quite a bit of merriment, and most of the men managed this feat of marching well enough, though a small number of men broke down, or developed blisters on their feet, and had to be carried on the service wagons for the latter part of the march. Rather to the surprise of Jonas, a number of women and children also managed to keep up the relatively hard pace, a couple of the women (who were 'sutlers') having their own donkey-carts. (There was also a horse-drawn coach accompanying them, which had been hired to carry the wives of the few officers who were married.)

On arrival at Tilbury, the detachment quickly 'shook out' into its various companies, each having its own officers, and with the most senior officers forming the nucleus of its 'headquarters group'. Arrangements had already been made by Horseguards in London for the transport of the detachment to the Cape of Good Hope, and it had been agreed that the different companies would board three ships then lying at Tilbury, in the berths normally allocated to outward-bound Indiamen, just abreast of Tilbury Fort. All three ships were bound for the East Indies. The largest of them was the Free Trader *Abraham Newland*, a vessel of 613 tons burthen.

Jonas had seen drawings of large ships, but he was still staggered by the ability of the *Abraham Newland* to just completely 'swallow up' whatever was put aboard from the mass of supplies of every sort on the dockside, most as being brought in by horse-drawn carts and wagons – but with lighters also coming along on the seaward side of the ship, bringing yet more stock. Jonas knew that his eyes were everywhere, trying to comprehend all the thousands of things that were going on. The dockside and the ships were so busy that it was a bit as though a sort of human anthill had been suddenly kicked over!

It was on the same dockside that Sergeant-Major Miller, with the active help of his orderlies, managed to clear just sufficient space to line up the three hundred men of the detachment in close order, ready for inspection by Colonel MARRIOTT. Having marched along the files, Colonel MARRIOTT climbed up on to a wagon, with the sergeant-major beside him, and the Colonel then raised his voice to command the men to gather closely around him. He then addressed the detachment. *"Well, men"*, he began, *"There's an awful lot for you to learn in a very short space of time! Pay full attention to what Sergeant-Major Miller here will have to say! He's done this all before, and he'll know what he's talking about! Right, carry on, please, Sergeant-Major!"* and Colonel MARRIOTT turned on his heel and marched up the brow on to the good ship *Abraham Newland,* to quickly disappear below. He was quickly followed down by several of the fellow-officers of his headquarters group, plus two of the wives from the group who had travelled by coach from Chelmsford. Most of the remaining officers and their wives had followed his lead, in principle at least, and were soon boarding the two smaller ships, the *Ocean* and the *Kingston.* Their soldier-servants followed them, carrying the officers' baggage aboard. Only a couple of officers remained on the dockside, watching events.

Sergeant-Major Miller now virtually had the stage to himself. *"RIGHT, LADS!"* he shouted at the top of his powerful voice, *"CLOSE UP TIGHT AROUND ME – MOVE! ...GOOD...NOW LISTEN UP, AND LISTEN GOOD!"*

Having got their full attention, and with the 300 men close-packed around his impromptu dais, he went on, speaking out very clearly, *"For most of you, this will be the first time you've ever seen a ship – let alone gone aboard one! You need to know that life aboard a ship is different to anything that you have ever experienced before! There are all kinds of strange fittings on a ship, especially on the Upper Deck. They are great for tripping up dozy soldiers – so keep yer eyes open at all times! I want you to be as sharp as needles! Wherever there is a doorway leading down into the bowels of the ship, there will be a so-called 'coaming' spelt 'C-O-A-M-I-N-G'. That is, a large sill across the doorway, put there to stop seawater from running down into the inside of the ship – which is exactly where we will be livin', and the last thing we'll want is seawater pouring down and wetting us and all our belongings! What's a 'coaming', Private GREEN?"*

"Er – a sort of door-sill, Sir?"

"And what's it for?"

"To stop seawater from pouring down, Sir."

"Good – glad to see that you're paying attention – even if yer eyes are looking everywhere but at me! – The rest of you had better keep paying close attention too! There's a lot to learn and precious little time to do it in!"

"Nah, you'll have two days to settle in an' to find yer way abaht the ship. She'll then put to sea. Once she does that, most of you will be as sick as cats for at least the first couple of days, due to the rolling and pitching motion of the ship. (He worked his arms for a moment to emphasise what he meant.) *You may think that you are going to die – or even wish you could – though yer won't! Some of you may even be taken sick whilst the ship is still just movin' gently at the dockside 'ere – long afore she gets to the sea proper!"*

"Nah, if you do feel really sick, the best place for you will be lying flat in yer bunks. When you vomit – as most of you will – I want the buckets which will be supplied to you by the sailors to be used. I do NOT want to see vomit honked-up on the deck – Yeah, by the 'deck' I mean the 'floor'. Should you be on the upper deck when you feel yer stomach start to heave – and if the ship is out at sea – I have no objection to a man honking over the side of the ship – but be bloody careful if there are waves washing along the decks – for if you are carried overboard by a wave there really is no chance of being saved – in effect, you'll be a dead man from that moment on! No matter what, always remember the sailor's ancient rule – 'One hand for the ship, and one for me!' You'll also need to remember to be sick on the <u>lee</u> side of the ship, with the wind at yer back – if you vomit facing the wind, you'll end up with the vomit all over you, or, worse, over yer mates! And they may never forgive yer!"

"Nah, a ship is a home which demands respect! It is a perilous place – fer, should one of you manage to set it alight by bein' careless say wiv 'is smoking equipment, or by knocking over a candle, well, there's nowhere for all the people on board to escape to if a fire takes hold! That is, nowhere except the sea – and the sea is a cold, watery place in which men quickly drown – even those men who reckon they can swim! And there's precious few such men in this here detachment!"

"So, we all have to take the greatest care to prevent the least risk of a fire breaking out! We will NOT have our own cooking fires. Our meals will be prepared by the Ship's Cook in the ship's 'galley' – that is, a special place well-protected from any risk of creating a fire. The Cook will be aided by fatigue parties of soldiers. He will use

rations provided from the ship's stores. A little money will be deducted from your pay in recompense. Your meals will be taken in our living accommodation below decks – specifically at the mess tables – which are large flat slabs of wood slung from four ropes fixed to the deck-head – that's what you normally calls 'the ceiling'. There will be one rope to each corner of the table. There will be frayed ropes-ends hanging by each table. As you eat, yer will wipe yer greasy hands on these frayed pieces of rope. Once well-greased, they will be used as wicks for candles which the sailors will make from the tallow they will gather from meats roasted in the galley. Yer cooked meals will be brought to the tables from the galley by fatigue parties, as appointed by yer corporals."

"Yer will each have yer own portion served into yer mess-tin from the large 'fanny'- that's a large metal dish – brought along by yer fatigue party. Yer Corporal will ensure that each man has a fair share."

"Lighting will be by oil-lamps and wrought-iron battle-lanterns, specially designed and fixed to stop them falling over no matter what the ship may be doing – an' she'll probably be standing on her head at times or rolling so that her lee side is well under the water! There will be no candles at all – apart from those protected in these special lanterns. The use of tinder boxes to make a light is strictly forbidden. All fires and lights are to be put out at 8.00 pm – and that includes the smoking of tobacco! You can chew tobacco after 8.00 pm – but you can't bleedin' smoke it! Remember, however, that spitting on the deck is regarded as a heinous crime aboard ship – so use the special buckets provided, which the sailors call 'spitkids'."

"There will be a few so-called 'smoking lamps', closely controlled by the ship's officers. Each will have a slow match beside it, which can be used to light your pipes or cigars – but only at times when the smoking lamps are lit. An' if yer do smoke, be bleedin' careful that you fully extinguish any cigar ends or fully put out the 'dottle' when you empty yer pipes. Put the 'ends' in the fireproof buckets half-filled wiv sand, that are positioned around the ship."

"It will be absolutely essential that the ship shows no lights at all, and that strict silence be maintained at night, so that our position is not revealed to any French privateers which may be lurking about. Sound can carry, and even a small light, such as from a cigar or a pipe, or the lighting of same, can be seen for a great many miles at sea – so just don't risk it!"

"We are at war, and any person found to be breaking these rules will be in for very severe punishment indeed. So, if you see a soldier breaking any of these rules, dissuade him immediately. If he does not respond favourably, and at once, report him to the nearest NCO, Officer or Ship's Officer. I know you may see this as 'snitching' – but it's the lives of all aboard which may be at stake – and, should you fail to report a man who is behaving wrongly, you will be held <u>equally responsible</u> for his crime! In its time, this ship has seen some frightful flogging of men's backs with the Cat o' Nine Tails, laying the flesh open to the bone – and I don't want to have to watch any repetitions o' that – wiv you as its victims! So think on!"

"For reasons which will soon become clear, you will each retain your paper cartridges – and you will do your level best to keep them dry and ready for use. Should there be any spillage of gunpowder – even a small amount – sweep it up immediately, put it in a bag and report wiv it to yer Corporal. Keep th' regulation thirty lead balls fer yer muskets always ready fer use in yer pouches. You must also use great care in regard to

any risk of sparks from yer flints. Keep 'em wrapped in separate folds of soft cloth, as you have already been shown."

"Our kegs of reserve gunpowder will be kept in the ship's own magazine, in the charge of the Ship's Gunner. Should there be insufficient space there, some of the kegs may be stored deep but dry in the ship's hold. Our grenades will also be stored in the ship's hold. Should we come into action against French shipping, the Ship's Gunner will arrange for the release of these stocks, as necessary."

"Whilst we are in northern climes, the ship's crew will maintain metal stoves containing hot coals. These will warm and air our living-spaces. No stove is ever to be touched or moved by a soldier."

"As you will realise, all these factors make the tight control of fires and lighting an even greater necessity. Potentially, each ship is a floating bomb. There have been a number of disasters at sea in recent times – and I do not want any of our three ships to become just another pathetic case of a ship lost with all souls aboard, due to fire and explosion."

"It may be airless at times down inside the ship, especially when we reach warmer climes. However, no 'deadlight' or 'gun-port cover' is ever to be opened by a soldier or passenger. Remember that a vessel may dip her lee side deep into the water – and her lee side may be either her port or her starboard side at different times. Hence this restriction is both to prevent the risk of water from flooding into the ship, and also, at night, for stopping any risk of a light showing inadvertently from the ship and imperilling our security. The opening of deadlights and gun-ports will always be controlled by the ship's officers. They will do their best to ensure a reasonable flow of air through the living-spaces. They may rig special air chutes when the weather becomes hot, to improve the ventilation below-decks – especially once we get into those more southerly and warmer climes!"

"We will have one bunk for every two soldiers, each soldier occupying it at different times. However, there are not enough bunks for the needs of every man, and those men who have no bunks allocated will have to sleep in hammocks. As you'll find, getting in and out of them can be a hard skill to master! You'll each be in a section, and each section will be in the charge of a Corporal. It will be yer Corporal who will tell off each of his men as to where each man will sleep. Yer Sergeants will advise the Corporals as and when necessary."

"Now, hygiene is very important. A contagious illness can spread like wildfire in a ship like this, with so many people crowded together. She may well be fumigated at times during the voyage. If she has men with contagious illness aboard when we approach our destination, we may not be allowed to land until the disease burns itself out. By that time a good many of you will probably be dead!"

"So, to avoid the risk of disease we will clean our berths every morning, and the deck and the woodwork is to be sprinkled with vinegar. Whenever the weather permits it, our bedclothes – straw-mattress, pillow, blanket and rug – will be carried to the upper deck every morning and hung neatly from the rigging to let the air blow through them. The same will apply to the hammocks, where the hammocks themselves will also be aired on the upper deck, in the special nets provided, again weather permitting. The stacked hammocks will provide a shield against small-calibre shot from enemy muskets and guns. Each hammock will be washed once a month.

Every man will wash himself and comb his hair every morning. The ship has pumps, and fatigue parties will be told off to work the pumps, so that every man can wash himself under the stream of seawater brought up by the pumps. Sea-soap will be provided, and a small charge will be made against yer pay in recompense fer it. You will each change an' wash yer undergarments and shirts once a week – or ask one of the women ter wash 'em fer yer. Yer trousers should be washed fortnightly. Yer garments can be hung out to dry during the day, on lines which the sailors will rig. Again, yer Corporals, working wiv the leading seamen, will supervise who does what – and when!"

"You will find that the days at sea can be long. So you will be divided into what are called 'watches'. Each watch will do four hours on and four hours off. During watches you will work with the sailors at various tasks which they will nominate to your noncoms. We'll also regularly practice wiv the sailors how best to defend this ship against the French! There is a real risk of being attacked by French ships and such practice is both urgent and essential! So, much more on that in a minute or two!"

"Nah, the water carried on the ship is not as 'sweet' as might be wished. Its quality will improve during the weeks ahead, and then really start to deteriorate. Rather than drink it freely, you will do better to just take it to the galley and ask the cooks to make tea or soup with it, or else drink wine or beer instead. You will therefore welcome the matter that you will be given a daily issue of small beer."

"You will find that the officers spend most of their time in the 'Cuddy' – that is, a very large cabin at the back end of the ship. The richer passengers will be there too. However. the individual officers and some of the passengers will also have so-called 'cabins' in which to sleep. The cabins will be sited around the sides of the ship. They are actually made up by thin wooden beams and canvas screens dividing one 'cabin' off from another.

All the 'Other Ranks', that is, you lot, will be kept in the middle of the ship. There will be some canvas screens to separate the women and children from you. You are not allowed in the cuddy, nor in the cabins. Perhaps most important of all, you are not allowed on the Quarter-Deck – that's the high bit of the Upper–Deck at the rear end of the ship. Only officers – and men on special duties – are allowed to climb the steps leading up to it. Sentries will be posted at all times to maintain all these separations. The sentries will also stop you from going on to the Upper Deck at all at certain times of the day, or when the weather has got up, so that it is dangerous to be on deck, or when the crew are working on a dangerous task – such as dismounting (or mounting) a top-gallant mast – or when there are French ships in the vicinity, so that total security has become of prime importance. Generally, though, you should try to get up on the Upper Deck for at least an hour or two each day, for the sake of yer health. I do not want ter hear of any man staying below fer days on end – that's a sure way to poor health and illnesses like consumption!"

"Nah, 'Action Stations' is denoted by a roll of drums. If you ever hear it for real, it will probably melt yer guts! Starting tomorrow, you will receive your first training in the defence of this ship against an enemy! In doing so, some of you will begin to learn how to work the big guns in combination with the seamen, whilst others of you will maintain volley-firing with your muskets. Others of you will probably be sent aloft, to snipe at the officers and men on an enemy ship's deck. There will be much more of all that to practice in the coming days."

"Some of yer may think that you know whither we are bound. Let me just remind yer that, should any of yer fall into enemy hands, the only information yer should give is yer name and rank. No soldier should ever disclose where he is bound, nor say from whence he has come, nor give away any information of any sort concerning his duties or the size and operations of his unit."

"Now, I know that some of what I have told yer will be hard to understand. Let me just add that the height of the deck-head – what yer might call the ceiling – is generally only 5ft 10 ins above the lower deck, and in some places it will be as little as 4½ ft. So the word is, 'Watch yer Head!' It's surprising how much it hurts when you crack yer head on a deck-beam! There'll be times when you're concentrating on lifting yer leg over a 'coaming' when passing through a doorway, and you'll forget about keeping yer head lowered. Then you'll get such a crack on it that you'll think the end of the world has come! Just remind us, Private Green – what's a 'coaming'?"

"Er - A sort of large door-sill, Sir!"

"Good lad! "What else? Well, I might just mention that each transport has a nurse, who is provided with bedding to accommodate any sick or injured members of the crew or passengers, including us. Like the youngest of you soldiers, she is paid at the princely rate of 6d per day. To see her, you'll have to report to the M.O. first, o' course."

"Right lads, that's it fer now. There's certainly a huge amount to take in, and me and yer sergeants and corporals will be talking to you more over the next few days, as we settle down to life aboard. We'll now set about boarding these here ships. To do so, we'll first ha' ter get back into our companies. There will be Corporals posted aboard to direct you to yer bunks or hammock positions, as appropriate. Good Luck! STAY VERY SHARP! Nah, BACK INTO YER RESPECTIVE COMPANIES – MOVE!"

In fact, as the Sergeant-Major had spotted, there were indeed a myriad of impressions which had struck Jonas – now about to be supplemented by the orderly files of red-coated soldiers boarding the three ships moored around him. Also the growing 'farmyard look' on the decks of those ships, where sheep were already installed in one of the rowboats, held in by netting stretched over the top, and where hens were held in coops. Clearly, a lot of fresh meat was being carried – he could see it in the form of sheep, goats and their kids, geese, piglets, chickens and other fowl. Stores of every imaginable shape and size lay all over the dockside – barrels of all sizes seemed to predominate – with teams of civilian workers and seamen busily getting everything aboard the ships, using cranes and slings to hoist the heavier and bulkier items and wheeling smaller but heavy items in hand-trucks of every size and description. The carts of two of the women sutlers were also taken on board – though, to the distress of the two women, not the donkeys to pull them!

There was also the very unhappy sight of groups of the women camp-followers of the detachment, wailing and begging to be allowed on board this or that of the ships. Sadly, as had been impressed upon the men of the detachment before they had even begun the march from Chelmsford, regulations stated that they were allowed only six women per company of 100 men, and not more than two children per woman, and the names of the women who were allowed to board these ships had already been drawn by ballot before they had left Chelmsford. Despite those facts, a substantial number of the other women and their children had taken the risk of accompanying their men down to

Tilbury. Clearly, the officers were sticking closely to the regulations, and they were actually allowing about twelve women from the camp followers – all allegedly wives – and the same number of children, to board each of the three ships in which the detachment of the 24th was to voyage. Unhappily, this left quite a number of women and children standing on the dockside, utterly bereft, as each of 'their' particular unlucky soldiers, his sad goodbyes said and his face set like stone, walked heavily up the gang-plank with its awkward transverse bars, on to the ship, keeping woodenly to his place amidst the men of his file – though tears were running down the cheeks of most of these men. The poor women, thus abandoned to their fate, screamed, pleaded and wailed desperately – but completely in vain.

Many pitied them, including the officers as well as the rank and file, but nobody dared do any more except to leave a few pounds and shillings from the 24th funds, to be shared between the women. None knew what the fate of the women would be – though it was to be expected that quite a few of them would eventually latch on to this or that 'time-expired' soldier returning by ship from service abroad (or to a man discharged early due to wounds or sickness), and become his common-law wife. Others might well end up in prostitution….Few had the ability to return to their parish of birth for succour, for the native parishes of these women were mainly to be found far away, in Ireland, Scotland, Wales or the remoter parts of England – and some even in the Americas, the West Indies or such other places – particularly in the case of those women who were the daughters of soldiers who had previously served abroad with the Army. The same great variety in birthplaces applied to the children of these women.

A member of the crew overheard Jonas talking quietly to another redcoat about the sad case of the women and children, and approached him, *"Excuse me, bor – but if I might make so bold – do I hear a Suffolk accent there?"* Glancing round, Jonas saw a well-built man with a shock of fair hair, heavy sideburns and twinkling blue eyes surrounded by the typical crow's feet of a sailor, set in a weather-beaten face. He was probably about thirty-five years old and dressed in a rather worn blue uniform coat with pinchbeck buttons and a white shirt, with white trousers and small black shoes. He looked open and honest, and Jonas took to him at once.

"Well, yes," said Jonas – *"I do come from the 'Land of the Hodmedods' and you'll hear precious few Suffolk accents from amongst my mates – who mostly come from Warwickshire, right on the other side of England."*

"Well, there's a thing," replied the sailor, *"I come from Ipswich in 'Silly Suffolk', and my name's Bill Hitchings – and I'm the fourth mate of this tub. It's great to hear a soft Suffolk accent like yours – reminds me of home, somehow – and I ain't bin there fer many years!"*

"Yes,", said Jonas, *"I know exactly what you mean about that feeling of 'home'. My mates in the company are fine – but – as I just said – they're mostly from Warwickshire and, naturally enough, they tend to stick together. So, it's great for me to hear your soft Suffolk accent, too! By the way, my name is Jonas Green, and I actually come from Great Bricett, which is quite near to Ipswich. You might know of Great Bricett? I'm a country-boy, and I know nuthin' about ships like this monster – can you tell me and my pals here something about her?"*

"Aye – certainly! Oh, Great Bricett – yes, that's near Somersham, ain't it? I had a cousin who lived there once, a Mrs Barnes, she were, a real motherly sort with splendid

big breasts – I liked her a lot…Well now, large ships like this here 'Abraham Newland'…I started learnin' about ships when I were just a young lad – working in the Barnard Shipyard at Ipswich, a'building East Indiamen.[3] They were fine ships, actually even larger and better-built than this one. You've probably noted the rich smell of cut Scottish pine still coming off her beams – because she's only two years old. But ships built of oak and elm, like those I used to work on at Ipswich, last much better. Knowing how they're put together – that's how I came to serve in ships, first as a Carpenter and nowadays as a junior officer, 'climbing up the hawsehole', at long last, I might say".

"Unfortunately", he continued, *"I ain't got long to talk just now, because we'll be casting off just as soon as the lading is complete. Our ships are going to form a convoy together. These ships lading alongside us are* (pointing one by one) *the 'Ocean' and the 'Kingston'. We talk of the 'Abraham Newland' as being of 600 tons burthen, the 'Ocean' as being of 560 tons burthen, and the 'Kingston' as being of only 400 tons. The bigger the ship, the more goods she carries and the heavier the guns she bears. As you can see, you and yer comrades are aboard the biggest one – though some of the East Indiamen are much bigger than her – 800 tons burthen not being exceptional and some even weighing-in at 1,000 tons and more! You'll doubtless learn a lot more about the guns of the 'Abraham Newland' in due course – 'cos some of you will have to help us to work 'em!"*

He went on, *"Anyway, because there's always danger from the French ships based on the south side of the English Channel, we're going to join other ships coming out of Portsmouth and the whole convoy is going to be escorted by the frigate HMS 'Magicienne' of the* Royal Nav*y – for a goodly part of the way south – including our passage down the English Channel and then on down past the west coast of France. It'd be better if there were at least two frigates or maybe even three protecting us, because, as just one example, the French corsairs which come out from St Malo are very fast and skilful at cutting out ships from convoys, and they sometimes run rings round single frigates trying to keep them at bay! However, the Royal Navy always seems to be short of enough ships to do the many jobs which face 'em. So, we may well have to defend ourselves to a large extent!"*

"Now, most of the ships will be bound direct for India, but these three are due to split off from the convoy and to head into Capetown (which, thanks to the 1st Battalion of your regiment and other regiments) is now again in British hands. Once there, these three ships will drop off yourselves and a few of the other passengers whom we are carrying – before we sailors set to sea again, to complete our voyage to India. Hope that all makes some sense – I see that your officers and sergeants have already imparted some of the shipboard rules and regs to you, with plenty more to come – Now, however, I must be about my duties! So long, Jonas – I'll see you again at some stage, I'm sure – for the voyage will probably take several months to accomplish!" A quick, strong handshake, a twinkle of his bright blue eyes, and he was gone.

In some ways the first three or four days at sea were ones which Jonas *preferred* to forget. Although he was not actually sea-sick, he had a hard knot in his stomach which came on soon after the ship began to gently pitch and roll as she met the open sea. The

---

[3] Author's note: Barnards had moved to Deptford in about 1800 – which may have been the cause of Bill Hitchings leaving their employment.

majority of the people on board – be they soldiers, sailors or passengers – were soon stretched out everywhere, some lying helplessly in their own vomit and with a powerful stench arising both from them and also from the iron buckets which were strategically placed all around the ship. These were all-too-quickly filled by those who were actively sick, but who managed a shred of self-control in not just spewing up unconstrainedly. 'Tween-decks, the smell of the vomit, which was aggravated by the ever-present stench from the bilges and the other shipboard smells, was enough to turn the strongest stomach, and Jonas nearly fell victim to it several times. The seamen did brilliantly in coping with emptying and replacing the buckets with clean ones, and in clearing up the vomit on the decks.

Jonas found that he did best when he was out in the fresh air of the upper deck, and that constantly nibbling whatever food he could manage, especially sweet things (rather than savouries) helped him to 'survive'. Lying down at times also helped, and having had the sheer luck to be allocated a bunk right on the centre-line of the ship, and more or less amidships (*so that the rolling and pitching of the ship were far less exaggerated than they would have been at one side, and/or at the bow or stern*) was a real boon. Indeed, by the fourth day, the knot in his stomach had eased off, and he actually began to enjoy the feeling of being at sea, with his legs braced against the steady pitch and roll of the ship. Soon he would really have his 'sea-legs', like a hardened sailor, and his full appetite would return. His good fortune in just happening to be on the upper deck on the second day also meant that he saw the magnificent sight of the frigate HMS *Magicienne*, with her towering 'pyramid' of white sails, as she imperiously closed with the convoy to 'speak' with the Commodore by 'loud hailer'. Thereafter, the frigate swiftly eased away to the south, and subsequently stayed about fifteen leagues off, still near enough to be in signalling distance by semaphore flags, but taking a parallel route to that of the convoy, and constantly ready to repel any French privateers threatening the convoy from the southward side of the English Channel.

Jonas was lucky that his new-found friend, Bill Hitchings, the fourth mate, had the time and the inclination to keep him informed of much of what was going on. Thus, during one evening, Jonas learnt that the blue light repeatedly shining from the *Magicienne* was a signal that her Captain was becoming increasingly dissatisfied with the slow rate of the convoy through the water, and angry that the ships would not close up on each other as much as he wanted – so that his task in protecting them from the risk of a French ship getting in amongst them, and cutting off a straggler was being made ever more difficult. As Bill well knew, the captains of the merchantmen did not like to sail their ships close together for fear of accidental collisions, especially at night when all the vessels were 'blacked-out'. Also, unlike the heavily-manned naval ships, the merchantmen tended to be under-manned with 'topmen', so that it was easier to keep up just a slow rate of progress rather than to be constantly trimming and re-trimming the sails, to catch every passing wind.

Somehow, it was quite entertaining to know a little about the bickering that was going on by signal between the smart and alert naval captain, and the sturdy and imperturbable captains of the merchantmen, who were all highly experienced seamen.

One thing which Jonas did find difficult to adjust to was his use of the ship's lavatories – known as 'the heads' because they were right up in the bows. For the 'Other Ranks', such as himself, a visit to the toilet meant a clamber right up into those bows, which were often plunging heavily up and down in the sea – to find one of the special 'bridged holes', and there to perch uncomfortably with one's trousers down until the job was done. In a really lively sea, one might have sea-spray splashing and soaking one. And, in heavy weather, it was often deemed too dangerous to go into the heads at all. So, there were heavy iron buckets stationed on the deck which could be used instead. The troops tended to use these to urinate in, at all times and conditions of the sea. The downside was that the buckets needed to be emptied over the lee side at frequent intervals, and this duty (which was sometimes highly dangerous as well as disgusting) was shared by fatigue parties of soldiers and ordinary seamen, with the seamen taking a lead when the weather was lively, usually by rigging 'lifelines' for the men involved, and by applying ropes to the buckets, to stop both men and buckets from being lost overboard. Jonas only had to participate in these fatigue parties a few times, and he was profoundly grateful for the clever skills displayed by the sailors whenever he did so.

He later discovered that there were special copper funnels situated on each gallery at the stern of the ship, to provide far less 'exposed' and much more convenient lavatories for the officers and passengers. Such are the privileges of rank…

By the fourth day, Bill told him that the convoy was about to round the Peninsular of Brittany (which was by now well out of sight to the south-east), and that they would next head far out into the Atlantic, keeping well clear of the dreaded Bay of Biscay which formed a large part of the western coastline of France. Not only was the Bay swarming with hostile French ships, but it was also renowned for its heavy storms and its frightening 'lee shores' which had wrecked a great many good ships.

There tended to be adverse westerlies blowing across the North Atlantic, against which the convoy would have to drive southwards, before encountering the strong North Easterly Trade winds once the ships reached the latitude of North Africa. The ships would use these winds to make their way right across the Atlantic, until they came across the sea-birds called 'gannets', and until 'trunk weed' was beginning to appear in the sea that the ships were passing through. These would be signs that the ships were on the 'Cape Bank' (that is, approaching the South American Coast) and that it was time to radically change course almost left-about but with a southerly element, keeping the South Easterly Trade Winds abeam, and hopefully to pick up the Westerlies a little further south and to use them to head eastwards for the Cape of Good Hope and thereafter (for a part of the convoy) on to the East Indies….. The whole voyage might last anything from 3 to 5 months from England to the Cape.

"My God!" said Jonas, *"Do we have sufficient water and food to last us for so long? There must be at least three hundred people on this ship!"*

"Oh, aye!" replied Bill, *"I've never heard of the water actually running out – though it's always possible that we might have to ration its use towards the end of a voyage. Certainly, as a precaution, it's the practice to regularly record the volume remaining as the later stages of a voyage are reached. Remember that we take at least forty tons of water aboard before we set out – that's about 50,000 gallons – and it comes straight out of the River Thames or wherever we may be – so it sure b'ain't the sweetest water in the world! But I 'spect you've already found that out!"*

"Yeah – it's pretty foul, right enough!" said Jonas, *"It gave me the gut-rot for a couple of days when I tried to drink it 'neat', so to speak! Now, me and my mates just get the cooks to make tea from it – or use it for cooking vegetables and in making soups and*

stews. Actually, call me a fool if you loike, but I reckon it's somehow beginning to become clearer!"

"Nay – you're nobody's fool Jonas Green – sure enough the water does become clearer as it ages, probably because it's so foul that it begins to ferment a bit as it gets older and that seems to purify it. There's a weird sort of stench coming off from the drinking water sometimes, when we go down to the huge butts of it deep down in the ship. We have what's called a 'dipstick', with a marked scale inbuilt into it, and the level of the water against this scale shows how much water is left in each butt. The fumes coming off the water have made me quite 'woozy' once or twice, and I've been glad to get back on deck, to clear me poor ol' head! Incidentally, some of the more experienced and wealthy of the gentleman passengers provide themselves with special filtering equipment before they come on board, and only use water which they have themselves filtered."

"Oho!" said Jonas, "Maybe there should be arrangements to do that for everybody – or at least for the officers and seamen of the ship! How do you and your lot actually get on?"

"Well, we tend to wait until the water sweetens before we use it much – and we're also wary of it at the later stages, when it starts to really deteriorate for ever after!" We carry a lot o' wine and small beer, and even brandy – so we tend to drink those sort of things instead – though we ha' to be careful, because to report for duty drunk is a flogging offence! You'll likely see various members o' the crew being flogged at the gratings for the offence of drunkenness as the voyage goes on – and I usually feels sorry for 'em, because it's all-too-easy to get well pissed by drinking the beer – and the hot weather of tropical seas can make a bloke remarkably thirsty! And drinking heavily can lead to a man becomin' an alcoholic. Incidentally, we also drink quite a lot of lime-juice which is a good thirst-quencher, and is said to keep down the risk o' scurvy."

"What the heck is 'scurvy', Bill?"

"I'll tell you more next time we speak – but it's high time for my watch and the 2ⁿᵈ Mate hates me being even a second late in relieving him – he can be a right sod! So cheerio for now, young Jonas!", and off he sped.

As the days went on, Jonas found that the rations were neither plentiful nor good. Officially, the weekly rations per man consisted of 2lb pork, 4lb beef, 2lb peas and ½ lb cheese, together with biscuits and butter. However, it was only in the early part of the voyage that fresh meat was issued. The 'farmyard' of animals on the upper deck swiftly declined in numbers, and it was clear that most of the fresh meat ended up on the plates of the officers and paying passengers. Soon the meat that men like Jonas were getting was mostly salt beef, preserved in casks. There were strong rumours that there were always rackets going on between the pursers of the ships, the dockyard 'maties' and (sometimes) the military quartermasters and the paymasters. Seemingly, the pursers were rather poorly paid, and the merchantile company was inclined to overlook them 'feathering their own nests' somewhat, to the detriment of the crews and the people being carried in the ships – especially the 'brutal and licentious soldiery'. Certainly, some of the salted beef and pork seemed to have been kept in cask for a remarkably long time – and, in the plain sight of some of the troops and seamen, and to the obvious discomfiture of the Purser, the Ship's Surgeon openly and roundly condemned two barrels of it as being totally unfit for human consumption! Those particular barrels were cast overboard under the Surgeon's eagle eye, with the Purser looking as mournful as if he were losing two dear friends!

Yet, strangely, there were also occasional 'delicacies' served up by the cooks, which they said had been passed out to them from the varied stocks maintained on board by the Purser. These included Essence of Malt, and Essence of Spice, oranges and lemons, peas and potatoes, onions, portable soup, port wine, sherry, flour, sugar, arrowroot, groats, pepper and rice – virtually all of which could be used to improve the flavour or constituency of the main course and/or of the desserts, as being prepared by the cooks.

There was indeed a 'galley' on the upper deck, cleverly built of bricks and metal so that it created no fire risk to the ship's timbers. The smells coming from the galley were often delightful – especially if one had been out in the fresh air of the upper deck, and one was beginning to feel a bit peckish. There was a breakfast at about 8.00 am, sometimes a cold snack available at noon, dinner at 2 pm, tea at 6 pm and supper at 8 pm. Yet, even this, sometimes seemed scarcely enough! The cooking of meals was supervised by the Ship's Cook – who was a highly emotional man and suspected of being a covert homosexual – and one who stood no nonsense from anybody! He was aided by soldiers of the detachment. Officially, they were regarded as being on fatigue duty. In practice, however, some men were gifted and quite dedicated to the task – and the Ship's Cook selected the types that he wanted – and shunned those he definitely didn't! So, men of a certain kind were almost permanently on the Cook's rosta.

They certainly needed to know what they were doing, for the motion of the ship was often 'lively', and handling saucepans of boiling water, or of meat coming out of an oven and spitting hot fat, were highly dangerous activities when at sea. The cooking facilities had 'fids' strategically placed to stop saucepans and the like from toppling over, but not always successfully so. Unsurprisingly, when the ship encountered really rough weather, cooking was regarded as simply too dangerous, and only cold meals would be served on board until the weather improved again. Such 'cold food' times were miserable for all concerned – especially as the men on the upper deck – particularly those on fatigue duty - often became wet and chilled on such days!

Jonas was just glad that he only had to act as a soldier-cook a few times. Perhaps he was too clearly a heterosexual to be truly acceptable to the Ship's Cook. He felt like a complete ignoramus amongst the 'regular' lads, who were steadily becoming well-skilled under the expert direction of the Cook. Even so, the small grounding in cooking which Jonas received, added to what he had previously learnt at the knees of his mother and his step-mother, would definitely help him in his future career as a soldier on campaign.

By this time some of the soldiers were learning how to aid the seamen in working the so-called 'great guns' of the ship. There were twenty of these guns, arranged around the gun-deck, most firing 'on the broadside', but with two forward firing - the so-called 'bow-chasers'- and two 'stern-chasers' to cover the rear. They were all 18 pounders, firing iron balls of that weight, and with 'flint-stock' firing mechanisms. (There were also seven 9 pounders on the quarter-deck.) There were so-called 'shot-garlands' near each gun, in which nestled balls for immediate use in each cannon. It was said that there were 30 rounds per gun carried here and there in the ship – making for a total of well over 600 balls available to be fired!

The gunpowder was kept in the magazine deep down in the ship. There were boys called 'Powder Monkeys' who wore special soft slippers to avoid the risk of accidentally creating a spark, and who carried the powder up from the magazine to the guns in small-sized bags, the best bags apparently being made of silk. The Gunner and his aides, who worked in the magazine, also wore special slippers designed to minimise any risk of creating a spark as the men moved about. Jonas only got to see into the magazine once, a strange, ghostly place in which the lighting was created by candles shining through glass from the outside.

All the men who were fit enough to stand had been paraded on the Upper Deck on the second day after embarkation, and appointed to their watches and duties in helping to run the ship. Jonas had hoped to be one of those chosen to work the guns – he liked the look of the discipline required to gain the exact rhythm and precision required for a successful gun-team, and hoped to learn to be a part of it – However, Sergeant-Major Miller had other ideas! Presumably, he had been talking matters over with Colonel MARRIOTT, who, with other officers of the 24th was watching events from the quarterdeck. On the first day they exercised, Jonas found himself in the ranks of soldiers practising volley-firing (without actual discharge of their weapons) from the Upper Deck. However, at the next exercise, and when the ship was already well out to sea, and with the officers again watching events closely, matters suddenly changed completely.

"Corporal Jones!" Sergeant-Major Miller had bellowed, *"You will take Privates Green, Silver and Simmons to the 'fighting-top' of the mainmast! Yes, you men will have to learn how to climb the ratlines! The first bit is exciting enough, as you'll have to step outboard of the ship – Yes – that does mean stepping out over the sea! Remember what I said about 'One hand for me and one for the ship! Make sure you always climb up on the weather side – and never on the lee side! You'll climb up about thirty feet, like you've already seen the sailors doin'. However, UNLIKE them, you can then use the 'Lubber's Hole', to climb INSIDE the ratlines, to haul yerselves up into the fighting top. DON'T try to climb wiv yer muskets. There's two seamen already told off to be in the fightin' top – yer can see their heads peerin' down at us now – and they'll drop a hempen line to which yer muskets can be tied, and the seamen will haul 'em up aloft for you. Corporal Jones, make sure each of yer men – and yerself – has 30 balls of shot wiv 'im, , a couple of good flints and thirty cartridges. In combat, yer duty will be to snipe at all and anybody on an enemy ship's deck – especially men in orficers' uniforms in the waist of the enemy ship, or on its quarterdeck.*

For now, however, I'll have men posted up in the bows, an' they'll set targets afloat in the sea when I give 'em the order. These targets will be old empty barrels. For practice, you'll be able to fire at 'em as they float past the ship and start to drift away astern. IS THAT ALL CLEAR?"

"Er, yes, Sir." Said Corporal Jones – but Jonas thought the Corporal looked ashen-faced at the prospect.

"Right – Up you four go!" said Sergeant-Major Miller, *"Leave yer muskets piled at the foot of the mainmast fer the moment. I'll have 'em sent up when you are all in the top – and the rest of you men watch Corporal Jones and his three men closely, 'cos some of youse will be told off to mount to the fighting tops of the foremast and others of you to the mizzen mast, in just a few minutes. That'll test yer guts! RIGHT, Jonesie – GO!"*

Under the direction of the Corporal, Jonas and his mates quickly piled their arms by the mainmast. They were by then several yards away from Sergeant-Major Miller, and Corporal Jones was very quietly whispering, *"The bastard – he knows that I hate heights, and last night in the Sergeants Mess he promised me that he'd never send me up a mast. Oh, shit! I must have upset him somehow! I'm sorry that you're involved in this mess lads!"*

Now, the highest that Jonas could ever remember climbing before in his life was a ladder taking him to the top of a haystack that he and others labourers had once built on a farm. But that ladder had been quite steady – not like this ship where the whole structure was rolling and pitching about, and where the taut shrouds and ratlines gave forth their own weird musical notes as the stresses and strains came and went on them. He never knew why, but he now saw that the Corporal was trembling uncontrollably and, frightened though he felt himself to be, he suddenly found himself saying, *"How about I lead the way, Corp? Let Silver and Simmons go next. You can stand beside the ratlines to see that we're "doing it right", so to speak – and then bring up the rear yourself."*

"Yeah. Good thinking, Greenie. Off you go then mate!"

And, rather surprised at his own audacity, Jonas found himself swinging outboard on to the tarry ratlines, holding on tight with both hands. It took a distinct effort of will to begin climbing, though it was not actually difficult once he started. He remembered that his father's advice in such situations was, *'Never look down, but only at your face-level with occasional quick glances slightly above you, just to ensure that you b'ain't about to bash your head on somethin'! Above all, NEVER LOOK DOWN!'*

However, Jonas simply couldn't stop himself looking down at the sea now and again, as he continued to climb – and it was indeed terrifying, because he had started off at 'hull height' (about 15 ft above the waves), and he had another 30 ft or so to go! A factor which he hadn't really anticipated was the way in which the rolling of the ship was causing him to be pressed hard against the ratlines at one moment, and then be almost thrown off into space as the ship rolled back, and when it was suddenly on the point of commencing its return roll! He promptly realised that he must just hold on very tight at that particular moment in the sequence, and keep on climbing hard in-between times. He was just lucky that the rolling from side to side, and the pitching of the ship back and forth was slow and gentle on that day – both could be serious dangers to be faced in more lively weather. He also began to appreciate why the weather side was to be preferred – he'd have been doing a lot more 'hanging-on' if he'd tried to climb the lee side, which overhung the sea far more.

Once he'd stared climbing it seemed little time before he was approaching the 'lubber's hole. This was the most frightening time of all, for the ratlines actually extended outwards into space here! To go on climbing them, would lead to one finding oneself taking one's full bodyweight on one's arms, and hanging with one's back facing down towards the waves. Jonas had seen the seamen casually carrying out this manoeuvre day after day, but it seemed to be far too risky for him to contemplate.

"Keep on coming! It's fine up here, Redcoat!" said a hidden and near-at-hand voice suddenly, taking Jonas all aback.

"Bloody hell!" cried Jonas, sweat pouring off him, *"You damn nearly made me lose my grip! Oh, my God!"*

But, in a twinkling, Jonas realised that the voice was from one of the seamen in the fighting-top just above his head, and that the man looking down and talking reassuringly to him.

"Oh, Wow! Yes – sorry! Um – What the Hell do I do next?!" said Jonas, his voice trembling and quite high-pitched with fear.

"Just reach through the shrouds right in front of you with one hand, to grasp the internal set of ratlines. Then swing your body through the outboard ratlines, and step on to the internal ratlines. These slope inwards, which make it easy. As you do so, transfer the grip of your second hand, to match the first one. Your body-weight will then be totally transferred to the internal ratlines. From there you'll easily be able to climb just a little more upwards and pull yourself up through the hole and up onto this platform, to make youself nice and comfortable here…That's the way!... Hurrah, you've done it!"

Jonas was soon followed by his two mates, with the seamen again prompting them in their movements, and, following on his men's heels, an ashen-faced Corporal Jones. As a matter of fact, the Corporal found it very hard to commit himself across the bit of space to the lubber's hole, and Silver and Simmons actually climbed back down a bit, to give him moral and practical support.

"Thanks, you lot!" he said, as he reached the sanctuary of the fighting-top, *"I'm getting too bleedin' old for japes like this! It'll be big toddies for all three of you if we ever get down safe again, and are free to visit the wet canteen! Now, I suppose we'd better introduce ourselves to these seamen here, get them to haul up our muskets and get ourselves ready for target-sniping at the barrels – once the other files have climbed into the fighting-tops in the foremast and the mizzen, so they can shoot too – Look, they're climbing up the other masts, afore and abaft o' us, and comin' level to our height, right now!"*

And, indeed, so other redcoats were. Sadly, even as they looked, one of the soldiers ascending the foremast was caught by the ship staggering in mid-roll, caused by an unusually heavy wave passing underneath her – and, with a terrifying scream he was thrown clean off the ratlines to plunge into the sea thirty-five feet or so below. So far as anyone could see, he never surfaced again. Private Josiah Smith would be the first of a number of men to be entered in the record-book of this voyage as 'D/D' (Discharged Dead).

So, it was with something of a gulp in the throat, and thereafter with rather heavy hearts that Corporal Jones and his men carried out their sniping that day from the well-designed and protected fighting-top – once they'd found how best to manage their muskets in the rather confined, though surprisingly secure-feeling space. To avoid accidentally hitting each other, a lot of teamwork and system was needed in swinging the long and heavy weapons about when loading and firing them. It was helpful that the weapons could be braced against this or that part of the structure of the fighting-top when pointing them downwards, helping for steadiness in aiming and also mitigating against one's stomach-churning fear of the dizzying height – and Corporal Jones and his men certainly had a commanding view! Under the 'old soldier' prompting of the Corporal, they adjusted the lengths of the slings of their muskets, and then kept their shoulders well tucked into the slings, to minimise the risk of the weapons accidentally falling out of their hands. They could well imagine the choler and bitter invective of Sergeant-Major Miller should a musket crash down on the deck, maybe hitting some poor sod as it fell – or, worse, splash straight down into the sea and be lost forever overboard! There was a heavy fine for such losses of equipment.

Jonas reckoned that he was quite a good shot, and his efforts that day caused splashes all around the target barrels as they passed quickly 'down the sides' of the ship, to rapidly vanish astern. However, Jonas reckoned that he had no actual hits – certainly, none of the barrels 'burst asunder' – and the splashes around the barrels seemed to be random rather than being 'grouped' in any way. He therefore felt that the problem of 'no hits' was mostly due to the inaccuracy of the musket itself, undoubtedly aggravated by the rolling and the slow pitching of the ship and the 'bobbing up and down' of the floating targets under the influence of the waves. They were very 'difficult' targets.

The Corporal and the two other redcoats in the fighting-top apparently had similarly erratic firing results to his own, and he and the other young soldiers had an interesting debate with the Corporal about the advantages and disadvantages of using one of the new-fangled rifles, as opposed to the musket. The seamen became interested and also joined in this discussion. The seamen felt that rifles would never become popular in ships because they were too complex, took too long to load, and could be 'finicky'. What naval ships wanted was more like a 'blunderbuss' – a reliable, tough weapon, not too demanding in setting it up to fire – and with a great blast of shot fanning out from it – ideal for felling a rush of the enemy in close-quarter combat. Thus chatting together the redcoats and seamen started to become pals, and what might have been a long watch in the fighting-top passed off quite quickly – and, in the event, having become reasonably accustomed to the height, climbing down (with their muskets being lowered separately by line) was not as bad as might have been feared.

During the next days, Corporal Jones was frequently ordered to lead his little team aloft, and they soon became inured to making the climb. The main disadvantage was that the tar on the ratlines fouled and stained their uniforms, and was the very devil to clean off. So far as they were allowed, they therefore left their best uniforms and gear on their bunks, and wore a mixture of their second-best and/or fatigue uniforms. All the practice was useful – but Jonas found that it was only by the greatest good fortune that he ever hit the odd target barrel floating past. He began to wonder how he might fare with enemy seamen or troops actually in his sights, should he ever become involved in an actual battle at sea.

These exercises at least served to break the monotony of sailing day after day, with only the vagaries of the weather to distinguish one day from the next. However, the weather was certainly becoming warmer as they headed south, and flying fish, about the size of pilchards, and sometimes manifesting in hundreds, were now often to be seen. Pigeon-like 'Pintado' birds with mottled backs and wings, and dark-blue heads also sometimes put in an appearance.[4] So, too, swallow-like stormy petrels – otherwise known as Mother Carey's Chickens, and also the occasional albatross, sometimes having the enormous wing-span of 7 ft or more. Sharks could also be discerned in the water now and again, well visible from a height due to the transparency of the water, and with their presence sometimes betrayed to a man at deck-level by a dorsal fin breaking the surface.

When the soldiers were confined below decks, as they often were, the boredom could become very oppressive. Some men took to playing card-games of various sorts.

---

[4] The name 'Pintado' probably coming from the Portugese word 'pinta' for a fleck or a spot.

They were not supposed to play for money, but a discreet amount of gambling certainly went on. Jonas, being well aware that some of the men involved were definitely well-skilled card-sharps, and that some men were already becoming heavily indebted to them, kept his distance from the 'card-schools'. Some men went in for wood-carving and model-making, using off-cuts of wood which they begged from the Ship's Carpenter, and spent many hours quietly working away at their self-imposed tasks – often showing remarkable skills. For some of the off-cuts of finer wood, Jonas suspected that certain 'favours' were expected by the Ship's Carpenter, either in money or in kind.

He was not strongly drawn to any of these activities – but he did find interest in the few games of 'Liar-dice' which were being played. These used Poker-dice, having faces running from 9 through 10, Jack, Queen and King, to Ace. The dice were thrown by the first player, but covered with a hand-shielded cup as they settled, so that only the thrower could observe how they lay after finishing their tumbling. The thrower would then make a 'call' – usually (though not invariably) a fairly low one, and pass the cup along with the dice fully-hidden – and the next player would have to make the mental decision as to whether or not the call was a 'fair one', i.e. under-called, exact, or overcalled.

If he accepted the dice under the cup, he then had to raise the call by at least one level, before passing the cup on. Before making his call, he was allowed to peek at the dice, and to throw as many of the six dice as he wanted – or even none at all. However, if the former player had called (say) "Four Aces", he would be most unwise to throw two (or more) dice and to call "Five Aces" – because the odds against throwing two Aces were very large. He might just get away with throwing only one dice (thus maintaining the impression that the four Aces were truly there) and by making a call of (say) "Four Aces, Jack", i.e. raising the call from the implied "Four Aces, Nine." (and also leaving a bit of scope for the next player to raise the call again).

However, if the next (third) player had formed the impression that the four Aces were never there when the cup had left the first player, there was a very good chance that the second player would be 'seen', by the third player lifting up the cup to expose the dice. There was also the matter to consider that the next player would have very little latitude, because the calls would be rapidly approaching the maximum possible of "Five Aces", when the cup would inevitably have to be lifted – revealing whether or not the dice had truly reached that highest level – or whether they were just a so-called 'bag of nails', with hardly even a pair amongst them! So there were a lot of 'probabilities' to consider.

Graft on to this general matter the little courtesies normally customary amongst the players – such as leaving just a narrow margin of 'hope' for the next player rather than always calling 'up to the hilt' – and then the ability of some players to lie fantastically well, without the least sign of their 'wickedness' on their countenances, sometimes coupled with the ability to pull off the most fantastic 'coups' and/or enormous luck in their throwing – and the counterpart of the downside in other people of regularly 'disbelieving' fantastic calls – but only to find all-too-often that the previous player had more than met his claim – and one had quite a game of bluff and counterbluff to while away the hours! It was also a game in which one could study very deeply and learn about the characters of one's fellow-soldiers – over and above the satisfaction of the process of the mental calculation of the odds involved with every throw of the dice (that is, provided that one was reasonably successful!).

Certainly, such factors led Jonas to regularly join in one or other of the 'schools' which grew up. There was little money involved, because they played for little slips of wood they had made (about the size of modern-day 'Swan Vesta' matches). Every time a player 'lost a life' by challenging a call unsuccessfully – or by himself being successfully challenged and defeated by another player – he took a slip of wood, which he placed in front of him. When a player gained a third match, he contributed a half-penny into the 'kitty' in the middle of the table, and it was 'Matches In!' for everybody – much to the relief of any of the other players who had two slips of wood standing in front of them by that time! The kitty went to buy drinks in the wet canteen, increasing the jollity and sociability of the whole group.

One day, a sergeant of the 'Light Bobs' company, whom they knew only by sight, idly wandered over and watched them playing for a while. He was a very impressive-looking man, with a shock of white hair surrounding a bald pate, and with a fresh, innocent-looking face. *"Would you fellers mind if I joined in for a little while?"* he asked mildly. *"Fine by us, Sarge!"* they chorused, as one man – but only to begin to quickly regret their decision, for the sergeant swiftly began to 'take them to the cleaners'. It was particularly bad for Herbie Johnson, the player sitting immediately downstream of the sergeant, because poor Herbie went into the 'timber business' in a big way! The school thought they were mostly good at the game, but the sergeant beat them hands down. When he made the most outrageous calls – and was seen – the dice would be more than there! When he looked most normal and innocent, he would be merrily passing on the most appalling rubbish! On each round, one or two slips of wood would soon be lying in front of virtually every player – especially poor Herbie – but almost never in front of the sergeant. Every time that it was "Matches In!", and the sergeant had no wood at all in front of him, he would leap to his feet, shouting out, *"I'm a virgin – I'm a virgin!"*. More like a bloody old whore, Jonas thought, sourly. However, Jonas had to relent, for, on leaving the school, the sergeant spontaneously put a florin into the kitty. *"Thanks lads!*, he said, *"I haven't had such fun for years!"*, and off he went.

Jonas later learnt that the sergeant had been a prisoner of the Americans for well over two years, and that he and his captors, almost bored out of their respective skulls, had played the game of Liar-dice virtually all the time. Clearly, the sergeant had a very charismatic personality and an excellent brain, and it could well be said that he had attained a 'professional' standard at the game!

Jonas and Bill, the 4th mate, met up again during what the seamen called a 'make and mend' period, on Sunday 28th May – basically, a time when all the men could relax. During their conversation, Jonas said, *"Apart from the other merchantmen sailing in company with us, and the 'Magicienne' which is nearly out of sight – all around us is just 'sea'. There's not even a hint of land – but just a bare horizon, wherever I look. Dare I ask you…How on earth do you know where we are? How do you know how far we yet have to go? How do you know which way to steer the ship?"*

"Oh, dearie me!" Bill replied, *"Now we are getting into 'deep water'! Sorry, pun only half-intended!"*

There was a little rumble of muted laughter, and Bill saw that a small group of the comrades of Jonas were beginning to gather around, looking quite interested. So, after a moment, he realised he was going to have to 'play the schoolmaster', and he continued, *"Where on earth do I start to answer those questions in a way which you lot will easily be able to understand?"*

"As to steering the ship – Well, we are heavily dependent upon the ship's compass, which, as you may have seen, is kept in a so-called 'binnacle' to safeguard it from the wind and weather – that is to say, a sort of protective box with a glass window inset in it, so we can see the face of the compass through it. The binnacle is placed near to the ship's wheel, so that the Quartermasters can move the steering wheel back and forth, as necessary, to keep the needle over the correct place on the compass card. I daresay you've heard the 1st Mate shouting at the Quartermasters once in a while – he's got a loud voice which carries well – 'Steer small, you bastards!' Well, that means that the Quartermasters are letting the ship 'fall off' several points, one way and then the other, from the true course that has been specified by the captain, so the ship is behaving rather like a badly-pissed bloke staggering about as he tries to make his way home after a long session in the ale-house. If allowed to continue for long like that, it means that the ship is travelling a much greater distance through the water than she ought – costing us both time and food!"

He looked around at the rather blank faces around him. *"H'm – I see that I'd better try to explain that all a bit more. Well, the compass itself is a special needle which is pivoted and balanced at its centre on a pivot – a bearing which allows the compass needle to rotate freely in what we call a 'horizontal plane' – Oh! Let's just call it in a 'horizontal way'* (And he spread his hands, back and forth, palms down, to show what he meant). *Now, the binnacle is a clever structure, because the compass housing within it is mounted on what are called 'gimbals', which tend to keep the whole structure pretty well horizontal even though the ship is rocking about, and the bearings on which the needle itself sits also help the needle to stay more or less horizontal, no matter whether the ship is standing on its bow or on its stern, or rolling all the way from one of its beam-ends to the other. This stability is vital, because we need to be able to stay on course, no matter how rough the sea may be. The binnacle has a light in it, too, because we must also be able to steer the ship reliably on the darkest night."*

"Now, the needle is 'magnetised'. Magnetism is a whole subject in itself, so let me just say that the needle will always point to the 'magnetic north', and there it will stay, provided that it is free to rotate. It does so because the enormous globe that we call the 'Earth' behaves as if it were a bloody great 'master magnet', with its magnetic North Pole near enough to the true North Pole at the very top of the Globe, and the South Pole near enough at its bottom. Strictly speaking, the Magnetic North wanders about a little from time to time – but it always approximates to the true geographic North. All the little compasses throughout the World are sort of slaves to the 'master magnet' and do its bidding".

"If we want to steer the ship to the north, all we have to do is to turn her until the head of the needle of the compass lies over the north which is marked on the so-called 'compass card'. The card is fixed permanently to the ship, and so we'll then be heading north. Similarly, if we want to head south, full and bye, all we have to do is to turn the

ship until the head of the needle lies over the South mark on our compass card – and we'll be heading southwards."

"Indeed, that direction is actually not far removed from our present course, which is very nearly true south. In the earlier days of this voyage we had to steer more or less south-west for much of the time, fighting our way against the prevailing westerly winds which are to be found in that region. We needed to be well out into the Atlantic, so that we could keep well clear of France and the danger of her warships. Once we get down to the latitude of the Cape Verde Islands, which lie off the north-west coast of Africa, we hope to pick up the North-East Trade winds. This should come about any day now. Once we pick them up, they will carry us far westwards, almost all the way across what is the narrowest part of the Atlantic Ocean, and take us nearly to the coast of Brazil. Once there, we will keep the South-East Trades coming from our port side. That is, we will head more or less southwards and hope to pick up the Westerlies which normally blow in the southern Atlantic. Then, using them, we will head east-south-eastwards, because the vast continent of Africa currently lies far out of sight to the east of us, and we need to offload you redcoats in the southern part of that continent."

"Now, Jonas, you asked how we know where we are, when the horizon is bare all around us. Well, let's start with the easiest bit – what we sailors call 'Latitude' – that is, how far we are travelling northwards or southwards. (He moved his arms up and down to emphasise what he meant by those terms.) *That is different from how far eastwards or westwards we are travelling – that's what we call 'Longitude'.* (And he moved his arms in and out horizontally, to emphasise what he meant by those terms.) *"Now, in regard to Latitude, as I imagine you know – you can actually just about see it from the masthead – the horizon ain't flat – even tho' it does look like it, certainly as seen from deck-level. In fact, it is gently curved. It's curved, because we all live on this damn great big globe flying through space. Contrary to the widespread belief of years ago – and what some cranks would still tell you now – the Earth is NOT flat! It is just the most enormous round ball and its outside skin is made up of the seas and the land – inside it is a huge mass of molten rock of the most fantastic heat! In your travelling abroad you may one day come across an active volcano – that is, a mountain spewing forth flames and red-hot molten rock – Well, that molten rock comes up from all the molten mass of it deep-down towards the centre of the globe - and the red-hot 'lava' as it is called can cause huge damage and be very frightening indeed when it breaks forth on the surface. It can sometimes spew forth in the sea, creating new reefs and islands, whilst the sea literally boils around it! Deep down, the molten mass is full of movement – which explains why the Magnetic North varies slightly from time to time."*

"Now, just for convenience, scientific men have, in theory, divided up the globe into so-called 'Lines of Latitude'. The most famous line is the 'Equator' – I daresay you've all heard people talk about it? Try to imagine it like a fine belt placed around the central part of the globe – the place where the globe is at its broadest – rather like the belt a very fat man might use to hold his trousers up! Then, you've got the two 'Poles'. As I've already said, these are at the absolute top and bottom of the globe. They are the coldest places, with ice and snow in profusion, whereas, give or take, the Equator is the hottest place, with burning sunshine. Also, whereas the Equator is the widest point, the poles are at the smallest points – in fact, at the precise points of each pole there really

isn't any distance at all! So, one might say that they really don't exist at all, except if one goes just a little way outside 'em! Ha, Ha!"

"Now, unfortunately, I now have to talk in terms of degrees, and I imagine that you've no idea what I mean by 'degrees'. "That is to say – I don't suppose you've ever done any geometry at school, Jonas? Have any of you other redcoats, here? No? – Well, I feared not. Geometry is a subject in it's own right, and it's not everybody who can master it! However, I expect that all of you have met aspects of it in daily life without ever really being aware about it to any depth.

"So, I want you to think, for a moment, of a ladder leaning against a wall, on level ground.

He went on, *Now, I think you will agree that a good wall will normally be built vertical, with each brick standing squarely on the ones beneath. That wall will be said to be 'perpendicular', and, if the ground is level, it will make what is called a right-angle with it."* And, he started to make made a simple little drawing, using a scrap of paper and a stub of pencil which he happened to have in his pocket . He went on;

"Now, take my word for it, a right-angle is said to contain ninety degrees. "Think now of the ladder. What happens if its foot is stood too far out from the wall, and some silly sod tries to climb it?"

And he showed Jonas and his comrades the drawing, which looked something like this:-

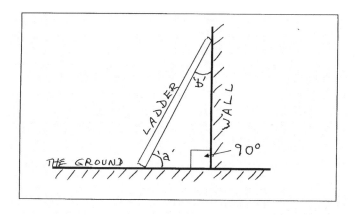

"YES – That's right, lads, the foot of the ladder will slide still further out as the weight of the man comes on it, and he'll end up flat on his face with the ladder underneath him. He'll probably be hurt as well as very embarrassed!"

"Right. Well now, what now if the foot of the ladder is too near to the wall, and the same silly sod tries to climb it again? I bet some of you have tried that! What happens? Yes – You're right, the ladder falls outwards, and the silly sod ends up by hitting his back hard on the ground, with the ladder on top of him!", adding, half-laughingly, when faced with some humorous protests from his audience, *"Ah, yes, all right – If he's very quick he MAY be able to step around the ladder as it falls, and end up on his feet as the ladder crashes down empty, so to speak! All right, smart arses – Well, at least I can see that you're with me so far!"*

And he went on, *"Yeah – well, this is all about 'practical geometry', as you've all experienced it in life. The main point that I wanted to make is that the angle between the wall and the ground is 90 degrees – provided that the wall is truly vertical and the ground is truly level. I'm sure that you can now understand in a practical sense what 90 degrees means. Similarly, I reckon that you will be able to understand what half of 90 degrees looks like, namely, 45 degrees."*

We <u>could</u> stand our ladder so that the other two angles, that I have called 'a' and 'b' on my little drawing, are each 45 degrees – because what are called the 'internal angles' of a right-angled triangle always add up to 180 degrees. PLEASE, just take my word for it – No, sorry lads, I don't think I can explain why!"

"However, were we to arrange the ladder with angles 'a' and 'b' at 45 degrees, we'd have the situation of the ladder sliding away as any poor sod climbed it – as we've just discussed – and, in practice, it has been found better to bring the foot of the ladder somewhat closer in to the wall than that, so that the angle at the foot is about 55 degrees – meaning that the angle its <u>head</u> makes with the wall will be is only about 35 degrees. I bet that quite a few of you lot know how to stand a ladder more or less safely – and pretty much just like that – but I bet that few of you knew how this related to geometry until just now!".

"Now, my reason for pointing out all that is just my long-winded way of ensuring that you know what a right-angle is. And that it's said to have 90 degrees. You'll also have a fair idea of what 45 degrees looks like."

"Now, if we imagine that we are some huge giant – like the mythical god Atlas, say – and if we were to cut the Earth in half like some ruddy great apple or orange, we'd have an object looking a bit like this, floating through space", and he began to develop another little drawing, showing the 'cut-through globe' and, at its very centre, a right-angle, like the one in his previous sketch of the ladder against the wall.

"In this case, he said, *"The "wall" is an imaginary line I have dropped down from the North Pole to the very centre of the Earth. As you can see, it meets the line of the Equator at a right-angle – like the wall met the level ground in our previous sketch."*

"We regard the Latitude of the Equator as our base-line. And, as such, we call its angle 'nought' or 'zero'. If we were to stand out on the line of the Equator at the point towards which I have shown our little ship as heading 'round the outside skin', so to speak – and if we were to crane our necks to look up high at the North Pole – we would say that it is at 90 degrees – rather like the vertical wall in my first little sketch. Hence, we call the latitude of the Pole 90 degrees."

"Here – have a look at what I've drawn!", and the sketch was quickly passed around the little group, before being passed back to him for further development.

He went on, *"Just as we might call the Equator a 'Prime Meridian – there is another so-called 'Prime Meridian', which we call 'The Tropic of Cancer'. This lies half-way up towards the Pole above the Equator, so to speak. That means that its Latitude is half of ninety – in other words, it is 45 degrees above where we would be standing".*

"There is another Prime Meridian, which we call the Tropic of Capricorn, also at 45 degrees, which I have now drawn."

Bill went on: *"However, there is something different about it. Can anybody tell me what?"* and he handed over the amended drawing, which was quickly passed around the group…

Jonas was looking at the composite drawing which Bill had now made. *"Well"*, he said slowly, *"The only difference I can see is that the Tropic of Capricorn is sort of upside-down. We would be looking <u>down</u> at it, were we to be standing on your imaginary base-line through the centre of the Earth."*

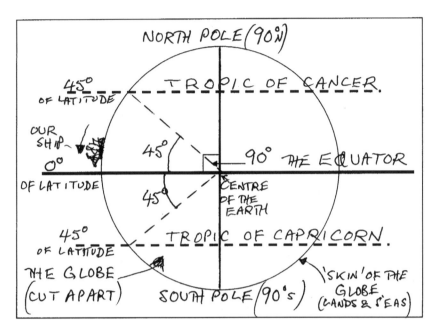

"Well said, friend!" said Bill, *"We call the Latitude of the Tropic of Cancer 45 degrees NORTH (that is, North of the Equator), and the latitude of the Tropic of Capricorn 45 degrees SOUTH – because it is south of the Equator. During this voyage we will be crossing the Equator very soon. The Equator is our 'base-line'. It has a latitude of zero degrees, and the pencilled positions which the Navigator of this ship adds day-by-day to our positions on the chart will change from showing an N for North, to S for South immediately we make that crossing."*

"As you have all seen, I've drawn our little ship heading down the skin of the globe from the north towards the Equator. Thereafter we'll be heading down towards the underside of the globe, heading for the South Pole. Everything will look the same, just the bare horizon all around us, but the situation is actually quite different. You'd be surprised how many watch-keepers get the N's and the S's mixed up when they plot our positions on the chart, day by day – especially around the days when we make the actual crossing of the Equator, when our latitude for a few moments will be exactly zero – and neither North nor South! It seems to throw everybody into confusion.

With a rather mischievous twinkle in his eye, which Jonas was coming to recognise, Bill went on; *"I have heard tell that, on some ships, 'King Neptune' and his various aides come on board from the Deep when we reach the Equator, and a great deal of fun and mischief is had by everyone as King Neptune's people set about shaving and ducking in a big tub of water all the people on the ship who've never crossed the Equator before! People have to appear before King Neptune's watery court to state whether or not this is their first crossing. He has huge power over the sea and Davy Jones' Locker, and that may be why confusion sometimes starts up in plotting our position at that time!"*

"What do you mean? What's Davy Jones' Locker? Who is this King Neptune?" asked Private Smithson, who was 'a bit straight', and something of a literalist, *"And* (rather angrily) *what gives him the right to cause all that disturbance?"*

"Oh, it's quite possible that you'll find out!" replied Bill, still rather mischievously and mysteriously, *"Though a lot will depend on whether my boss, Captain HOWLETT, will welcome King Neptune aboard – or not – and I really don't yet know the answer to that. Let 'Sufficient unto the Day' be your watchword for now!"*

Then, more seriously, Bill went on; *"Now, lads, just to finish about latitude – Between the Equator and the Poles, in total, there are ninety different lines of latitude north, and ninety lines south – that is to say, one line (or 'degree') for each of those ninety degrees ranging from the Equator up to one or other of the two poles. And – just take my word for it – the distance between any two lines of latitude is called sixty minutes."*

"We measure the position where any ship is located in the sea – in terms of its latitude – by using a sextant. They're complicated bits of equipment made out of shiny brass. I daresay you've noticed little groups of the ship's officers assembled together at noon each day the sun can be seen, playing about in setting their sextants to catch the sun's rays in little mirrors, whilst they peer at the horizon and twiddle with the setting-screws on their instruments, and so forth. The end results are measures of latitude. The officers then cross-compare their results – because they seldom match <u>exactly</u>. The average result of the best ones is recorded as the ship's latitude at noon. Officers who are badly in error are disciplined, and made to repeat their readings until they are more nearly correct. That makes good sense, because one fine day they may eventually find themselves in sole command of a vessel, and it will then be essential that they can calculate their Latitude accurately! The lives of people may well depend on them."

"Right – Getting a reading of Latitude tells us where we are, coming 'southwards DOWN the globe from England' as it were – but it also begs the question as to how far towards the west or the east we have travelled! Or, if you prefer, how far ROUND the ball we have come. (and he used his arms in a horizontal and circular motion to emphasise what he meant.) *That measure is called 'Longitude'. On that matter I'll just say for the moment that England has the great honour that the 'Prime Zero' of Longitude passes through an arbitrary pointer permanently set in the ground at Greenwich in London (so, in a sense, an imaginary vertical line through that point is a bit like an 'Equator' stood on its side), and every other point on the globe is recorded as being either 'East' or 'West' of Greenwich, again with the 'distance' being measured in degrees and minutes, though 'East' or 'West' of course, rather than 'North' or 'South'. To actually measure 'Longitude' is far from easy – but every ship needs to know where it is when out at sea, and the 'position' as it is called, has to be given in both Latitude and Longitude. That is, so many degrees and minutes North (or South) of the Equator, and so many degrees and minutes West (or East) of Greenwich.*

"I've got a little suggestion," said Private 'Shiny' Silver, *"How about posting up on a slate our position at noon each day, so that we soldiers can see how we're doing? There could be further writing to show where we're headed for in Latitude and Longitude. We might even be able to run a sweepstake on it, guessing where we'll be on the next day – or sumphin' like that. It could be a good diversion for us redcoats!"*

"All right, said Bill, *"Fair enough, that's not a bad idea at all. I'll have a word with the 1ˢᵗ Mate about it – See if he's willing to 'play ball', so to speak".*

"Now, I'll tell you lot more about Longitude next time I'm free. Just as we use the sun in estimating Latitude, we use the Moon in determining our Longitude – though some of the wealthiest captains use very clever, beautifully-made and expensive clocks! I'll also say something about charts – because it's vital for the captain of a ship to know where the sea ends and the land begins, or where dangerous reefs may exist out in the sea, maybe invisible beneath the surface, but just waiting to tear the bottom out of a ship! However, I think that's more than enough stuff for your heads to cope with for the time being – it sure is for mine!"

And off he went, with a warm smile to Jonas, broad-beamed and apparently very confident in himself, humming gently *"Hearts of Oak"*...

On Saturday, 5ᵗʰ June 1808, there was a flurry of excitement on board when a strange brig was sighted, closing with the convoy. Their escorting frigate seemed content to let the brig come on. Then Captain HOWLETT was observed to be exchanging signals with her, and their ship, the *Abraham Newland,* moved out of the convoy, so her captain could speak by loud hailer with the captain of the brig, whilst the other ships sailed majestically on. The *Abraham Newland* subsequently made full sail to catch up again.

On 11ᵗʰ June, by which time the convoy was at Latitude 9° 15'N, Longitude 27° 42' W, just over 9 degrees above the Equator, the frigate *Magicienne,* her escorting duty safely done, hoisted her ensign and parted company, swiftly heading away to the north-east. The convoy was now on its own, though by now well past the latitude of the Cape Verde Islands and far away from the shores of France.

However, it seemed that not all was sunshine and smiles aboard the *Ocean* in mid-June. She happened to be sailing in near company with the *Abraham Newland* in the morning at about this time, when the whole ship's Company of the *Ocean,* and the detachment of soldiers aboard, were brought up on deck to witness punishment. This punishment was of two of the crew who were to be flogged that morning, after being confined in irons for two days. One of these men was a caulker, who was flogged for disobedience and for striking out at the Ship's Carpenter, receiving 18 lashes. The other was a seaman, who was given six lashes for neglect of duty.

The men aboard the *Abraham Newland* who happened to be on deck at the time were close enough to the *Ocean* to hear and see most of the happenings which ensued.

Jonas was one of those men. He, for one, had never seen men thrashed with a cat o' nine tails before, and he found it an appalling punishment, laying open a man's bare back. Blood and flesh adhered to the leather thongs of the 'cat-o'-nine tails' wielded by the Master at Arms, and he squeezed out the thongs each time he came to give the later blows to the wreck that had been the first man's back. (The second man's back was not in quite such bad case, as he had fewer lashes to contend with.) Leather strops had been put in the mouths of the men, for them to bite on, but the strops fell out as the blows continued to rain on the men, one after the other, and then they screamed with pain as each of the subsequent blows landed. The Surgeon of the *Ocean* was present, checking on the physical state of the men – and he actually managed to get the last two blows of the 'eighteen' cancelled, because the man under punishment had fainted with the pain. The sight of buckets of salt water being thrown over the mutilated backs of the men, to wash away the worst of the bloody mess, before they were carried down into the Orlop by the surgeon's so-called 'Loblolly Boys', was fearsome.

Bill later discussed the matter with Jonas, saying that he had hated the whole business of flogging, and was just glad that it had taken place on a ship other than his own. *"I've heard it said that flogging makes a good man bad – and a bad man worse!"*, he said. Jonas agreed – though he knew by repute that flogging was sometimes – even if only rarely – carried out in the 24th. It was therefore with some relief that they heard the following day that a seaman of the *Ocean* who was due to be flogged for drunkeness, had been liberated from his irons after 12 hours, following his promise to the Master at Arms of future good behaviour. *"As I've said before, Jonas,"* said Bill, *"It's all too easy for us to get drunk, because we consume so much wine, spirits and small beer – due to the water really being unfit for us to drink. If a man is a bit of an alcoholic, and likes his tipple for its own sake, so to speak – he lives in great danger in a ship. I can recognise that drinking tendency in myself – especially as I am a sociable sort of animal, and I like singing sea shanties and being in merry company!"*

The convoy passed the latitude of the Equator on the 26th June. There was no 'Crossing the Line Ceremony' on any of the ships. Perhaps there was a feeling amongst the captains that the number of 'Shellbacks' (men who had already crossed the Equator) was much too low in relation to the great number of men who had not yet crossed the line – so that the 'tables might be turned', when the sometimes rather brutal 'initiation ceremonies' started up – and that chaos might then reign. So, seemingly, they took the simplest course, in having no ceremony at all. They were probably very wise to do so. (Jonas had noted quite a few signals being exchanged between the captains of the various ships in the convoy, and had suspected that was the subject of their discussions.)

On Sunday 4th July, the Ship's Cook of the *Abraham Newland* had all the potatoes remaining in stock brought up on deck. There was still a good ton of them left, and they were brought up by a fatigue party of redcoats. Evidently, the Cook had spotted that some of the potatoes were going mouldy, and that a repugnant liquid was oozing out of some of them. He organised the fatigue parties throw overboard all the mildewed potatoes and the 'wettest' ones – and to wash all the other potatoes in potable water that was frequently-changed. They were then carefully dried, before being re-stored below decks – once the storage area had been well-washed and dried out. His actions started quite a debate amongst the soldiers as to how best potatoes should be stored. It was generally known that they should be kept in darkness, but it now appeared that they needed a circulation of air around them rather that just being stacked in heaps. As some of the soldiers who were former Agricultural Labourers expressed it, *"Them taters is like folk – they're living creatures and they likes to breathe, and they'll live and spawn if they possibly can – just look at the way them's a'puttin' out roots – feeling for the soil that ought to be around 'em! No wonder they likes to be kept in the dark – just like in the cosy darkness of the soil."*

Throughout July the seamen and soldiers continued to be regularly exercised at the great guns, mostly in 'dummy runs', hauling the cannon in and out, and training them round with 'so-called 'marlin spikes' – but with the exercises occasionally involving live ammunition, and then creating a lot of noise and a huge 'smoke haze round the ships'.

67

The soldiers told off to assist the naval gunners soon learnt, like them, to tie scarves round their heads and over their ears, to provide at least some measure of protection against the explosively concussive noises of the guns firing.

Now that their escorting frigate had gone, their defence against any attack was totally down to them, and this training was even more important. As a further precaution, fatigue parties were assigned to make a so-called 'boarding netting'. This was a large net, capable of being extended over a large part of the ship in such a way as to make it very difficult for an attacking boarding party coming alongside their ship, to try to swarm up and over the sides of the *Abraham Newland.*

There were more mundane tasks for the fatigue parties, too, such as 'picking oakum' (teasing out short lengths of old rope into its constituent fibres) ready for the Ship's Caulker to use when packing out the seams of the ship – especially on the Upper Deck – to stop water-leaks. In rough weather – due to her deliberate design, intended to make her more resistant to the stresses imposed by the action of the waves – the ship 'worked' slightly (flexing back and forth, and from side to side), and the flexing tended to gradually open up the ship's seams. In prolonged periods of hot, dry weather there was a also certain amount of shrinkage of the ship's timbers, especially the deck-planks on the Upper Deck and the Quarterdeck, again opening up the seams. So, one way and another, the skilled services of the Caulker and his helpers were in constant demand, using heated 'caulking-irons' to pack the seams hard with a mix of oakum and tar. (There was also regular washing-down of the decks, partly for hygienic reasons, but also to keep shrinkage at bay.)

By now, the vessels in the convoy, including the *Abraham Newland* were 'pumping ship' now and again. The longer the voyage continued, the greater and more frequent would become the need. All the ships were sheathed in copper, which greatly slowed-down the growth of barnacles and weed, and prevented the extensive and damaging boring of ship's timbers by the Teredo worm in tropical seas. However, individual sheets of the copper sometimes became torn away and contamination did gradually build up, promoting some leakage. Further to that matter, any seams which opened below the water-line were inaccessible to the Caulker until the ship was hove-to and careened in sheltered waters – or brought into dry-dock – and so the only remedy whilst out at sea was to keep the ship regularly 'pumped dry'. The rather mournful note of the clanking of the pumps as the fatigue parties worked away, would become increasingly evident in the remaining days of the voyage. The ship would also become relatively slower through the water, due to the inevitable growth of weed on her bottom.

They had been making only slow progress south, due to the calm weather. They now encountered what seemed to be the Doldrums – though, if they were truly the Doldrums they were located further south than usual. Be that as it may, the winds now died right away, and they lay like a 'painted ship upon a painted ocean'. The sun scorched down from day to day from a clear blue sky. It was a frightening time, for a feeling grew, more and ever more insinuatingly, that they were accursed and would never move through the water again. Having lost all way, their ship gradually 'boxed the compass', swinging very slowly and randomly around the compass points according to the vagaries of the sea and its currents. Although the men only moved languorously, sweat simply poured off them in the oppressive heat.

Below decks, the stifling heat was almost unsupportable. The crew had rigged air-ducts to convey a draught of air below – but the total absence of any movement of air nullified the intended effects. It was only on the upper deck, in the early morning, and under the sea-water hoses, that Jonas and his comrades gained any real sense of relief. Even to eat was an effort, and often made the men feel nauseous. Jonas sought out Mrs Murphy again, and purchased samples of her strong liquors to get him through the worst of this period. She was not in the best of states herself, though Jonas found that the dew of perspiration on her half-exposed breasts caused a special sort of respectful admiration within himself. She was well aware of this, and, though she had a certain affection for the young soldier, as a married woman she ensured that their friendship was restrained only to the business of selling alcohol, whilst being careful (as we might say nowadays) not to bruise his ego to any extent.

The convoy lost about ten days of August to the nightmare of intense calm. When a few cats-paws of wind began to breathe over the surface of the sea the men cheered each and every one of them – but it took another two days before the breeze summoned up enough energy to gradually put way on to the three ships again. The mood aboard lifted enormously as the ships began to heel at last under the influence of the wind, and their voyage continued.

On a different aspect related to water, each ship was now regularly checking the amount of drinking water it had still aboard.

On Sunday 26th August there was another flogging on the *Ocean* this time the culprit having been confined in irons and then receiving 12 lashes for insolence to the 3rd Officer and neglect of duty. It was said that the indiscipline of the man was a token of the malaise that the heat and unnaturally calm weather had been causing throughout the people on board the ships. It was therefore a blessing that the weather had now totally changed, with squally rain and high seas, albeit that the conditions increased the frequency required for pumping ship. By now they were picking up the vigorous Westerlies which were bringing them swiftly eastward across the Atlantic.

By now the soldiers were inured to shipboard life, but becoming almost desperate to set foot ashore once again, to stretch their legs and to explore horizons new.

Their wish began to be granted on 10th September 1808, when the log of the *Abraham Newland* read *"at latitude of 34° 52m S, parted company with the convoy, continuing with Ocean and Kingston. Headed into Table Bay on the 12th September, mooring ship at 10 am. Noah's Ark SE, Roman Rocks east, the jetty head SW ½ W. Draught 17ft 6ins and 17ft 3ins aft."* They had arrived, and the journey had taken about four and a half months.

As indicated by the ship's log, the Batavians had built a jetty at Capetown (and they had also begun to construct some dockyards), so the newly-arrived ships were able to go alongside the jetty, and, on 23rd September 1808, they each disembarked their troops 'dry-shod'. Jonas just had time to bid goodbye to Bill Hitchings. *"A pleasure to have known you"*, said Bill, *"I hope that our courses will meet again in the future. Here's all the luck in the World to you, Young Jonas!"*

"And the same to you", said Jonas, *"Keep a sharp lookout for French frigates, mind!"* *"Sure will"*, replied Bill, with a broad smile…

Chapter Five

The Year 1809:
With the 1st Btn at 'the Cape':
(News of the 2nd Btn in Combat in Spain.)

The docks at Capetown were not as large as the docks at Tilbury, but they were teeming with life, and bore similarities with what had been happening at Tilbury when the fleet had left – though the ships were now unloading their passengers and cargoes rather than embarking them. The first thing that Jonas noted were that there were soldiers wearing similar red-jacketed uniforms to his own, with the same green facings, already paraded on the dockside before his own company had got ashore. The faces of these other soldiers were not familiar to him – and he guessed that they had to be men of the 1st Btn of the 24th – men who were veterans of combat with the Batavian settlers, and who, together with the other troops under General Sir David BAIRD, had now taken over possession of the Cape, and had been running it for about 15 months.

There were also brown-skinned men – negroes – who were acting as stevedores under the direct control of white-skinned men. The white men were armed with ox-hide whips, and were not shy of using them on the backs of the negroes whenever they felt that the negroes were shirking. Jonas guessed that these white men, who were dressed in homespun dark clothes and who wore straw-plaited slouch hats against the hot sun, were the tough Batavian settlers.

Overlooking the whole scene was the magnificent backdrop of Table Mountain, which was approximately 3,600 feet high, with the unusually-shaped 'Lion's Head', another considerable mountain, off to the right as one looked at the panorama from seaward. On this day Table Mountain had a long flat cloud over it, *rather like the most enormous 'table-cloth'*, as one of the pals of Jonas quite wittily remarked – though Jonas later found that this was an expression that was commonly used locally. In fact, the local people used the presence or absence of the 'table-cloth' and other associated cloud-formations as a sort of 'barometer' of the weather-conditions about to come over Capetown on a day-by-day basis.

There were plenty of light, horse-drawn carriages available, and the impedimenta of the 24th were quickly stowed in them, by a mix of fatigue parties of the 24th, and by negroes under the direction of the Batavians. Some of the negroes wore similar clothes to the Batavians, but others wore little more than what might be described as a 'loin cloth', with a sheep-skin cloak called a *kross,* together with a decorative head-dress (often made from ostrich feathers) and anklets made of metal or of feathers and beads. Some of the little groups of these workers chanted a strange, haunting melody when there was a heavy object to be hoisted up, the song evidently helping the men to co-ordinate their efforts

Jonas learned that the veterans of the 24th who were lined up on parade in the bright South African sunlight were headed by the Adjutant, Mr WARD, astride a so-called 'Cape Pony' - that is, a small horse bred by the Batavians, of a type which was reasonably immune to the horse-flies and other biting insects to be found in the area of the Cape. The veteran soldiers were paraded as a welcoming gesture to the reinforcements, and it was not long before the veterans were stood at ease. It was then possible to have some communication with them, conversations springing up where one or other of the newcomers had known one of the veterans before the departure of the first contingent from Chelmsford.

Thereafter, the word quickly began to spread as to what exactly had happened to the 1st Btn thus far. The account ran in this fashion:

In 1805 the 1st Btn had been embarked in East Indiamen for an assault on Rio de Janiero.[5] However, that operation had been cancelled just after they left English shores, and they had then been held in the large bay called 'The Cove of Cork', in south-west Ireland. Here, the days had stretched into months before fresh orders arrived, whilst the men stultified on board, with virtually no shore leave – though a few recruiting parties had managed to get ashore and had recruited a few Irishmen into the battalion.

The new orders had led to the East Indiamen setting forth in convoy in August 1806, bound for South Africa. By that time they were part of an Army of 6,000 men, under the command of Sir David BAIRD, the officer who, a few years earlier had attacked Seringapatam in India, and whose forces had killed the notorious and murderous Tippoo Sahib. Now, they were going to invade the Cape of South Africa, and to take over the trading station which had been successfully set up in 1652 by the so-called 'Batavian' settlers from Holland. Rather like the earlier British Puritan settlers on the east coast of America, these Dutch settlers had wished to find a sanctuary where they could practice their religious faith free from European control or restriction.

Both the British and the Dutch governments had been toying for many years with the idea of setting up a trading station at the Cape, to supply the needs of ships making the long voyage to India and the Far East – and especially in combating the ravages of scurvy – a problem which was not then well understood. However, the Batavians, under the leadership of Jan van Riebeeck, a former ship's surgeon, were the first to establish commercial gardens at the trading post which was set up there in the 1650s. The Batavians were very religious but also very tough men, farmers who also soon became skilled at hunting wild animals for food. The Batavians had entered into agreements (or suppressed such opposition as they had met) in regard to the dark-skinned native Africans, and nowadays used numbers of them as near-slaves – indeed, at one time, when they were short of manpower, and in commercial agreements with Arab traders, they had actually imported slaves from other parts of Africa. The British had captured the Cape in 1795, but had ceded the territory back to the Batavian Republic in 1803, under the terms of the European Treaty of Amiens. The start of the abolition of the slave trade in 1807, in which the British played a leading role, would not go down well with the Batavians, who were not only short of manpower, but who also needed cheap labour to make their farming profitable. (By 1834 the British would have abolished slavery throughout the Empire, increasing those strains.)

Back in 1805, the conventional course followed by the convoy had taken them westwards right across the Atlantic and back, as they followed the trade winds. This voyage had taken several months to accomplish, and the men had badly-needed the

---

[5] The main substance of this report has been derived from the regimental histories as currently maintained in the Museum at Brecon. Some fragments of additional data have also been acquired from sundry contemporaneous accounts.

stopover ashore they had made for three weeks at the beautiful bay of San Salvador, in the Bahamas, after adverse weather had driven their ships in there.

Having continued its crossing of the Atlantic back to the east, the bulk of the Army had eventually landed north of Capetown on the 6th January 1806, initially meeting no resistance, but with some men of the 93rd Regiment being drowned in the surf after their boat had struck a rock as the invading force had disembarked. However, the 1st Btn of the 24th had got ashore safely the next day. The Army had disembarked its stores and, on 8th January 1807, had advanced towards Capetown, with teams of sailors using drag-ropes to pull the force's six field guns and two howitzers 'with aplomb, through deep sand, uphill and downhill'. The speed of the movement of the Army seemed to have taken the Batavians by surprise, and General Baird's advance guard had seized the majority of the Blauberg Ridge before the Batavians had managed to fully occupy it, and despite some accurate rifle-fire from its few defenders.

General BAIRD's advance guard then found that, under their commander, General JANSENNS, the main force of the Batavians had established a defensive position in some foothills to the ridge, astride the road into Capetown. When the main British Army had come up, a successful assault had been made on the defences, though casualties had been suffered by both sides. The casualties had included Captain Andrew FOSTER of the 24th, and three privates, who were all killed outright, and one who later died of his wounds. Fifteen other privates had been wounded. There had been significant losses in the other regiments involved, and the total of men wounded was close to 200 for the invading army as a whole.

The Batavians themselves were good soldiers and, certainly, very good marksmen. However, their numbers were comparatively small, and their army had of necessity had an addition of Javanese artillerymen, Hottentot infantrymen and other Non-Batavians, many of whom were regarded as 'highly unreliable'. The burghers had also recognised that no help was going to come to them from Holland. So, being practical men, and on the understanding that they would be able to continue with their smallholdings and with the sale of foodstuffs, goods, wine and merchandise to passing ships, they had surrendered to the British on the 18th January 1806. Thereafter, the Batavians had caused no trouble, with the two sides settling down together in running the Cape station, primarily as a British possession. Indeed, a number of the men in the Batavian Army had actually transferred to the 24th, though they had subsequently been moved to the 60th Regiment.

Currently, the Colonel of the 24th was Lt-Col G MacDONALD. The Cape had a reasonably good climate, and the sick-list of the 24th had been low During the early months, an average of only nine men had been on the sick-list each month, out of the near 1,000 men then available to it for duty.

There was a Regimental Hospital, together with a General Hospital for the more seriously ill cases. As time had gone on, the sick-list had increased somewhat, with up to 28 men sick at each muster, though most less seriously so, and hence with the majority being treated at the Regimental Hospital. Currently, the 24th were losing about three or four men to fatal illnesses per month.

Having thus buried some 90 men, and with a further number of men unfit, and needing to be repatriated, the 1st Btn were therefore very glad to welcome the reinforcements. Basically, however, their peace-keeping duties were minimal, because the Batavians had settled down well, and there was no trouble.

It seemed likely that the Colonel of the 24th had already sent a message to that effect to 'Horseguards', back in England, saying that the 1st Btn would probably be better employed on active service somewhere else in the World. Indeed, none of the rank and file seemed sure of it, but there was a rumour that a detachment under Lieutenant Parsons had already been sent to South America on a secret mission, but had failed. The fate of the men who went with him was unknown. Currently, some of the officers seemed 'restive', and a few of them were now apparently trying to wangle their way back to Europe, where active service with the newly-formed 2nd Btn in the 'Peninsular Campaign' against the French, , was apparently a real possibility.

For the present, however, the men of the 1st Btn of the 24th could enjoy themselves, insofar as their duties (and their officers) would permit. Nominally, Jonas was now under Captain Richard GUBBINS, in No 10 Company, based at a camp near Newlands, at the foot of Table Mountain. However, Jonas soon volunteered to be a member of a working party of ten men under Corporal Jones, helping with the farming on one of the larger estates, which was owned by a certain Meinheer Jan der Beek. The speciality on this farm was the growing of oranges and citrus fruits – though apples were also grown and harvested. On the southern slopes of a nearby estate, grapes were grown in profusion, and wine was produced from them.

Jonas, who was instinctively aware that his body had been starved of fruit and vegetables whilst on the ship, simply loved the taste of the various fruits on the estate. He was free to help himself to them to some degree, and thrived physically, marvelling at the climate and the profusion in which the fruits cropped. Some of his days with the working party he found quite magical. For instance, at one time of the year, when marching over what was normally the rough green grass of the 'veldt', to his day's work at Jan der Beek's farm, he found that his party were going through stretches of the most beautiful wild flowers, apparently called 'trefoils', of every colour and hue imaginable – but especially yellow and orange. The abundance of wild life in terms of animals and birds was also amazing in its scope and variety.

He had to leave the working party in November 1809, for his Company was moved to Wynberg Camp for a while. This lay about ten miles to the south of Capetown. Wynberg was an old garrison town, originally established by the British in 1795, during their first occupation of the Province. Wynberg stood astride the hilly north-south wagon-road from Capetown down to False Bay and Simonstown, False Bay being generally regarded as a safer anchorage for shipping than the more 'open' bay at Capetown. Due to the steepness of the local roads it was customary for the wagons to be pulled by very large teams of oxen, the drivers having long ox-hide whips with which to control their beasts. (There were no bridges to speak of across the rivers at the Cape, and any driver worth his salt was also expected to be able to control his oxen at the fording-places across the rivers – the various fords each creating their own individual problems.)

Jonas enjoyed being at Wynberg – despite the greater formality of military life there – but he was relieved when he was posted back to Capetown in the early part of 1810, and especially when Corporal Jones permitted him to rejoin the working party on the farm.

As a soldier and a former farm labourer from England, Jonas found the way of life of the Batavian farmers rather hard to identify with, albeit that they were clearly good at the main tasks of their farming activities. As opposed to his rather light-hearted and slightly cynical view of life at that time, Jonas found that the Batavians were mostly dour, solemn-faced and deeply religious. They observed the Sabbath Day punctiliously, with the men doing virtually no work that day. *(True, the Batavian womenfolk were expected to cook a full lunch for the family on the Sabbath Day – but they were otherwise entitled to do no work on that special day apart from the absolute essentials, like feeding the chickens and gathering their eggs.)*

Yet the Batavian men, on Sundays as on the other days of the week, used their ox-hide whips quite ruthlessly on their wagon-drawing oxen and on their black servants alike. The Batavians were hard men indeed. The soldiers tried to form friendly relationships with them, but it was far from easy, because there was so little common ground in their attitudes to life, and the sense of humour of the British soldier found no real echo in the rather dour minds of the Batavians. There was also the problem that most of the Batavians spoke only *Afrikaans,* a language derived from Dutch and incomprehensible to the Englishmen. The Batavians did not willingly open their houses to the British soldiers, and, by pre-arrangement with the cooks of the 24th, Corporal Jones and his working party found it best for each man to take along a pre-packed lunch and a bottle of porter, to see him through the day.

Generally speaking, despite the related difficulties of communication, the soldiers found it easier to relate to the black men, who were of the *Khoikhoi* race – and especially to their children, the so-called 'piccaninnys' – because it was so easy to get smiles out of them, and Jonas would long remember the sound of their laughter, the flashes of their white teeth, and the strong whites of their eyes, contrasting so vividly against their dark skins. (To avoid any problems with the men-folk, there were standing orders forbidding the soldiers to have any contact at all with the women of the Province, be they black or white. In fact, the men were specifically warned against the temptation of having sexual relations with black prostitutes, due to what was said to be the grave risk of 'climatic bilbo' – a disease against which there was then no known cure.)

The *Khoikhoi* lived in native villages called *kraals.* Their huts – perhaps twenty or so in number - were arranged in a circle, with their entrances facing inwards. At night their cattle were driven into the central ground and boxed-in with a wall of thorns, to protect them from predators, such as lions.

Ostriches – large flightless birds standing perhaps seven or eight feet tall – were also to be seen in the area. They were valued by the *Khoikhoi* for their beautiful black and white plumage. The very large eggs of the ostriches were sometimes sold to the soldiers as curiosities to be taken home to England.

It became abundantly clear that the merriment which was often to be observed between the soldiers and the black folk did not go down well with the Batavians. The Batavians wanted to retain their superiority over the black races, and saw the easy relationships which were developing between the soldiers and the black folk as dangerous.

Corporal Jones was in conversation with Jonas one morning when the elderly and grey-bearded Jan der Beek came up to them. Later, in talking to other members of the working party, Jonas would try to imitate what Jan then said. Jonas reckoned that it sounded something like this:

"Eeet is all ver' well for you an' your mensch", said Jan to Corporal Jones. (Jan was one of the few Batavians who spoke comparatively good English, albeit often well-larded with German. His past was never fully revealed, but it was clear that he'd lived in England at one time, long before he'd settled at the Cape. He was married to a stolid German *hausfrau* who stood no nonsense from anybody at all – including Jan himself! Rumour said that Jan had originally been banished to the Cape from Holland for losing all control and beating somebody to near death in a quarrel.)

According to Jonas, Jan said, *"You English soldiers vill probably only be in strength here in South Africa for a few more months – whereas ve vill be here forever, and ve haf got to keep all ze black tribes in total submission zu uns. It is true that ve Batavians haf got superior veapons to their 'assegai' spears, and our bullets can pierce their oxhide shields. But ze day may not be too far off ven dey start to buy und use muskets against us. At present, the Arabs are masters of the slave trade, raiding African villages, taking the inhabitants prisoner und confining them in chains, an' zen selling zem at a gut profit at slave auctions around ze Weld. However, should the slave trade begin to dwindle away – an' you Eenglishe are verking at zat - the Arabs might well start up an arms-smuggling trade with ze Africans in der future."*

"Remember that the black tribes outnumber us by many thousands to one! In our history, we have managed to make agreements wiv certain of the tribes, whereby we have our farms here. Other tribes, like the 'Kaffirs' in South-East Africa, we are alvays having unrest and trouble with. Ve are lucky that the different tribes tend to have long-standing disputes and wars between zemselves. One day they may form a general alliance, and seek to kick us Batavians out of their country. Ve just cannot afford to let zem develop any sort of parity with us. Instead, to survive, ve must always keep zem in the role of second-class members of ze population, in both a mental und a physical sense. To have you soldiers giving them the least sense of a sort of 'equality' with white men is simply fraught with danger for us – and it must stop! Zu halten – ja!"

After a moment he went on, *"I'm sorry Corporal Jones – but I intend to speak to your sergeant about it, to request that he arranges an interview for me with your Colonel – so that I can arrange for an order to be issued, totally forbidding fraternisation of you soldiers with the natives!"*

Corporal Jones did tell his men to 'ease off' from their developing relationships with the black Africans on the farm – but, so far as ever Jonas heard, there never was a standing order issued by Colonel MARRIOTT which forbade fraternisation of the soldiers with the natives. Indeed, from what Jonas could see, the British policy seemed to be to give more or less equal justice and fairness of treatment to black and white men alike. This might well become a serious 'bone of contention' with the Batavians in the future.

However, for the present it was clear that the 24th Regiment of Foot was pretty well wasting its time on the South African station, because the Batavians had currently accepted the British occupation, and it certainly seemed that the officers of the 24th were 'champing at the bit' for a move elsewhere. Indeed, more officers now felt that they had made the wrong move in transferring away from the 2nd Btn., because rumours had begun to circulate that the 'new' 2nd Btn., which included a few of the officers who had stayed on in England, had now been in hectic action in the Iberian Peninsular against the seasoned troops of France. It was on active service that officers stood to gain experience and accelerated promotion – even if it had to be 'in dead men's shoes'. Some of the officers of the 1st Btn had now definitely started to seek a transfer to the 2nd Btn in Portugal. This situation continued to gain strength as the weeks turned into months.

The dissatisfaction of the officers further increased when a circular arrived from England, early in 1810, detailing something of the recent affairs of the 2nd Btn since the reinforcements for the 1st Btn., including Jonas, had left England. The 2nd Btn had indeed seen some hectic action, and the circular had carried interesting information. The substance of it quickly spread amongst the rank and file of the 1st Btn:-

"In April 1809, the 2nd Btn had marched from Chelmsford to Tilbury.[6] There they had embarked for Guernsey u/c Lt Col George Duncan DRUMMOND (who had exchanged with Col MacDONALD in Feb 1808). The Officers in the 2nd Btn had included Major POPHAM, Major CHAMBERLAIN, 5 Captains and 14 Subalterns. Recruiting had been difficult, and the 2nd Btn had still only mustered 839 rank and file, rather than the standard of just over 1,000, when it had embarked at Guernsey for Portugal.

Having landed at Lisbon on the 28th April 1809, the 2nd Btn had moved to Santarem and thence to Cordegas. By that time, reduced through sickness, the 2nd Btn had only 774 rank and file, though it still had about twenty-two officers. Being so short of numbers, the Battalion was amalgamated with the 27th, 31st and 45th Regiments, and they were formed as a Brigade under Major-Gen MACKENZIE's 'corps of observers', to maintain a watch on the movements by the French Army, which was under General SEBASTIAN.

Seemingly, General WELLINGTON had considered that the corps was still too weak, and, after he had reviewed Major-General MACKENZIE's men, the Brigade had been further reinforced by the 87th and 88th Regiments and the German Hussars, and also by the 14th/16th Light Dragoons and by a brigade of artillery. This composite Brigade had then marched to Talavera as the advance guard for WELLINGTON's Army.

In so doing they had also covered the retreat of Spanish Army under General CUELT, and they had crossed and re-crossed the Alberché River on 27th July. This had been a very severe and testing march for them.

The Brigade had subsequently halted in a very thick wood. It was suspected that an Army of 50,000 Frenchmen was near to the British Army and that another French Army, under Marshall SOULT, was manoeuvring to cut off any possible retreat of the British Army to Placencia. Consequently, picquets were set to observe the situation.

The 24th was ordered to pile its arms, the 24th then being on the right of the Brigade. The other regiments in the Brigade also piled their arms, and took off their packs, the orders coming from the left. The 24th then also began to remove their packs. A further order then came, to cut down wood and bushes, and it was assumed that a bivouac was to be established. In no time, the British soldiers were dispersed amongst the trees, busily cutting wood for the bivouac.

---

[6] The main substance of this report has been derived from the regimental histories as currently maintained in the Museum at Brecon. Some fragments of additional data have been acquired from sundry contemporaneous accounts.

Suddenly, the ALARM was sounded – French light troops had been observed in the wood! Fortunately, the picquets of the 24th had not taken off their packs and had time to run to the front of the Brigade and to join some of the 60th Regiment firing and skirmishing.

The wood was too thick for proper manoeuvring, so the Brigade retired from it and formed up on the plain outside. The 24th quickly had its three right companies moving towards a large building called the Casa Salinas, but a large French column was observed to be also heading towards it from the woods. Thereupon, General WELLINGTON ordered the British companies back, their withdrawal being conducted under French grape shot which caused some casualties.

Following that skirmish, no rations had been issued for three days and the men of the 2nd Btn had been suffering from dysentery and the heat of the weather. The troops were exhausted. The officers were as badly off as the men.

In fact, the 24th had been forced to abandon their baggage, which had been pillaged by the French Army. The officers' money, the company books, ammunition and so forth were all gone. The supplies of the women sutlers of the regiments, which were normally available (at a fairly low cost) to help out the troops in adversity, had also been plundered by the French. The men, still unfed, lay down to sleep with their muskets placed under their greatcoats, to protect them against the heavy dew which was falling.

On the 28th July 1809, the BATTLE OF TALAVERA had opened. Soon after daylight, enemy artillery had started to fire on the small arms units on the left of the British Army. The Brigade was thereupon ordered to lie down to minimise casualties. The French fire had ceased at 0900 hrs and the wounded men in the British lines had then been removed. The firing resumed at 1300 hrs. General CAMPBELL's Division in the British centre was hard-pressed by the French, and General McKENZIE's brigade was brought forward to support them. This support included the 24th, whose independent fire caused serious casualties in the French infantry as the French deployed from column into line. Indeed, the French were so cut up that they retired.

The Btn was then ordered to support the Coldstream Guards on its former ground. The 24th faced left, and moved off at the double, in the direction of the front line. The Guards charged and the 24th took up the ground vacated by the Coldstreamers, wheeling first into line and keeping up a steady fire against the French line which was following up hard on the Coldstreamers. The French artillery and musket fire was severe and reduced the 24th to only one rank to show front – and even that with long gaps! Sadly, General McKENZIE was killed and all the field officers were wounded with the exception of Major CHAMBERLAIN, who took command of the brigade. Captain EVANS was also killed. The wounded officers included Lt-Col DRUMMOND, Major POPHAM, Major AYLMER, Captain COLLIS, Lieutenants GRANT and VARDY, Ensigns JOHNSTONE, SKEENE, and JESSMAN and 355 other ranks out of 710.

Sad to relate, despite this huge 'butcher's bill', precious little credit was given to the 24th. Instead, the 48th Regt, who'd supported the 3rd Footguards, picked up the credit in the dispatch. Unfortunately, a detailed letter from Lord WELLINGTON was lost in the 'Marlborough', Packet. The letter never appeared in print. One additional problem was that half of the men had militia clothing on, with light-coloured facings instead of the green of the 24th, i.e. 300-400 men from Tipperary, West Meath, Nottingham, Warwickshire and other militia regiments which had yellow or other light facings had *arrived as reinforcements just before the battle. Nearly one-half of the 24th Regt had been killed or wounded in supporting the Guards. Severely wounded men in the 'transfer' area had been burnt to death in flames from the long dry grass set on fire by the shells. Men who had tried to save them were forced back, their clothing burnt and ammunition pouches blown up on their own backs. Not fifty men were left with the colours after fatigue parties had been sent off to escort the wounded*

The British Army had marched off from Talavera on the 3rd August 1809, to face Marshall SOULT and his 40,000 men at Plascencia. The Spanish were left to cover the battlefield – but unfortunately abandoned it. Thus, Major POPHAM, Captain COLLIS, Lieutenants GRANT and SKEENE and Ensign JESSMAN, who had all been wounded and left on the field, were all made PoWs by the French. Ensign JESSMAN later escaped, and joined the guerillas. However, he was captured again and subsequently shot by the French at Madrid. (His fate, which would otherwise have remained unknown, was reported by some English soldiers who subsequently managed to escape.)

The Btn had again suffered much from dysentery on the march from Talavera to Truxill and on to Guadiana. The temperature was 100°F in the shade and dragging the artillery up the mountain passes was hard work indeed.

The 24th were formed into a Brigade with the 2nd Btn of the 42nd/83rd regiments – and later with the 1st Btn of the 61st. General CAMERON had replaced General MacKENZIE (KiA) at the head of the Brigade. However, General CAMERON had left the Army at the year end and Colonel H E STOPFORD of the Guards had taken command. Contagious fever had broken out whilst the Brigade was on the banks of the Guadiana – the 24th could not parade even 100 men when the regiment left camp and marched to winter quarters at Arroyo de St Savan. Adjutant TOPP died of this fever. Captain STRAWBENZEE was sent to Lisbon sick and died from sickness and debilitation. Often 8-10 graves were being dug per day for the Btn.

All men shown as PoWs or missing were ordered to be struck off the strength. The Regiment had been near 1000 strong when it left Portugal in May: by the year's end it had lost about 600 other ranks."

Jonas was present when one of the junior officers read aloud the substance of the above communiqué. He was one of those who spontaneously gave forth a groan of sympathy when the death of his former Company Commander, Captain STRAWBENZEE, was read out. Jonas was probably just one man of many who nursed strange feelings about the whole matter. *"Just suppose that I hadn't volunteered for the 1st Battalion,"* he thought to himself, *"and that I'd gone off to the fighting in the Peninsula with the 2nd Btn instead. Would I now be dead meat from the hectic actions that the 2nd Btn have been engaged in? Could I have stood the strain? Looks like my chances of dying would have been higher than 50-50! Fancy just being a name struck off the strength – as if I had never existed at all. Ye Gods above!"*

In June 1810, orders at last arrived from Horseguards in England. The 1st Btn were to serve in India, in support of the Honourable East India Company. Arrangements had been made in London for the Btn to embark in four HEIC ships expected to arrive at Capetown shortly. The Btn was to load at an average of about 280 men per ship, though the *Euphrates,* due to her smaller size, was to take only half that number.

Chapter Six

The Year 1810:
The 1ˢᵗ Btn Sets Forth for India:
The Sea Battle of the 3ʳᵈ July

Like his comrades, Jonas was ordered to parade in his full kit on 10ᵗʰ June 1810, when every fit man of the 24ᵗʰ was marched down to the dockside at Capetown. Their band led the way, and the men of the battalion were accompanied by their wives and children, who straggled along behind. The heavy baggage of the Btn was carried to the dockyard in horse-drawn 'Cape Carts'. The 24ᵗʰ, with its bright red jackets (and their green facings), and its white trousers and cross-belts, topped up by their black shakos, made a splendid sight, when lined up in its companies, ready to board ship.

The ships which were present were all attractive East Indiamen, and four of them were considerably larger that the *Abraham Newland,* on which Jonas had sailed out from England. Those four were the *Ceylon*, the *Astell*, the *William Pitt* and the *Windham.* All these ships were of about 800 tons burthen. The other ship, the *Euphrates*, was of only 600 tons burthen.[7] For this voyage, it seemed that the Commodore of the convoy would sail in the *Ceylon.* There would be no escorting warships of the Royal Navy – the Indiamen would have to be self-sufficient in warding off any enemy ships – though they were now far from France, of course. Still, with five of them, they should be a fleet to reckon with. By leaving in June, they should be well within the season for picking up the South-West Monsoon winds to carry them across the Indian Ocean to Madras.

After arriving on the dockside, there seemed to be some interesting dialogue going on between the officers, to which the rank and file 'had their ears pricked'. There always seemed to be one or two ordinary rankers who somehow managed to hone in on such conversations – and some of the men appointed to be servants to the officers were also remarkably quick-witted at 'putting two and two together' from scraps of overheard conversations and by looking at clues stemming from their own officer's behaviour and requirements. Rumours could then ramify quickly throughout the whole battalion.

In this instance, there were two rumours. There had long been a belief amongst the rankers in the battalion that Major FORSTER was better company in the Mess, and much more popular with his fellow-officers, than was Lt-Colonel Randolf MARRIOTT. Certainly, one strong rumour today was that no less than six of the Captains had managed to accompany Major FORSTER aboard the *Astell*, whereas only two Captains had accompanied the Lt-Colonel aboard the *Ceylon*.

However, no less than six of the sixteen Lieutenants had accompanied the Lt-Colonel into the *Ceylon*, maybe to safeguard his good opinion of them. Perhaps for the same reason of self-interest, the *Ceylon* carried Sergeant-Major Miller and the Quartermaster-Sergeant, together with the Armourer-Sergeant and the Surgeon (with the Assistant Surgeons being carried in the *Astell* and the *Windham,* respectively.) Jonas thought that these rather negative rumours were all unreliable, and that at least some of

---

[7] The author has drawn heavily on what survives of the logs of these vessels within the British Library, and especially upon the remarkable log of the *Astell*, to write this chapter. (See Appendix.)

the reason might have been that the *Ceylon* was, effectively, carrying the Headquarters Company of the 24th, including her Colours and the regimental account books and the money-chest, all items which he'd personally seen go aboard.

Another rumour concerned the *Windham*. She was said to be an unlucky ship, having twice been captured by the French – although twice won back from them! She had only recently been recaptured and brought into Capetown for refitting – which meant that she was still short of her normal complement of seamen and had been forced to take aboard a larger-than-usual number of 'lascar' seamen (men of Indian origin), to make up her numbers. The French had plundered the ship of her provisions, though not of her guns, prior to her recapture. (She was, in fact, well-armed, with twenty 18 pdrs and ten carronades.) She had been re-stocked to an extent at the Cape, but her comforts would not be of the best. There was said to be considerable rivalry amongst the officers <u>not</u> to be quartered in the *Windham*.

The ordinary rankers absorbed all this information and tried to do a bit of 'duck-shoving' themselves. As was to be expected, the *Euphrates,* being a significantly smaller ship, had a smaller party going aboard her – but the smallest detachment of all the soldiers was actually on board the 800-ton *Windham,* which had only 143 rank and file soldiers, as compared with about 280 in each of the similarly-sized ships, the *Ceylon,* the *Astell* and the *William Pitt.* (This made a total for the Btn of about 1,140 other ranks.)

Similarly, each ship carried about 12 women and 12 children – except for the *Windham*, which had only half that number.

It was later established that the parties of officers boarding the ships worked out as follows:-

In the *Ceylon* there was Lt-Colonel MARRIOTT. He was accompanied by two Captains and six Lieutenants (Making 9 officers in all). In the *Astell* was the second-in-command, Major FORSTER, with six Captains, namely CRAIG, GUBBINS, LANGWORTHY, SMITH, TAYLOR and WHITE, together with four Lieutenants and an Ensign (12 officers in all.). In the *William Pitt* were Major HICKS, Captains MALKIN and GREEN and four Lieutenants (Making 7 officers), and in the (smaller) *Euphrates*, under Major ROBISON, were Captains LANGWORTHY and STEWART, two Lieutenants and 2 ensigns, plus the Quartermaster: she also carried the Adjutant and his wife. (Making 7 commissioned officers). As compared with them, the *Windham* had a <u>total</u> of only two humble lieutenants as its Army officers!

This, despite the fact that the master of the *Windham*, Captain STEWART, had a most remarkable record. During November 1809, whilst sailing alone south-east of Ceylon, his ship had been attacked by two French frigates, the *Venus* and the *Manche*, supported by a corvette, the *Creole*. Despite putting up a doughty and prolonged resistance, the odds were far too great, and Captain STEWART had eventually been forced to surrender. The French had put a prize crew aboard the *Windham*, and Captain STEWART and his men were subsequently held captive below decks in the *Venus*. However, a tremendous gale had blown up as the *Venus* was on passage westward across the Indian Ocean to the French-held Island of Mauritius, and she had lost her three masts overboard. Soon there was 7ft of water in the well and the ship was near to foundering. The crew had given up hope, and had withdrawn into the hold to await their fate. In his desperation, the French Captain, Commodore HAMELIN – knowing that Captain

STEWART was a seaman of the very finest standing – had asked him, if he could possibly save the situation.

Legend said that Captain STEWART, still angry at the loss of his ship and seeing the French as the natural enemy of his country, had almost told Commodore HAMELIN to 'go to the devil'! However, he then thought of the dreadful fate which was about to overwhelm his imprisoned fellow-captives, and, reluctantly, he had agreed to try to save the *Venus*. By a superb and determined piece of seamanship, and with the aid of his men, whom the French released *pro tem*, he had restored what appeared to be the most desperate situation and thus the lives of all those on board. In gratitude for his services, the French had freed him, and put him on a 'cartel', which had duly delivered him, safe and sound, at the Cape. The downside of this was that the *Venus* was once again back in active service with the French!

Meantime, the *Windham* had been recaptured when at anchor through a bold 'cutting-out' expedition by boats from the Royal Navy frigate HMS *Magicienne*. This successful action had taken place on 10 Dec 1809, and she had been brought to the Cape by a prize-crew. Captain STEWART had therefore been able to 'reclaim' his ship on his return to the Cape – albeit that she had previously been well-pillaged by the French. He now had the disadvantage that only a dozen of the new crew he had hastily recruited at the Cape were white men. Some 100 were Lascars of Indian origin, as compared with the usual figure of about 30. His fighting ability was now correspondingly reduced. He was now busily re-stocking his ship using all the services available at the Cape – and, having had his previous business schedule totally disrupted, he was looking for all and any trade and hence he was more than ready to add his ship to the fleet which was to convey such officers and men of the 24th who were available, for onwards transit to India. Once there, he could hope to begin to pick up the business threads of his normal schedule once more.

Be that as it all may, according to regulation, the troops were given just two days to 'sort themselves out' and to settle down aboard their respective ships. Jonas was in the company commanded by Captain Richard GUBBINS, whose men were quickly settling down aboard the virtually brand-new *Astell*. Jonas was one of those men who was up and about early on the 11th June 1810, when *Astell*'s men hoisted in the launch, and carefully stowed and secured it on its mountings in the well of the Upper-Deck. They then unmoored the ship, which was temporarily hove-to.

There was some sort of 'kerfuffle' at this time aboard the *Ceylon,* which apparently delayed the departure of the whole convoy from Capetown. (Rumour later said that a couple of seamen had deserted from the *Ceylon* that day, making off in her large cutter – which had been alongside – when doing so. The Captain wanted both the cutter and the two seamen back – though it was probable that the latter had 'gone native' and would in all likelihood be sheltered by the local population. Jonas got to hear about this from one of the seamen, and he also heard that one soldier had collapsed and died in the *Ceylon* on the day of embarkation, and that another had deserted – probably again 'going native' – probably further contributing to the overall delay.)

Due to the problems in the *Ceylon,* the *Astell* had to be re-moored, and the departure of the convoy was delayed until 7.00 am the next day. Its leaving that day took place in rain and what the sailors called 'very thick weather'. There was just a modest north-west wind to help to carry the convoy out of the bay. At 8.00 the *Astell* passed the

Noah's Ark rock which Jonas remembered from their inward voyage to the Cape, back in 1809. Two hours later, some of the seamen told Jonas and his pals that the *Euphrates* was clearly in trouble, because she 'was down in the water' and she was flying a signal of distress. In fact, it later transpired that she had hit a hidden reef and that she was making water fast. Seemingly in vain, she was trying to signal to the Commodore aboard the *Ceylon*. Jonas soon heard some of the *Astell's* seamen being called on deck to man one of the guns, and the gun then crashed out three shots, to emphasise the *Euphrates'* signal, which the *Astell*, being a little nearer to the *Ceylon*, was repeating

However, the *Ceylon* still made no response, and evidently did not see or hear the signals, due to the adverse weather. Soon, the *Ceylon* was out of sight to the south-west.

At 11.00 am the *Euphrates* started to fly another signal, which *(the seamen said)* indicated that her condition was worse, and that she was now in serious danger of sinking – albeit, as could be seen and heard, parties of soldiers were actively aiding her seamen to work her pumps. The *William Pitt* then flew a signal which *(the seamen again said)* meant that she would stand beside the *Euphrate*s to rescue as many as possible of the people aboard her, should the *Euphrates* sink as she tried to struggle back into Capetown. Once there, the *Euphrates* would attempt to go into dry dock – or try to be safely beached if docking was not immediately available.

The *Windham* then started to fly a signal which indicated *(the seamen yet again said)* that her Captain wanted to discuss the situation with the Commodore – or with the second in command of the convoy. The Commodore being out of sight, Captain HAY of the *Astell* took the responsibility and called for his gig. He was rowed to the *Windham* and went aboard her, returning after about twenty minutes. Seemingly, there had been a debate between the captains about what best to do. The *Ceylon* being out of sight to the south-west, it had presumably been agreed between the two Captains that they had better continue on their present course, and to try to catch up with the *Ceylon*. The convoy would be seriously weakened by the absence of the *William Pitt* and the *Euphrates*, but sail they should – and must. Assuming that she reached safety at Capetown, the *Euphrates* would need time to be repaired. The *William Pitt* could follow on just as soon as her escorting duty to the *Euphrates* was done - preferably then sailing in convoy with other ships – but alone if necessary. Signals were exchanged to this effect, with all the Captains apparently being in agreement.

In the meantime, the weather had freshened. By the 17th the *Astell* and the *Windham* had caught up with the Ceylon, and, using the prevailing westerly winds, were proceeding in company with her, the three ships having made their way around the Cape of Good Hope, and now shaping a course up the south-eastern coast of Africa. Once again, there was much sea-sickness aboard the ships, which were well battened-down, for fresh gales, high following seas and hard squalls were now being experienced. These gales were not entirely unexpected, for the area to the east of the Island of Madagascar was prone to tropical storms – but it looked as though they had found themselves a real corker, and one which was raging further south-west than usual. Due to the adverse weather, the *Astell,* like her consorts, was under close-reefed topsails.

By the 20th June, the wind was blowing even harder, the clouds were heavy and gloomy and there was much lightning. St Elmo's fire, once a cause of fear amongst ancient mariners, could be discerned crackling around the mast-heads. At the risk of their lives, the seamen handed down the top-gallant yards, took in some of the sails and close-reefed the mainsail. Below decks the scene was appalling. Only the seamen were allowed on deck – it was deemed to be far too dangerous for other people – and Jonas found no escape from the misery and stench below-decks. Vomit was everywhere – soldiers, women and children lay in it, their bodies limp and tumbling about with the constant and violent motion of the ship, which was pitching heavily and often rolling nigh on to her beam ends. Some people were thrown out of their bunks, or against deck-beams, etc., leading to serious contusions and a few broken limbs.

Mrs Murphy saw that Jonas was one of the few soldiers who was just about surviving in this holocaust of a gale, in their dark, candle-lit and violently-tossed about accommodation, *"Would youse be after joinin' me in havin' a wee drop of me potcheen, me darlin'?"*, she asked him, *"Here's me husband sleepin' like a wee baby and dead to the World – the poor soul is exhausted – for he ha' been so dreadful sick these last four days, bless him - an' I've niver a soul to exchange a friendly word with! All the other good ladies is sick as could be – an' here's me truly terrified o' the sea! Come now, me darlin' Jonas, the potcheen is home-made from years ago – t'wont cost you a penny me treasure, and it'll do you a real lot of good!"*

So Jonas found himself drinking the fiery spirit, which, as Mrs Murphy warned him, needed to be just touched to one's lips and very gently sipped. Even so, it seemed to set his breastbone afire, and the warmth of it, expanding through his body, did indeed make him feel a lot better. *"Oh, Mrs M"*, he said, *"You are truly a jewel amongst women! This is wonderful stuff! The sergeant is a very lucky man to have you as his wife. I'm not surprised that he looks like a 'doggie with two tails' at times, and I'm sorry to see him laid so low at the moment. Let's hope that this storm blows itself out soon, so that he and all our other men can quickly recover themselves."*

"There's roight y'are – may the Good Lord safeguard us all, and bring us to a quick calm!", replied Mrs Murphy, *"Now, p'raps you'll be arfter letting me have a sixpenny piece from your foine pocket, and I'll be passing you some good Oirish whuskey!"*. And so Jonas began to settle down for a remarkable afternoon with Mrs Murphy, in which a certain amount of his money changed hands, and the two of them each consumed a remarkable amount of good, strong spirit, whilst the storm started to gradually blow itself out. During that time the two of them exchanged their life-stories, wept over this and that nostalgic reminiscence, laughed hysterically over this and that amusing recollection, swapped jokes, clung to each other at times – helpless with joy or sadness, or just thrown about by the mad gyrations of the ship – but ended up by bidding each other a very fond farewell at 'Lights Out' – both as drunk as lords and never to have any but the vaguest memory of what each had said to the other. Just a permanent feeling of great mutual respect between the two of them, partly induced by the fact that, although almost pathologically drunk, the two of them were still not only more or less 'conscious', but still able to walk – even if they had to hang on to more or less solid objects to do so!

Sure enough, by the 23rd June the weather had eased, and there were only light winds. The men of the 24th were paraded on deck and Sergeant Kipling, as the senior NCO, detailed the men to their various duties in defence of the ship. In essence, these were the same as those when previously aboard the *Abraham Newland* on the voyage out from England. This quick allocation of duties was just as well, because many of the men were still too ill to stand for long, and the parade was soon dismissed.

Thereafter, Jonas was permitted to stay on deck, to clear his still-fuzzy head. Once again, the seamen were brilliant, and, joined by the few redcoats who felt up to the task, they set about cleaning up the 'tween-decks area, and washing-down the gun deck.

Sad to say, Private Jeremy THOMPSON had injured himself by a fall during the storm. He had also been one of the worst affected with seasickness, and, despite all that the surgeons could do, he died. His body was sewn into a hammock, with a heavy iron shot at his feet, and his body was committed to the deep in an impressive funeral service, with Major FORSTER reading movingly from the Good Book.

It was their salvation that the ship was still sailing under reduced canvas, for, that same evening, another squall suddenly hit the ship and her two consorts, and a heavy swell quickly developed, causing extreme motion in the ship. During the evening, a further heavy squall split the foretopsail, which quickly began to thrash itself to tatters. The seamen managed to get it down. The weather improved somewhat the next day, and the Sailmaker washed and set a replacement for the foretopsail, before (the day after), setting about a repair of the badly-damaged one. Once again, the seamen washed the Upper Deck and fatigue parties of soldiers and sailors cleaned the 'tween deck areas.

The ship had been taking such a pounding from the heavy seas that, on the 30th June it was considered advisable to stay the foretopmast and the top gallant mast, and to re-set the rigging – so Jonas and his comrades were not allowed on deck whilst that dangerous repair work was in hand.

By now the ships had travelled some 133 nautical miles – but they were still hugging the east coast of Africa with the crossing of the Indian Ocean still lying ahead of them.

Until this time the seamen had been extraordinarily busy. However, Jonas had a shock on the evening of the 1st July, when a familiar shape suddenly loomed up in the twilight. *"How are you, bor?"* it asked in a soft Suffolk accent. *"Well, damn my soul!"* said Jonas, *"Whatever are you doing here, Bill?"*

"Ah, well", said Bill Hitchings, *"I was paid off from the Abraham Newland when we got back to England, and I managed to get the position of Fourth Mate on this fine East Indiaman, which happened to be in port at Tilbury at the time! I was very lucky to do so, for the previous holder of the position had suddenly fallen ill, right on the eve of her departure for India, and Captain HAY needed an immediate replacement. Normally, the positions of the mates are only open to a select few, as pre-organised by the captain – usually with quite a bit of money changing hands. Anyway – here I be, and happy at that – and truly delighted to re-make your acquaintance!"*

The two men quickly fell into conversation, and Bill mentioned to Jonas that the question now looming for the Commodore was whether or not to risk the Mozambique Channel. This would offer more sheltered waters, and be better for the comfort of the passengers, but possibly put the convoy at a greater risk of interception by hostile warships than might have been the case in the more open waters to the south of the Island of Madagascar. It seemed likely that the Commodore would decide to risk the channel route. *"What's this about 'hostile warships', Bill"*, asked Jonas.*" What nationality are they?"*

"Aha," replied Bill, *"Well, by all accounts there's a remarkably clever French naval captain around. I reckon he must have played at 'conkers' when he was a schoolboy. That is to say, arriving in this area from France with just one or two*

warships of his own, he seems to be gifted at capturing our merchantmen one by one, adding further guns and large crews of his own men to 'em, and thus converting them into fighting ships. In that way, he's managed to build himself up quite a little fleet, and it's said that he's striving to build it up even more. It seems likely that his fleet is based at the Isle of France – otherwise known as Mauritius - which is not too far from here! I just hope that we don't meet him in force – especially as we're now down to only three ships, instead of the five which was originally intended...I'd have felt happier if we had a naval frigate as an escort...and I've been hoping that we might fall in with one."

"I've never heard you talk as dismally as that!" said Jonas.

"Oh – Sorry!", said Bill, lightening his tone, *"I didn't mean to sound off! I bet that Captain STEWART of the 'Windham' is just hoping against hope to get his hands on the Johnny Crapauds again and to wreak his revenge on 'em! He's a real old warhorse and a living example to us all!"* (Bill deliberately chose not to tell Jonas of the awful and disturbing premonitions that were haunting his very soul.)

On the 2nd July all hands were called on deck to witness punishment, and the officers and soldiers of the 24th were also paraded. A William JAMES seaman, had been confined in irons for disobedience. Now, a court of enquiry was being held upon his case. He was found guilty by the ship's commander, Captain HAY, and he was sentenced to receive 36 lashes. In fact, he was given only 24 lashes, taking his punishment with some dignity, and with the captain forgiving him the rest. On that same occasion, John PERKINS, one of the quartermasters, received 12 lashes for desertion and two other seamen each received six lashes for neglect of duty. This was the closest that Jonas had come to witnessing such brutal punishment. He wondered if the behaviour was a token that these men had actually been worn out from their continual exertions in the stormy weather the ship had been passing through. Once again he doubted the wisdom of the savage treatment – though he could see that the men's crimes did need to be expiated in some way as an example to the rest of the crew.

Meantime, the convoy had entered the Mozambique Channel and, aided by the still-stiff cyclonic winds was proceeding north-eastwards through it, towards the open seas of the Indian Ocean. The weather was fine and flying fish were often to be seen, leaping briefly out of the sparkling blue sea. On another occasion Jonas also witnessed dolphins which were dashing through the clear water just ahead of the ship's bows, and now and again leaping clear of the waves. It was a fine sight to behold and one which Jonas would keep forever in his mind's eye.

Jonas had come on deck early in the morning of the 3rd July, when he noticed that the ship's officers were grouped together on the quarterdeck, peering through their telescopes well ahead of the ship, towards the north-east. Shading his eyes with his hand, Jonas could just discern three sailing vessels out there.

The call was made for 'All Hands', and Jonas immediately heard the insistent noise of the drum calling the men to quarters, and the rumbling noise of the cannon being made ready. *(As Sergeant-Major Miller had told his men at the time of their departure from English shores, the noise of the drum 'beating men to quarters' was indeed 'gut-melting'!)* The flintlocks for the cannon were being rapidly issued to the gun-captains, the decks were being soaked with water, and then sanded, and barrels of water, with swabs, were being placed all over the ship – both for dousing any fires and for refreshment. There were also shouted orders stemming from below decks, and, in response, redcoats were spilling on to the Upper Deck, still pulling on and straightening their uniforms and accoutrements. Jonas promptly sped down in the reverse direction, against the stream of his comrades, bumping into some and receiving mouthfuls of good-humoured curses in response! However, he reached his bunk, quickly donned his cross-belts, complete with his bayonet, grabbed his musket, and headed swiftly back to the Upper Deck, finding Corporal Jones already at their preliminary Action Station, together with 'Shiny' Silver and Tom Simmons.

The seemingly imperturbable Sergeant Kipling was nearby, standing with the Company Officers, including Captain Richard GUBBINS who was still in charge of the Company in which Jonas and his colleagues were serving. Major FORSTER was on the quarterdeck, in close conversation with Captain HAY. Seemingly, the Commodore had signalled from the *Ceylon*, that, despite flying English colours, the three strangers might well be French and that all three ships of the convoy should prepare for action against them. The *Ceylon* was now sailing under topsails only, having furled her mainsails. The *Astell* and the *Windham* were manoeuvring to get in her wake, whilst the Commodore flew interrogative signals to the strangers – apparently without any response, which indeed seemed very ominous – especially as the strangers were now closing with the convoy, and were now only six or seven miles distant.

By 10.00am the breeze was increasing, and the ships hove-to briefly. *Astell* took in the 3rd reef of her topsail, with the wind now freshening further, and with sudden rain squalls. The seas were running high and the ships were heeling to such an extent that they could not keep their deck-gun ports open on the lee side. By midday the word going around was that Commodore had been discussing tactics with the other two Captains (by heliograph for some of the time), and they had agreed that they could not outrun the strangers, but must fight. Indeed, the Captain of the *Windham* had suggested that they get close into the protective lee of the land, and actually let their own speed fall right off, so that they could engage well before dark, and this, too, had been agreed

It was therefore not surprising when their own seamen were ordered to take in the mainsail. Meantime, the strangers had continued to close, and, at about 2.15 pm the leading ship, a frigate, hoisted the French tricolour in place of her English flag, and promptly opened fire. Shortly afterwards, the second ship, a fast corvette of 22 guns, came into action on *Astell's* lee quarter, then bore up, crossed *Astell's* stern, and raked her, causing considerable damage. It was very fortunate that her guns were of small calibre – otherwise the damage might have been terrible within the *Astell*!

By that time, in response to the orders being issued throughout the ship, Corporal Jones had led his little team, including Jonas, straight up to the fighting top of the mainmast. From there, as opportunity offered, they had begun to snipe at the men on the French ships, especially at the officers. However, accuracy in shooting was difficult, owing to the plunging of the respective ships in the choppy sea, and the manner in which the French ships surged ahead at one moment, only to veer off or fall back at the next – and the manner in which the *Astell* herself pitched and rolled. In fact, Jonas became so engrossed in the technical difficulties and ingrained discipline of what he was trying to do, that he almost forgot he was shooting at human beings for the first time in his life – and, despite the French cannon-fire, which caused débris from aloft to fall around their position from time to time, he also half-forgot that the French were hell-bent on killing him and his mates in return, using every means at their disposal!

Glancing at the quarter-deck below and astern of their position, Corporal Jones saw that there was a sudden commotion near to the ship's wheel. *"That's bad luck, lads!"*, he exclaimed, *"Captain HAY is down. I think he's been hit in the thigh!"* , and a few moments later he added, *"Yes – they're carrying him below – Looks like the 1st Mate – that's William HAWKEY – is taking over – That's a hell of a responsibility to suddenly drop on his shoulders. Never mind, keep on firing as best you three can, and as much as you can – That's the best thing we can do!* And, a few moments later he added, *"Good shot, 'Shiny' – I distinctly saw your bullet rip up the deck just by the feet of that French officer – that must have shaken him up a bit! – Keep it up, mate – We'll frighten the buggers off yet! You, too, Jonas – keep up the fusillade – that's the way, my son!"*

Meantime, however, the French frigate (the *Minerve*) was keeping up a continuous fire of both cannon and grapeshot from her heavy 32-pounder guns, mainly at the *Astell* - and she also appeared to be firing bar shot, expanding link shot and 'Langridge' shot from time to time – that is, twin cannon balls with a short rigid bar of steel joining them, shells packed with scrap iron, or thin-walled casings containing rough-edged lengths of iron linked with chain, which burst apart on discharge. The former balls tended to spin noisily and furiously in the air, and were designed to cause havoc amidst the masts and rigging of an opposing ship. So, too, the Langridge shot. Becoming more conscious of the return fire, Jonas fancied that he spotted out of the corner of his eye just such vague dark shapes thrumming and whizzing amongst their mastheads and wreaking serious damage. Certainly, there were now more of the alarming twangs and clangs coming from above their heads, and torn-away fragment of spars and ropes and fragments of wood – some quite large, were now constantly crashing down all around them. Thirty feet below them, the protective net spread over and above the Upper Deck was peppered with rips and tears and well littered with thousands of pieces of débris. There was by now much noise and gun-smoke coming from the six ships involved.

Suddenly, there was a particularly loud crash, and Corporal Jones yelled above the by now almost continuous din, *"They've hit the fighting-top on the foremast and virtually obliterated it! I fear that the fellers there are all dead! And just look at the mess down on the Upper Deck – I can see several guns upended, some with bodies underneath – the bulwarks are shattered here and there – and I have seen several men carried below. This is hot work – but keep right on firing, lads – the Johnny Crapauds must surely be suffering too! Well done – Keep right on going!"*

The corvette was now ranging down their weather side and also firing furiously, so that smoke-clouds were often hiding the *Astell* and the two French ships. Now, however, the frigate suddenly shot ahead and engaged the *Ceylon*, the two ships exchanging broadsides at close range.

The third French frigate, had meantime closed with the *Windham*, and was pouring both cannon and musket fire into her. The French firing, especially of muskets, considerably exceeded that of the under-manned *Windham*. The poor old *Windham* was on a loser in this battle, thought Jonas, though her captain was fighting his ship well and with spirit.

At this stage, as Jonas learnt much later, Captain MERITON of the *Ceylon* received a severe grape-shot wound in the neck and the 2nd mate took over – but only to be himself quickly and severely wounded, whereupon the 3rd Mate, Tristram FENNING took over. It seems that, by that stage, the masts, rigging and sails of the *Ceylon* were badly damaged, as was all of her upper deck. Five of her lower-deck guns had been disabled, and, due to shot-holes below her water-line, she was making 3ft of water per hour.

However, as Jonas could see from his vantage-point in the fighting-top, the French were not having things all their own way, and the largest frigate (the *Bellone*, armed with 42-pounder carronades, as it turned out) – which had not long entered the fight – suddenly hauled out of line, having lost her main and mizzen top-masts and having also suffered considerably from the musket-fire of the British troops which had almost swept the gun-crews from her upper decks.

Astell was now re-engaged by the *Bellone*, only for Jonas to suddenly find that he was lying flat on his back on the deck of the fighting top, all the breath knocked out of him, gazing dazedly at the broken stump of the topmast swaying back and forth above him. It dawned on him that he had lost consciousness, though he did not know for how long. His brain was gradually returning to him. Looking to his right, he realised that what remained of the late Corporal Jones lay close at hand. The body had no legs at all and Jonas was lying in a vast pool of blood which had pulsed out from it. Of 'Shiny' Silver there was no sign – except of his badly smashed musket. Of Simmons there was absolutely no evidence at all. The two seamen had also disappeared and the fighting-top was a ruin, with all its surrounding woodwork smashed to smithereens – clearly, a Langridge shot had swept nearly all of it away.

Still part-deafened, and as if in a dream, Jonas could hear a distant voice calling to Corporal Jones. *"Jonesy! – Jonesy! Hi, there, Corporal Jones – are you all right? How are your men, Jonesy? Report your damage!"*

Jonas realised it was the indomitable Sergeant Kipling calling up to their position from the shambles of the Upper Deck. Jonas part-rolled and part-crawled to the splintered edge of what was left of the fighting-top, spat the blood out of his badly-bruised mouth, took as deep a breath as he could, and, peering down through blurred vision, and taking advantage of a brief lull in the cannon-firing, he croaked as loudly as he could, *"Yes, Sergeant! There's only me, Private Green, still alive here! Very sorry to report that Corporal Jones is dead - and Privates Silver and Smithers are missing – presumed dead! The fighting top is a shambles. Two seamen who were here have also - vanished, presumed dead! Sorry, Sergeant."*

"Right Jonas! Message heard and understood. Are you wounded?"

"Only lightly, I think, Sergeant. I'm covered in blood – but I don't think that too much of it is mine! I still have my musket, and I think I can still fire it!"

"Good lad, Jonas! Stay in action if you can – we still need to fight the ship for as long as we can. I'll get some help up to you just as soon as things ease down!"

The firing of heavy weapons and musketry now re-commenced, with the French seeming to concentrate on the masts and rigging, so far as the *Astell* was concerned. Jonas observed just then that the HEIC pennant had been shot away – but he also saw that a brave seaman (he later learned that his name was Andrew PETERS) had now climbed to Astell's maintop masthead, and was just finishing nailing the pennant to it. Sadly, however, even as Jonas watched, he saw the brave man shot and killed as he started to make his descent, the body plunging into the sea.

Through his still-watering eyes Jonas then saw that the *Astell* had now steered under the stern of the *Ceylon*, which was hove-to. *Astell* had spilt the wind from her sails as she did so. He later learned that the time was just after a quarter to eight, with the tropical evening soon to descend. There was a momentary lull in the firing, and he could just about understand a shouted dialogue between the officers of the two ships.

"Ahoy the Ceylon! Why are you stopped and why have you ceased firing?"

"Ahoy, Astell! We have surrendered to the French!"

"Ahoy, Ceylon! – What the bloody hell for??!!"

"Ahoy Astell! – Group decision by the senior HEIC and Army Officers – Sorry! We have surrendered to save unnecessary loss of life! We have already cast the regimental colours, the books and the records overboard to prevent their capture, and we have now ceased fire and hauled down our ensign!"

As Jonas could just about see, there then followed a rapid debate between the deputy Mate of the *Astell* and Major FORSTER, which took place some thirty feet below him and near to the stern of the ship. The two officers came to a sudden decision, and each started shouting orders to their men – and then there was the sight of the quartermasters throwing their weight on the ship's wheel, so that the *Astell* 'turned on her heel' and started rapidly making her way to the westward under the vigorous influence of the strong east wind which was blowing – getting the maximum benefit from it by using it as a 'soldier's wind', that is, by having it coming from dead astern of them. (The *Astell* would modify her course to the north-east when out of gunshot.)

Their move was immediately accompanied by harsh shouting and what sounded like strong cursing from the French ships, together with a further blast of cannon-fire from the *Bellone* to speed them on their way. The French ship *Victor* promptly set more sail and started out in chase of them.

From the sounds that could be heard in the evening air, it seemed that the *Windham* continued in action against the other French ship for a little while longer, but she too had ceased firing long before they were out of earshot of her, and she, too, had presumably hauled down her ensign in token of surrender. Remembering how few were the soldiers aboard her, with the *Astell* making off and with the *Ceylon* already out of the fight, that was scarcely surprising. (It was later learned that Captain STEWART, swiftly recognising what the *Astell* was attempting to do, tried to give her covering fire for the first few essential minutes before himself being forced to surrender, as his ship was a total wreck.)

By now, dusk was falling fast. *Astell* had put out all lights which could be seen outside the ship and now made various changes of course, in the hope of shaking off the *Victor*. (Blue flares from the French ship would be seen during the early part of the night, but, come the morning, the horizon would be providentially clear.)

Sergeant Kipling was as good as his word, and, as soon as the ship made her escape he arranged with the Boatswain for three of the best seamen to carefully climb up the badly-damaged and therefore hazardous ratlines to check on Jonas. By that time Jonas was not feeling at all good. The three seamen swiftly contrived a large sling, whereby they lowered him to the deck, showing surprising gentleness and consideration in doing so. It was clear to Jonas that he was an appalling sight, being saturated from head to foot in the blood of the late Corporal Jones and with splinters and shards of wood and rope and dust covering all his person. He was also badly scratched and abraded, especially on his bare head, and somewhat scorched. His shako was gone heavens knew where, and his uniform was in tatters. Sergeant Kipling seemed amazed that Jonas could still walk with just a little support from two of the seamen. *"Right, Jonas! Off with you to the Sickbay! Escort him down there please, lads. Well done, today, Jonas! I'm very sorry to hear that Corporal Jones and your two pals – and the two seamen – are all gone. Sad to say, they are by no means alone! Off you go, chums!"*

As Jonas later learned, the *Astell* had suffered the loss of four soldiers and four seamen killed outright, and twenty soldiers and nineteen seamen wounded, the latter including Captain HAY and Mr HAWKEY, the 1st Mate – and no less that five of her young cadets. (They would much later learn that theirs were the heaviest total of casualties aboard any of the ships involved! The total 'Butcher's Bill' of the men killed in the French ships had actually matched that of the British ships, but they had only half as many men wounded.)

Very shortly after Jonas had been stripped of the rags of his uniform, cleaned up, bandaged and dressed in a nightshirt, one of the Surgeon's 'Loblolly Boys' came up to him. *"How are you doin, me ol' Jonas?"* he asked, *"Are you up to a short walk if I give you a bit of a hand? – Somebody's been asking for you."*

"Who – what?" said Jonas, *"Can it be that one of my mates from the fighting top has somehow miraculously survived?"*

"Sorry, Jonas – I don't know nothin' about that. Nay, friend, this is Mr Hitchings as has been asking for you. I'm very sorry to have to tell you that he has been very severely wounded and the Surgeon has told me that Mr Hitchings has not long to live."

"Oh, Dear God, No!" exclaimed Jonas, *"Not Bill too!"*

"Yes, but please keep the seriousness of his wounds to yourself, Jonas – Don't let on to him about it!"

And, minutes later, Jonas found himself standing beside Bill's cot. Bill was bandaged from his chest down to his groin, and blood was steadily seeping through the dressings. Bill's face was ashen white, as if he were already exsanguinated – but the spark of life was still there, although the voice was faint and Jonas had to bend over Bill to hear his words.

"Hello, Jonas – thanks for coming to see me. I heard you had been in the wars, too – and it sure looks like it! What have they done to you, dear friend?"

"Yes, Bill – the French blasted our position in the fighting-top apart, killing everybody there except for me. I've no idea why I was left alive…But, tell me, what has happened to you?"

"Ah – well, we weren't doing too badly on the foc'sle – just the odd gun here and there overturned and a few men killed or wounded, but the French were really smashing up the sides of our ship…and I suddenly found myself down on the deck with a damned great splinter of wood driven through my belly…and a musket-ball had struck me in the chest at the same time… So, they carried me down to the Sickbay…The surgeon has done his best – but I'm afraid these wounds have done for me, Jonas!". His eyes closed, and Jonas feared he had gone. But, after a few moments Bill's eyes flickered open again. *"Jonas"*, he murmured, *"I can't see too well – Are you still here?"*

"Yes", replied Jonas, *"I'm right here beside you"*, and he took Bill's near lifeless hand in his own, receiving just a shadow of return pressure from it.

"I'm sorry, pal", murmured Bill, *"Seems like I'll never be able to tell you about charts and longi-tude..."*, and he gave a sort of shuddering sigh as he died. Jonas stared at Bill's face for long moments – it seemed quite impossible that this powerhouse of a man and his fine brain was gone forever. Suddenly, involuntarily, Jonas began to weep – and he wept as he had never wept before, with the tears simply streaming down his face.

The Loblolly Boy had been watching discreetly from a little distance away. He gently closed the staring bright blue eyes of Bill Hitchings, then slid his arms under the unresisting armpits of Jonas, lifted him to his feet, and led him, like a loving father with a son, back to his bunk, helping him in and arranging the bedclothes around him. Jonas was still weeping, with great sobs shaking his rather battered frame from time to time.

"There, there, old lad!", said the Loblolly Boy quietly, *"I'll get you a nice hot mug o'kye with a slug of Navy Rum in it – That'll make the World seem just a tiny bit better. You've had one helluva day, and I think you'll sleep the clock around once the rum takes effect. Now rest easy, dear lad – You're duty is more than done for today!"*

Jonas was indeed fast asleep when Sergeant Kipling and Captain GUBBINS later made their rounds of the wounded, though the courses made by the tears through the scorch marks and pock-wounds on the face of Jonas were very evident. *"Young Jonas did incredibly well today, Sir!"* said Sergeant Kipling. *"Yes, I think that every man-jack did, Sergeant,"* replied Captain GUBBINS. *"The next question is what the morrow will bring? Will we have to stand to our arms yet again, I wonder?"*

Jonas slept right through the next day (the 4th July), whilst the ship and her exhausted company fortunately remained unmolested, and she gave formal naval burials to her dead – but Jonas began to take notice of the world around him on the 5th July, and, despite feeling incredibly stiff and bruised, with the help of one of the Loblolly Boys, he actually managed to get dressed. He had been wearing his 2nd best uniform jacket during the engagement two days earlier, and that was totally ruined. However, his best uniform jacket had somehow survived intact in the ruin of the 'tween decks, and somebody kindly fetched that for him to put on. He then managed, with some assistance, to stagger up to the Upper Deck.

There was much damage to be seen, both 'alow and aloft' as the seamen put it. Due to the havoc the French had created aloft, the foretop yards and mast were in a parlous state, and had had to be brought down. Already, however, the seamen were at work, preparing a replacement foretopmast on the Upper Deck. The Gunner had a party at work, getting those guns which had been overturned back onto their trunnions, and making such repairs to them as was possible. The Carpenter could be heard over the side, working off a staging which was moved along from time to time. He was plugging the many shot-holes in the hull, above the water-line. Some of his aids were neatly patching the smashed parts of the bulwarks and the gun-ports. Two sails had already been fothered over the worst of the shot-holes below the water-line, to slow down the inrush of water. Fatigue parties of soldiers were working two-hour shifts in constantly pumping ship, with some of the passengers helping at that and other tasks, the clanking of the pump merging with the other sounds of the repair work proceeding busily on every hand.

There was still no sight of any other ships – French or otherwise – but land was in sight. This was apparently the Island of Johanna.

There was much conversation as to the fate of the men who had been aboard the *Ceylon* and the *Windham* – men who were now all presumably in the hands of the French. There was curiosity as to how the French would treat them, and where the French might be taking them. It was presumed that the officers would be 'exchanged' ere long, but it seemed difficult to say what the fate of the rank and file would be. Sergeant Kipling was not very forthcoming when Jonas summoned up the courage to ask him about the matter, *"I don't know that I can tell you much, Jonas,"* he said, *"I suspect that I would be in despair at the prospect of being held prisoner by the French for a long period. There is no exchange system for the ordinary rankers like you and me. I'd just be hoping for the best, I suppose – but I don't know what that would be – maybe a reasonably cushy billet workin' on a farm or on a plantation, or something like that. Just to be kept behind bars could be very demoralising. I sure hope that the French are being considerate to our lads – they must be holdin' well over four hundred of 'em from the 24th alone!"*

From what Jonas could understand the forty or so of his fellow-wounded in the *Astell* were generally doing well – though he understood that the danger of possible infection of their wounds would not materialise for a few days. As for himself, he not only felt battered, sore and bruised, but he was also emotionally drained, and deeply affected by the loss of Bill Hitchings, Corporal Jones, 'Shiny' Silver and the others. Jonas kept having mental flashes of the bloody horror of the fighting-top after it had been hit, and he was glad to regain his bunk that afternoon, where he quickly fell into an exhausted sleep.

The weather remained changeable, but the next day, despite some squally rain showers, the seamen fidded the new foretopmast to the foremast, and set up the new rigging. In the early evening, as Jonas watched, they bent the 2nd best foretopsail on the new foretopmast. Then they got down the main topgallant yard and mast – got up a new topmast and exchanged the damaged main topsail for the 'second-best' one. Now, the ship was at last beginning to get into a fit state to sail and fight again, and they now began their risky voyage to cross the wide expanse of the Indian Ocean, and so to India.

However, as the Carpenter established, the *Astell* was still leaking, and making up to 14 inches per hour despite the constant pumping. This remained a real danger for them all. Some of their boats were still damaged, and there was far from sufficient accommodation for all the people on board – should the *Astell* start to take in even more water.

Almost frantic activity was now taking place on board, the work continuing through the Sabbath day. The mainmast had been damaged by shot, and the Carpenter fished a heavy spar to it, to improve its strength, before the mainsail was bent on the mast. He then set about repairing the partially-shattered large cutter, whilst the Sailmaker made a new jack out of the fore topsail, and the Gunner had a team busily making wads to replace the many used in the combat of the 3rd July. These skilled men were certainly earning their pay.

On the 16th July the gun-deck was washed down. The Carpenter was now turning his attention to repairing the jolly boat, and the Sailmaker was preparing a mizzen royal topsail. By this time infection had started up in some of the wounded men, and, on this day, two of the wounded seamen died of their wounds and were reverently buried at sea.

They were Michael GRAB and Peter MacDONALD. On Sunday, the 22nd July, the first of the wounded soldiers died and was also committed reverently to the Deep. He was Private William WRIGHT. However, the Surgeon had done a superb job in keeping so many of the other wounded men in life, and the policy of frequently bringing those who could be moved up on deck for air and sunshine seemed to be working well.

Although his various minor bodily wounds were healing cleanly, Jonas was still in a very depressed state of mind. However, he was proud to be present with some of the other wounded at the ocean burial of Private WRIGHT, when all the fit men of the 24th were paraded. The twelve wives who had sailed with the men were also in attendance, prominent amongst them being Mrs Murphy. *(Happily, and almost incredibly, all the women and children had survived the action of the 3rd July unharmed. They had been put into the Bread Room for the duration of the action, and they must have been scared almost out of their wits by the roaring of the guns and the constant bangs and crashes jarring the ship's timbers.)* At the conclusion of the impressive burial ceremony for Private WRIGHT, Jonas saw out of the corner of his eye that Mrs Murphy was making her way over to where he was sitting, more or less disconsolate.

"How are you doin' Jonas my angel?", she asked him gently, with a kindly smile in her eyes. *"Do youse mind that foine arternoon which we two spent together weeks ago, at the very hoight o' that devilish ould starm? My God, but I was frightened – for them waves was so huge, and the ould ship was plunging all over the shop – but you made me feel so very much bether, bless you!"* and , despite his lack of response, she took a deep breath and then plunged straight on,

"Now, I've bin a'hearing as to how you was so very nearly killed, up in that dreadful foightin-top – where my husband's friend – that poor Corporal Jones – was so sadly taken from this loife – an' your two buddies with 'im. I know for a fact that Sergeant Kipling was deeply impressed by your valour that day – because he ha' told my husband, Sergeant Murphy about it all.

Now, I can see that you're still a'pinin' about the loss o' your dear friends, my Jonas. But, don't take on too much – a soldier's life is full of hard knocks, an' it don't do to reflect too much about the deaths of friends – no matter how close they may ha' been. Just know that they have gone to a better place – somewhere where we will all go at any toime – so best, as people say, to 'gather ye rosebuds while ye may'!

I might as well tell thee – indeed, ye may already know – that Sergeant Murphy ain't by any means my first husband – I've already buried two others in my loife – and two darlin' children as well. I loved them all as deep as the sea – but we just ha' to carry on, best we can – an' hope that the next chapter of our life will be just as good as may be. So, 'Cheer up for Chatham – Dover's in soight!' as people say – Well, if not Chatham – at least Madras will be loomin' up shortly! And who knows what new adventures and marvels lie in wait for us, eh? – To say nothin' of all the new hardships!"

Jonas, couldn't help himself – he just had to smile a bit at this doughty woman, even if she was bringing the tears back into his eyes again…

And, seeing she was getting a glimmer of positive response from the poor, hunched and battered figure that was Jonas, Mrs Murphy continued softly,

"Here, now, me lucky lad, oi've brought this wee drop of potcheen along especially for you – just take it in small sips mind!...There, that's better – now you just wipe away those tears – take a deep breath, and think that you've been saved by the

Good Lord for some special reason. There's a lot more loife for you to live yet – and plenty of new chapters, so to speak! So brace up, my hearty! St George for England – and St Paddy for Old Oirland!", and heaving herself (and her handsome and half-exposed bosom) upright, she continued,

"Righto, Jonas, well that's the end of my sermon for today!", and off she went, her self-imposed task done, for the mental depression which had lain like a leaden cloud over Jonas had begun to ease from the moment that Mrs Murphy had started to speak so encouragingly to him.

Sure enough, the navigation of the *Astell* having been aided by the south-westerly Monsoon winds which were now prevailing, the Malabar Coast of India <u>was</u> looming up on their their larboard side, and they would soon be rounding Cape Comorin and making their way through the Palk Strait which separated India from Ceylon before heading northwards up the Coromandel Coast. On Thursday 2nd August the *Astell* came at last into Madras Roads. As was normally the case, there was a considerable swell running. The officers and men were elated at their safe passage, and fired a salute of 13 guns to celebrate the action of the 3rd July, followed by the regular salute of 11 guns for Fort St George. They were boarded by a boat from HMS *Russell*, with her naval officers curious as to why they had run the gauntlet of the Indian Ocean alone, keen to check out their credentials and then quickly agog to learn more of the action of the 3rd July.

The first priority was to get the seriously wounded men ashore, and into the hospital. Jonas and the other lightly-wounded men stayed aboard, and were disembarked with all the 240 fit men of the 24th, commencing at daylight the next day, the 3rd August. Due to the heavy surf, the landing at Madras was by *'mussulah'* boats, commanded by *'tindals'* (coxswains) who expertly directed the rowers from a platform in the stern. It seemed strange to see these rather primitive-looking boats in full use against the splendid backdrop of the beautifully-constructed and brilliantly white-coloured 'traders and directors' buildings and well-kept gardens which formed the waterfront at Madras. Fort St George itself was a truly massive structure with strongly-built gun-batteries.

After the sun came up, the awnings of the *mussulah* boats were spread out to provide welcome shade. Jonas found it fascinating to travel by one of these boats, which were swept boldly in on the surf. In fact, during the trip which Jonas made, there were three successive banks of foaming and thundering breakers to negotiate and profit from, each of which towered over the supple mussulah boat, thrice lifting it almost to a vertical stance as it careered its way in three great surging pulses to the shore, yet with the tindals somehow always seeming to keep the apparently unwieldy craft upright, bows pointing ahead, and safe. Under the directions of their *tindal*, the crew dipped and swung the oars just as needed to 'catch' each big wave, and to stop the boat from broaching-to, often timing their swings to a weird maritime chant to Allah, so different in tone and rhythm to an English sailors' sea shanty. (In case of accidents on the way in through the breakers there were small catamarans, crewed by lone natives, constantly on the lookout to save any persons who happened to be thrown into the sea. Luckily, there was no need for their services on this occasion.)

At the end of the run, as their boat was being hurled up onto the shore amidst the foam of the last broken wave, a horde of natives seized the boat before the backwash of the wave could drag it back into the ebbing but still raging foam of the breakers. The natives quickly dragged the boat well up the beach, so that Jonas and his companions could disembark dry-shod. Immediately the soldiers did so, they were surrounded by a motley crowd of natives flourishing sundry credentials and certificates and each vociferously begging to become the humblest of servants – seeking out especially the officers, though some of the NCOs and even a few of the ordinary rankers elected to choose a servant too.

The lightly-wounded men (including Jonas, to his chagrin) and the ladies of the 24th were individually helped to climb out, once the *mussulah* boat had been hauled well up the beach, it usually needing two of the thinly-framed rowers to provide the help needed by each white person.

Once ashore from the boats, the men of the 24th formed up, and marched inland with pride, behind Major Thomas Watkin FORSTER, their six officers and their five drummers and five fifers.

One of the first impressions to strike Jonas was the heat. It was quite different to the heat of the sun as he had experienced in South Africa. It was more like being in a sort of gentle oven, where the very fabric of the surroundings had absorbed the sun's rays for millennia, and were now just releasing the heat of them, bit by bit. True, there was light and shade, in itself somewhat less stark than it had been in South Africa, but there was only a little perceptible escape from the all-pervading heat by just finding the nearest area of shade. It was well into the normal time of the Monsoon, but the weather chose to be sultry but quite dry on that day. The eastern breeze off the sea was itself a blessing, though Jonas was warned about a wind from the south which could blow at any time from July to September. It was called a 'Long-Shore Wind' and it could be unpleasantly damp and not at all cooling.

Perhaps the second impression to strike Jonas was the huge variety of smells, many of which were totally alien to him and hard to identify – especially in the crowded native part of Madras. Almost everywhere was the smell of cow dung – which the natives made into flat, circular 'cakes' to use as fuel. And the third impression was one of a huge range of dazzling colours, of which subject more presently. For the moment, Jonas just let these almost overwhelming impressions wash over him as his feet carried him on.

The detachment was given a warm reception by the authorities as its men marched through the Main Gate into the huge and commanding structure of Fort St George. The Main Gate was located in the North Wall, facing the 'Black Town' where the majority of the natives lived. The fort was built as a huge rectangle, with a glacis protecting each of the walls on its three landward sides. The imposing structure of the fort stood right on the edge of the sea, and there was a strongly-defended 'Sea Gate' into the fort. A small 'postern' gate on the south side was the only other entrance. The stout walls of the fort had guns mounted on them, and there were lofty rounded defensive 'bastions' at each of the four corners. Having arrived at Fort St George, the men of the 24th were temporarily housed in the vast and echoing 'King's Barracks' aligned along the internal face of the western wall, opposite to the old Portugese Church, and near to the strategically important points of the Guardhouse, the Governor's House and the Magazine. *Charpoys* (instead of bunks) were set out in orderly rows in the barracks, each *charpoy* having a large mosquito net hung around it. Here the troops immediately began to make themselves at home.

The Adjutant-General, W GRANT, issued a General Order, *"Offering His Best Thanks for their highly Gallant and Meritorious Conduct during an action of Several*

Hours Engaged by a French Squadron of Superior Force". The 24th were told that *"His Excellency has pleasure in forwarding to England a Report on their Honourable Conduct to be Laid Before the King."* Later, the men of the 24th learned that Captain HAY of the *Astell* had received a pension of £460 from the HEIC, and that the crew had received 'Prize Money' of £2,000, to be apportioned between them. (The seamen had also received certificates giving them three years of 'protection from the Press Gangs of the Royal Navy'.) However, the soldiers had received no such pecuniary rewards at all!

Talking strategically, Jonas found that the British 'held' a large area in the south of India around Madras. Also a much larger area to the north, in Bengal, nearly 700 miles to the north of Madras. This area extended out westwards along the huge valley of the River Ganges which ran to the south of the Himalayan mountains, and embracing other provinces, such as Uttah Pradesh. The two large areas in the south and the north were connected by a fairly narrow strip of land running continuously up the east coast. The British also 'held' the city and port of Bombay, on the west coast. By the term 'held' one needed to understand that the British were only present due to 'business and/or protective agreements' which had originally been drawn up by the Honourable East Indies Company with various of the rajahs and princes of the related localities – but the British 'occupation' was now being slowly strengthened by a few battalions of various regiments of the British Army. These had been sent to India as a back-up for the native regiments under British officers which had long been formed by the Honourable East Indies Company – mainly with the intention of keeping out possible French and Russian 'intrusions'. Overall, the political scene was a complex and dynamic one, with the HEIC and the British government back home in England not always seeing eye to eye on policy. Complications also arose due to the lawlessness which broke out from time to time in the territories where the British currently had no representation.

Jonas played only a muted part in the celebrations surrounding the safe arrival of the *Astell*, for he had been put on 'light duties' until his 'surface' wounds were really well-healed. He found that there were a myriad of impressions to take in, and that a whole new language was swiftly developing amongst his fellow-soldiers – in an effort to deal with living amidst the Indian people – who, of themselves, spoke a variety of languages. Some of the first people he personally encountered were the so-called *'nabobs'*, most of whom were nominally white men, and most of whom were making quite a good living by trading. It was said that certain of these men 'had a lick of the tar-brush' (to quote the vernacular of the period), meaning that although one of their parents had been of European origin, the other had been of Indian origin – usually a Hindu woman. This was scarcely surprising, since there were a fair number of white men around, but comparatively few white women. (Such white women as were around were mostly married or otherwise related to the more senior army officers or to the senior officials of the Honourable East Indies Company. These women tended to regard themselves as much 'superior' to the private soldiers and as 'infinitely superior' to all but the richest of the native population.) The *nabobs*, sometimes top-hatted and in European clothing, tended to ride small ponies, or to be carried in *'palanquins'* by native bearers – symbolic of the status which they themselves felt they deserved.

The native Indians enormously outnumbered the white people – and were sometimes to be seen in incredible multitudes – especially when they assembled together for a festival or to worship one of their gods – as for the festival of *Mohurrum* which was held by the Mahommedans in August. As Jonas learnt, there were various races of the natives, each with its own religion. There was also a caste system, whereby some races of people were regarded as of lower status than others, with the lowest (who had the poorest, and often the most insanitary of jobs) being regarded as *'untouchables'* by the people of higher caste. A few of the Indians had enormous wealth, but most were poor – many incredibly so, and just living from hand to mouth. The Mahommedans of Madras hated the Mahommedans who lived in the area of the Ganges and in Oude with an animosity of long-standing origin. The Hindus of the native army of Madras were antagonistic to the Mahommedans of Madras. All hated the Christians. Homosexuality was well-tolerated amongst the Indians – though (officially at least) it was regarded as a serious crime by the British military and civil authorities.

Cows wandered freely on the streets – even in the populous cities like Madras – and were venerated. At some times of the year the people decorated them in vivid colours. Indeed, as a general matter, bright colours were to be seen everywhere, often accompanied by the gaudiest of metallic decoration. The women wore *saris,* usually of brilliant colours. Most native men wore simple, loose, white clothes, often with a coloured turban. Widows wore white – and were not allowed to re-marry. In fact, widows of Hindu men were expected to throw themselves upon the funeral pyres of their dead husbands in a ceremony called *'suttee'*. To the minds of the British inhabitants this seemed to be the most appalling fate – and they were trying to get the practice of *suttee* stopped, although to do so would involve a great risk of upsetting the Hindus.

There was a great deal of loud talking and laughter amongst the native people, intermixed with their religious practices, the temples being highly decorated with frescoes and sculptures illustrating the various myths and legends of the various Indian religions. To European eyes many of the statues seemed to be highly erotic – especially as the *lingam* (the male organ) was an object of worship in some Indian religions. According to what Jonas heard, the people in the different regions roundabout spoke in several different languages, including Tamil and Kannara, and others he'd never heard of before. There was no modesty such as one would expect to find in England, with the native people urinating and passing motions in the streets, without reserve and quite unconcernedly. The chewing of betel nut was also widely practised, with people spitting out the red juice everywhere.

Elephants – with *'Mahouts'* on the elephants' backs – were to be seen, sometimes performing feats of great strength (as in lifting huge logs of wood), and sometimes carrying people in gaily caparisoned *'Howdahs'* on their backs. A few camels, water-buffalo and other large beasts unfamiliar to English eyes were also to be seen. The attitude of the Indians to the animals was quite different to a European perception – because the Hindus (who formed by far the main part of the population in India) believed in the caste system. That is to say that, after death, a person would be reborn as a person of higher or lower caste, or maybe as an animal, the status of person or the type of animal depending upon the quality of life and religious observance the person had led. The races of India other than the Hindus had slightly different concepts, but all treated animals with some sort of respect.

Yet, a high-born Indian would think nothing of severely kicking a lowly servant for some dereliction of duty, imaginary or real. Jonas soon became used to the unedifying sight (to European eyes) of seeing 'a master' raving at one of his servants, and the servant prostrating himself on the ground with his hands over his ears, in an effort to beg forgiveness and thus not to be kicked too severely.

There were a huge number of matters to consider, and a great danger of inadvertently causing offence by accidentally committing some slight. For example, it *might* be acceptable to touch a man's hand on first meeting, but *never* for a man to touch a woman. Generally, it was safer to greet all people with the *namaste*, that is, with the palms and fingers of one's hands placed together and pointing upwards, as if in prayer, and accompanied by a slight bobbing action of the body, rather like a shallow bow. The fact that there were so many different languages spoken by the different races in India also led to complications in understanding.

From the point of view of nature, it was obvious that there were snakes living in the territory – cobras were particularly feared by the soldiers, who liked to have a mongoose or two living in the barracks to 'keep the snakes down' – but the only snakes that Jonas actually saw at this time were in baskets, and owned by so-called 'snake-charmers'. These were natives playing on flute-like pipes, who seemed to have the ability to make their snakes undulate in time with the wailing notes of the pipe. These men appeared to make a reasonable living by performing in public and passing a bowl round into which their listeners were expected to make small donations, their audiences including both the native population and the soldiers of the garrison. There was a lot of argument amongst the soldiers as to whether the snakes were still venomous and dangerous, or whether their 'keepers' had extracted the fangs or stitched up their mouths in some subtle way. It was also said that there were non-venomous 'rat' snakes which resembled the cobra, though they had no hood. Generally, however, any snake found in or around the barracks would be quickly hacked to death by any soldiers who found it. The soldiers also developed a sort of ritual of carefully holding their shoes upside-down and hitting them against something, before donning them in the morning – lest a krait or other small venomous snake had crawled into one or other of them overnight.

There were many Indians who were obtaining some sort of living by performing various services for the soldiers. These included Indian servants of the lower castes who seemed to be part-resident at Fort St George. For a few *pi* (or *annas* for the more laborious tasks) they would sweep an area, their *dhobiwallahs* would do a soldier's laundry, their *charwallahs* would provide hot tea, their *punkawallahs* would operate cooling overhead fans, and so forth. The NCOs were quick to learn how easy it was to boss them around and the ordinary soldiers soon began to follow suit! By now, small numbers of the ordinary rankers and most of the NCOs had hired personal servants.

It was the officers of the 24th who mingled with the senior European traders and officials, and also with the higher and wealthier castes of the Indians, some of whom were *rajahs* – sometimes (though not always) of great wealth and power, and then commanding the devotion of huge numbers of their people. As time went on, Jonas would see a number of such high-caste people, though only at a distance – as when he was posted on guard at a dinner or some other official function. He did, however, get to meet a number of natives going under the title of *Dubash* – men who acted as servants and interpreters for the officers – and from whom he began to pick up a smattering of Indian words.

On Sunday the 5th August, only three days after their own arrival, and to the pleasure and surprise of the men of the 24th who'd arrived in the *Astell*, the *William Pitt* arrived safely, making the numbers of 'other ranks' up from about 240 to 500. The *William Pitt* had followed a very southerly route across the Indian Ocean and had experienced no contact with French ships. It was not until the 17th September that the *Euphrates* also arrived safely, her repairs at Capetown having taken a long while to complete. This made the numbers of the rank and file of the 24th up to 650 or so, implying that some 400 rank and file were PoWs of the French – and about fifteen of the officers.

In the meantime, on the 8th August, a 'cartel' from the Isle of France had arrived, bringing some PoWs. These were mostly officers of various regiments being exchanged, for the French ships were still enjoying some notable successes around the Indian Ocean and they apparently had acquired more prisoners (and thus more mouths to feed) than they felt to be desirable. So it seemed that they had also 'freely' returned a number of other ranks – though, unfortunately, none from the 24th. One inference that could be drawn was that the men of the 24th who had been taken prisoner by the French were almost certainly being held on the Isle de France – otherwise known as Mauritius.

Chapter Seven

The Years 1810 to 1814:

Outbound from Madras and then at Calcutta
(Further news of the 2ⁿᵈ Btn in Combat in Spain.)

There were still a number of repairs to be made to the *Astell,* and Jonas heard that she was surveyed by the master and carpenter of HMS Russell on the 17th August 1810. This was evidently by way of finalising and approving the many repairs which had been made (and re-defining a few others which had yet to be done), because, on the 12th September, Captain GUBBINS' company, including Jonas, re-embarked in the *Astell* – together with the men of the 24th who had arrived in the *Euphrates* and a detachment of the 37th Regiment, who had arrived earlier at Madras. The related women and children of the 24th accompanied them. Once again, there was the excitement and danger of negotiating the heavy surf in *mussulah* boats, though all went well. The *William Pitt* had already departed from Madras, and the men of the 24th who had arrived in her now embarked in the HEIC ship *Sovereign.* The next day the baggage was got aboard the two ships, together with supplies of water. The *Astell* also took on board some despatches. Meantime, the seamen stayed the mizzen topmast and set the rigging up.

The two ships sailed the next day, carrying a total of about a dozen officers and 564 other ranks, and proceeding northwards up the Coramandel coast, heading for Bengal. There was a scare on Sunday 16th September, when a strange ship was seen. As a precaution, the *Sovereign* made the interrogative signal and, together with the *Astell*, beat to quarters and 'cleared ship for action'. So, once again, Jonas heard that 'gut melting' sound, and hurried to his action station (This time a firing-position in a file on the upper deck, rather than being up aloft in a fighting-top.) However, the stranger appeared to make no response to the *Sovereign's* signal, continued on her course and was out of sight by sunset. The troops had long been stood down by that time.

The weather continuing fine, on Tuesday 16th the two ships put studding booms on their foreyards, and spread extra sails, to speed their progress through the water. The seamen also washed the upper deck and fatigue parties of soldiers were put to picking oakum, ready for use by the Caulker on any seams which began to open-up in the sunlit heat.

On 27th September, ahead of them, the two ships now had a coastline extending as far as the eye could see to west and north, and, although invisible to them because of the distance, actually round to the east as well. Directly ahead of them lay the many inlets to the Ganges Delta. They were now at latitude 20° 51N, and each took on a pilot, to guide them safely up to Diamond Harbour, part-way up the largest inlet in the huge delta. This was a wise precaution, as there were dangerous shoals, called 'The Braces', at the mouth of the delta and other shoals further in to the delta.

There was a sad duty for the seamen to do at this time, for, after a long struggle, Gunner James MINGUS had died of his wounds, and his body was taken ashore for formal interment in the European cemetery at Diamond Harbour. Jonas was not a part of it, but the 24th provided a firing party to fire a commemorative volley over his grave.

It was at Diamond Harbour that they landed their delta pilot, and took aboard a river pilot, and then continued their voyage northwards up the Hooghly River from Diamond Harbour to Calcutta, through the northern part of the enormous Ganges delta. The delta seemed to have lush grasses and high banks of dried mud just about everywhere, with constantly shifting muddy shoals. The river was seldom free from floating detritus – half-burnt corpses and scorched wood, parts of trees, small 'islands' of large clumps of grass, and the occasional dead animal… There were 'bunds' in places – large banks of earth constructed in an effort to control the tremendous 'excesses' of the river when it was in flood.

On Sunday 30th September 1810 the ships emerged from the delta to enter the thriving harbour for Calcutta, nearly ninety miles upriver from the sea. The city had an impressive appearance, for the houses, especially at the western extremity of the city, were finely built and decorated in white stonework, and each was surrounded by flourishing gardens. The crew moored ship abreast of the Culpher Monument, and put out a gangplank to the shore. Here most of the passengers left the ship, including the men of the 24th.

The detachment now entered the huge barracks in Fort William, the headquarters of the Honourable East Indies Company. This was a sprawling structure on the east bank of the River Hoogly, built in the old traditional 'star' design and with its central core dating from 1781. All its slopes and ramparts were covered in well-maintained green verdure, the heavy morning dews helping to sustain the greenery through the dry heat of the day. There was a large park-like *maidan* in front of the fort, stretching between the Chowringhee Road and the Hoogly River. The *maidan* was surrounded by dusty trees, and was the place where parades were held. From the fort one could see the river stretching away inland towards its junction with the great River Ganges, the sacred river of the Hindus, whose source lay some 1,500 miles to the north-west, in the distant Himalayan mountains. As seen from the fort, the river was dotted with many isolated trees and the alluvial plain around it headed far, far away. Jonas was told that the river was so broad and mighty that, in places, even far upstream, it resembled an inland sea.

In fact, the vast River Ganges emptied not only into the River Hoogly, but also into a number of other rivers and streams which wound their way southwards through the huge Ganges Delta, to empty into the Bay of Bengal. Indeed, an arm of the River Ganges continued eastwards to link up with the massive Brahmaputra River which flowed into the Gangetic valley from the east, the two then breaking up into further rivers and streams which flowed southwards through the eastern part of the Delta to the sea. The whole area of the Delta was intensively occupied by native families, living in grass-roofed shanties which were mounted on rickety poles, with some families making a precarious living from the farming of land which regularly flooded, others by making salt, and yet other families by fishing. The high mud banks of the rivers and streams were prone to collapse, especially during the rainy season, when floodwaters inundated the river-banks and the delta, with the rivers then sometimes totally changing their courses and radically changing the surrounding landscape.

The 24th quickly settled into their new surroundings at Calcutta. Once again they were in barracks in a huge, echoing building. Here the men again slept on comfortable *charpoys* with mosquito netting. Some men relied on keeping a mongoose against snakes, but there were always large birds called *'adjutants'* strutting about outside the walls of the fort. These birds performed a scavenger role and also attacked any snakes. The *adjutants* were officially protected by the Honourable East Indies Company, and there was a considerable fine for anybody who harmed one.

The soldiers' meals began to acquire a few Indian characteristics, especially in the use of curry and other spices, and often in the replacement of potatoes with boiled rice. The military activities of the troops consisted of parades on the *maidan*, usually conducted before the heat of the day became intense. By now the troops were wearing white cloths suspended from their rear of their shakos to protect the back of their necks from the sun. There were regular route marches and practices at manoeuvring, such as quickly forming into line from column. There were also routine practices at arms training, including volley-firing at targets and standardised exercises with the bayonet. When in barracks, the life of the men was made easier by the employment of native Indians to do the more mundane of tasks, including latrine duty and the polishing of brass-work. Perhaps the most vital task was carried out by the servants who operated the *punkas* – in effect large cooling fans - which created a current of air through the barrack-rooms. The constant wetting of fibrous screens placed across many of the external doorways also helped to keep the air somewhat cooled.

Although the western part of the city was made up of many fine buildings interspersed with trees and flowering shrubs, in stark contrast, there were also many native hovels made of mats, grass-thatch and bamboo, scattered 'higgledy-piggledy' amongst them, and many impoverished native bazaars were dispersed amongst the avenues leading off from the principal streets.

Jonas found that boredom could be a serious problem. It was not helped by the fact that so many of the menial tasks could be performed by the Indians for such small amounts of money – so that time tended to hang heavy on the hands of the soldiers. One escape lay in wandering around the native bazaars, where all kinds of knick-knacks were available at remarkably low prices, especially if one was prepared to haggle a bit. These knick-knacks included native jewellery of all descriptions – bangles, beads, rings and bracelets. There was also food to be had, which some soldiers risked, though Jonas felt it was rather unwise – especially as their rations at the barracks were quite substantial. For his own part, Jonas found that some of the native crafts were fascinating, and he became quite friendly with a Hindu family engaged in the manufacture of metal pots and pans of various descriptions – even to the extent of sometimes 'trying his own hand' under 'native supervision'. These attempts at metal-working also led to his extending of his small vocabulary of Hindi words and, as he gradually became a little more involved with the family he began to understand something of their social life and interactions.

The barracks were shared with an infantry battalion of fine-looking Rajput Indians of the Honourable East Indies Company. The battalion had Indian NCOs but British Officers. Sometimes the 24th carried out route marches and manoeuvred together with the Rajputs, though there was little social integration between the different nationalities. The difference in language and culture did not help, though, like Jonas, many men of the 24th were by now beginning to pick up a small vocabulary of native words.

As Jonas found on the more distant route-marches, the landscape had its own luxuriant attractions, with mango and tamarind trees, and the crimson splendour of wild cotton-trees. There were also belts of palmyras, groves of coconuts and isolated banyan trees, interspersed with shrubs bearing masses of multicoloured flowers. Villages, usually heavily-populated, were tucked away in the heavily-farmed landscape. When the rains came, the extensive flooding all along the lower reaches of the huge Ganges valley meant that the only houses of the natives which survived were those built on platforms raised about ten feet off the ground. The rooms of these thatched houses were arranged around a small central courtyard, there being one room in which to live, one in which to cook, and, usually two cattle sheds. During the periods of flood, the houses were cut off from each other like little islands and travel between them was by boat, or by rafts of plaintain trees, or simply by hanging on to the tail of a bullock driven into the water. The flooding could be a real problem for the soldiers too, and there were times when considerable skills with boats needed to be exercised, particularly in the rapids which resulted in various places. It could be all-too-easy for men to be swept away to their deaths.

During their route-marches along the Ganges valley, and also in Calcutta itself, the soldiers often came across native *fakirs*, who were frequently the cause of much lively discussion and speculation amongst the troops, sometimes indecently so. These so-called 'holy men' often appeared to practise self-abuse and torture, such as (say) hanging head-downwards from trees, or lying on 'beds of nails', or carrying metal grills on their bodies, or covering themselves in white ash, or growing their hair to immense lengths, some maintaining a permanent silence, some stalking about and continually calling out the names of their gods. Some of the *fakirs* acted as seers and fortune-tellers, and most appeared to live under the most basic of conditions. All seemed to expect to receive freely-given food and money from the native people – and most were not shy of verbally abusing people who did not come forward to aid them. Rightly or wrongly, the soldiers generally perceived them as religiously-inspired freaks, on the fringe of madness.

Regimental musters were regularly being taken, usually on the 24th of each month. On the 24th August Jonas had received £2 3s 2½d., representing 61 days back pay at a rate of 8½d per day. (The reason for this temporary 'rise' was unclear, for some of that time had been spent at sea, when a sum of 3½d was normally <u>deducted</u> per day for the cooked rations provided on board.) Jonas was also present at the muster which was taken on Christmas Day, the 25th December 1810, being recorded as still serving in the Company under Captain Richard GUBBINS, and in good health.

Nearly all of the ORs who had been PoWs had returned by that time, but Colonel MARRIOTT and eight of the other officers were still absent from the muster – and still officially recorded as being PoWs of the French. So, too, were the Surgeon and an Assistant Surgeon. Currently, therefore, the 1st Btn consisted of 51 Officers, 54 Sergeants, 50 Corporals, 21 Drummers and Fifers, and 974 Privates – making 1,150 men in total. The muster roll showed that the birthplaces of the men included Ireland and Scotland, and ranged all over England – though Suffolk, the birth-county of Jonas, seemed almost non-existent. It therefore remained rare for him to hear a homely Suffolk accent.

Some news concerning the fate of the missing officers and of some men began to filter back during the opening months of 1811, when the muster rolls showed entries for Thomas BRADBURY, who was shown as KiA on 3rd July 1810, and Corporals Reed NOBLE and Bennett WINDSOR, and Privates Thomas BLACKWELL, Peter FENNERMANN and Jeremiah REYNOLDS, who were shown as Died of Wounds.

Clearly, these were men who had been captured by the French in the action of the 3rd July, and who had died in captivity.

Lt Colonel MARRIOTT had re-appeared on the scene by March, and he took the muster parade on the 24th March 1811. Several of the other officers who had been captured in the *Ceylon* were also present, and it seemed that they had travelled back independently after their separate captivity in Mauritius. Presumably, they had brought further news with them, for a further ten privates were now recorded in the muster roll as killed in action on the 3rd July. However, a number of privates were still listed as PoWs. There also seemed to be some sort of tragic shame surrounding the fate of some of the men, and the officers appeared to be loath to recount the things which had happened. There was also some reluctance to discuss what seemed to have been an assault by the Royal Navy on Mauritius. Perhaps the officers of the 24th had been told to keep their mouths shut *pro tem.*

It was only when the last batch of private soldiers who had been held captive returned during April, that the full happenings at Mauritius began to be revealed.

It was a somewhat chequered story. Perhaps the first thing to note was that the French ships had been extremely well led, as the late Bill Hitchings had once mentioned to Jonas. The leading Frenchman was Captain Victor Guy DUPERRÉ. Unfortunately, Captain DUPERRÉ and the other senior French authorities were convinced that the *Astell* had lowered her flag in token of surrender on the 3rd July, just prior to effecting her sudden escape (It will be recalled that Jonas had seen the late Andrew PETERS climb up and nail the colours to the mast after the colours had twice been shot away – the French had evidently – though wrongly - seen the fall of the colours as a deliberate act of capitulation by the British.) This, coupled with the precipitate flying of the *Astell* from the scene, meant that the officers and possibly also the men who had been aboard the *Astell* at the time might be regarded as shameful renegades if ever captured by the French – and thus eligible for summary execution! The reason for the 'loud and abusive shouting' from the French ships at the time of the *Astell's* escape had now become clear!

The next thing to note was that, after their capture on the 3rd July 1810, the men of the *Ceylon* and the *Windham*, held captive in their own ships, had been taken to the Island of Mauritius. There they had been disembarked, the officers and paying passengers in the ships being held separately from the rank and file. The conditions for the officers and paying passengers were bearable, but they were much less so for the rank and file. Also, whilst the officers could look forward to an 'exchange' (and thus to their eventual liberty), the rankers had no such guarantee. Persuaded by French propaganda, 22 of the soldiers of the 24th had quickly deserted to the enemy rather than stultify as prisoners, apparently without hope of release.

Then, at the end of August, at about the same time as the arrival of the 24th as prisoners, the Royal Navy had made an assault on Mauritius, initially having some success with operations by parties of seamen on land, but eventually losing the fine frigates *Magicienne* and *Sirius* in an impetuous seaborne attack on Grand Harbour. Also with the *Néréide* and the *Iphigienia* being captured by the French, and with the naval forces altogether being soundly defeated. During this prolonged action the French had created a defensive crescent-shaped formation of several ships 'en flute' (i.e. stripped of their main spars and much of their rigging, but still well-armed.) This formation had included the *Ceylon* and the *Windham*, as well as the *Bellone* and the *Minerve.*

The French had hoped to stave off any further limited British assaults of this type. However, the British had assembled the almost amazingly large force of 10,000 troops, and the British had totally overwhelmed the French defenders when they landed on 29th November 1810. The numerous British PoWs were therefore quickly released, and were being returned to their proper stations in India or elsewhere, as and when opportunity afforded.

Nobody in Mauritius had foreseen that the British would arrive in such numbers to conquer the Island. Sadly, the 22 men of the 24th Foot who had gone over to the enemy, had actually taken part in the earlier defence of the island against the British Navy. Clearly, they could only be regarded as traitors. The muster roll for the March 1811 contained the names of these 22 men, who had mostly survived the action unharmed, and who had then been put on trial. They all risked being hanged, but, understanding the awful position to which they had been subjected as PoWs, the authorities commuted their sentences to serving in India permanently, which was the heart-breaking equivalent of 'Banishment from England For Life'.

All the other surviving officers and men of the 24th who had been PoWs, were now returned to the 1st Btn. This permitted certain of the remaining gaps in the muster roll to be filled, especially in regard to deaths. Thus three soldiers were recorded as 'killed on the prison ship' (presumably when the Royal Navy had made their initial attack on the Isle of France), one was shown simply as KiA, two men were shown as 'missing', and four others simply as 'dead' – presumably from natural causes.

It was, perhaps, inevitable that a degree of uncertainty still prevailed, for a separate list was then compiled and signed by Colonel MARRIOTT of 32 men who had 'died, deserted or became missing'.

At this time, a draft of twenty-one men from England 'joined for service', to help to make up the losses in the ranks. In fact, as Jonas well knew, there was a steady drain of men, with an average of five men per month dying from tropical diseases or other causes. There was also a steady drain of men being 'invalided home'. From now on, the strength of the 1st Btn would always be short, even of just the nominal 1,000 mark, let alone of its full 1,047 or so. As Jonas observed at first hand, the chances of the men of the 24th making sufficient length of service to gain a pension from Chelsea Hospital were steadily diminishing!

In May 1811 a terrible hurricane devastated the shipping then lying off Madras, driving some seventy ships ashore with the loss of most of their crews and passengers. Jonas and his fellow-soldiers heard of this with dismay, thinking how easily such a disaster could have overwhelmed them when they were laying off Madras in the previous year – and thinking of the potential perils of the return voyage they would each have to make at some time in the years ahead – if they lived so long!

In the meantime, further news arrived from Europe concerning the hectic battlefield activities of the 2nd Btn, and leading to further feelings of frustration amongst some of the officers. Jonas was present when one of the officers read the substance of a communiqué to a group of rankers. The text seemed to be rather garbled at times, but this was what Jonas understood the officer to say. From the point of view of an ordinary soldier, it all sounded hard going indeed;

The Battle of Busaco had taken place on 27 Sep 1810.[8] Sick men left behind after the Battle of Talavera had rejoined the 24th, and the Btn had been able to muster about 500 men – approximately half of the normal strength of an infantry battalion. Only the light company had been directly involved in the costly battle. Captain MEACHAM had been very severely wounded. A number of men had been killed and a good many wounded.

The 2nd Btn had then been employed, turn by turn with other units, to cover the retreat to the lines of Torres Vedros, defending Lisbon. There had been a sharp affair involving their picquets on the 14th October, and the rearguard of the 24th had been involved in a skirmish near Sorral on 24th October. There had been very heavy rainfall, the roads were in a dreadful state, and there was a general lack of shelter from the weather during the retreat.

Thanks to General WELLINGTON's retirement of the British Army behind very strong natural fortifications, and his 'scorched earth' policy of the country in front of those fortifications, the besieging French had been desperately short of food throughout the winter. As often happened when the respective armies were relatively inactive, there had been some conversation between the French and English picquets. According to what was said, the French officers were short of accurate information about the war, and therefore always very pleased to obtain English newspapers!

There had been great disappointment in the English Army in 1811, when the French Army, instead of attacking, had suddenly started to retreat. The brigade had immediately started a pursuit as the French retired from Santarem and Thomos. By this time the brigade was under the command of Major-General NIGHTINGALE, and consisted of the Brigade of Guards, a Brigade of Germans and the 24th, 42[n] and 70th Regiments. They were often called the 'Scottish Brigade', because the 42nd and 70th wore kilts – though the 24th certainly didn't!

NIGHTINGALE's Brigade was ordered to follow-up the French General Reynier's 'Division of the East', as it retreated on the mountain road of the Estrella to Espinhal. The French rear guard was soon overtaken by the 24th, who were now engaged in one of the most active pursuits of a flying enemy ever recorded in the annals of British warfare. The most disastrous scenes occurred in regard to the French – and truly brilliant successes for the British. The French did not make a stand until 14th March at Espinhal, whereupon the 2nd Btn of the 24th got on left flank of the French via a mountain pathway, and had some sharp fighting. They were also hotly engaged on the next day, and halted on the 16th March. On 17th March the brigade were detached to find a ford over the Alva near Pombiero – succeeding in their task at daybreak and unobserved. The 2nd Division followed immediately, and the left flank of the French was turned. It is believed that the French were not aware of the existence of the ford. They were surprised and severely defeated. They lost all their artillery, baggage, stores and provisions – and fled for their lives. Foraging parties which they had sent out were captured as each returned. (The British had been fortunate. Had the ford been defended, the Pointe de Murcella was indeed one of the strongest defensive positions in Portugal.)

---

[8] The main substance of this report has been derived from the regimental histories as currently maintained in the Museum at Brecon. Some fragments of additional data have been acquired from sundry contemporaneous accounts.

The Brigade was actively employed on these days, performing as light infantry and being active on the flank of the enemy. The British Army halted briefly on the 19th, having out-marched its supplies. However, after a forced march by the Brigade, Reynier's Corps at Suugal was nearly surrounded by three divisions of the British Army. It was only owing to very heavy rains that the French escaped – albeit with great loss.

In fact, the French retreat from Santaren to Spain was marked by an immense amount of abandoned baggage and animals littered along the routes, their panniers and pack saddles stripped and destroyed. The roads were strewn with dead men. Every small village was crowded with French wounded, collected together in houses to defend themselves against the Portugese, from whom they could expect no mercy – due to the atrocities committed by the French during the previous year.

On the 1st May 1811, the British Army began to assemble at Fuentes d'Oro. Maj-General NIGHTINGALE's Brigade were stationed at the rear of the village during a three-day attack on this position. The Light Companies of the 24th, 42nd, 79th (and other) Regiments got into the village. In fact, it was taken and re-taken three times. By the 5th, only our light companies remained in Fuentes d'Oro, on the British left flank. They nobly defended it. Coming to their support, the remainder of the Brigade, at first hard-pressed, made a good stand behind some stone walls. The riflemen of the 60th were also hard-pressed, and drove in on the 24th, who were ordered to change front by throwing back their right wing, and told to occupy a stone wall. However, a heavy column of the French got possession of the wall first and opened flanking fire on the (now) exposed 24th. Major CHAMBERLAIN, commanding the 24th became at extreme risk when his horse refused to jump the wall. Men dismantled and threw down stones – made a gap in the wall – and saved the major. Fresh British troops came up – and the French column retired. Lt IRELAND was killed. Capt ANDREW was wounded and made a PoW. About 400 French dead were brought out of the village. Many more lay dead in its environs.

Colonel KELLY had arrived from England on the 5th, but he did not take command until the next day. By that time the Btn had again been greatly reduced, now to only 300 men.

On the 8th May the Btn was in a village in Spain called the new Aldfa-de-Ponte. Colonel George Duncan DRUMMOND, severely wounded at Talavera, had gone home, but returned to Portugal early in 1811 – and took command of a brigade of the Light Division. Sadly. however, he died of a fever (and his wounds) in August. His death was much regretted.

The SIEGE of CIUDAD RODRIGO took place in January 1812. The weather was very cold – there was no camp equipage – and no cover near the town – so the troops remained cantoned in the nearest villages. The duties of the siege were taken by light troops of the 1st and 3rd Divisions, alternating in 24 hour spells, to guard the trenches and working parties. However, the bad practice soon developed of the guards and working parties withdrawing from the trenches as the relieving division was seen to be approaching. The French observed this from the steeple of the cathedral. Thereupon the French made a swift assault the next time the same tactical error was made by the British – but were eventually repulsed by a working party of the 24th under Lt STACK (Who lost 1 sergeant and 2 ORs killed and 15 ORs wounded). Had the French succeeded in spiking the guns, the siege would have had to be abandoned. As it was, Cuidad Rodrigo was successfully stormed by the 3rd and Light Divisions on 19th January 1812.

In Feb 1812 the 1ˢᵗ Div marched to the South of Portugal to cover the Siege of Badajoz, which was stormed and taken in April. On the way, the Brigade had halted for a few days at Abrantes to receive new clothing – since the old was in rags – with its patches of red scarcely visible. A supply of 'necessaries' was also issued.

At the abortive Siege of Burgos (which followed the Battle of Salamanca, fought on 22ⁿᵈ July 1812) the 24ᵗʰ formed a part of the storming party, and Captain HEDDERWICK, although wounded, distinguished himself in still urging his men on. They lost 10 men killed, and one officer and 57 men wounded. Little was now left of the 24ᵗʰ. One has the feeling that the men who remained were all virtually 'worn out', and some may well have been in a weird mental state.

This could account for the sad fact that two men of the 24ᵗʰ were court-martialled and executed after the long and frightful Battle of Vittoria, which took place on 21ˢᵗ June 1813, ending with a decisive victory for General WELLINGTON, but at the fearful cost of nearly 500 killed and 2,640 men wounded on the Allied side. The two men were charged with having looted Lord AYLMER's tent on 16ᵗʰ July 1813 – It was said that several valuable items had been stolen and that Lord AYLMER had been 'put in bodily fear'. Lord AYLMER was in command of the 2ⁿᵈ Brigade and these same men had often mounted guard over him. Possibly as a sign of the stress to which the men were being subjected day by day, it was said that Lord AYLMER had permitted the guard to lie down and sleep – or was it perhaps the case that they were so tired that they just fell asleep anyway?

There was no reprieve. After the proceedings of the Court Martial had been read out, the sentence had been announced and the two men had each confessed their guilt, they were cleanly and efficiently hanged by the Provost Marshals in front of several regiments, of which the men were formed into a large square. This square was surrounded by the women of the 24ᵗʰ Regiment, all lamenting and protesting. The aura of the situation was aggravated, because, on seeing such a large body of troops assembled together, the French thought that an attack on them might be imminent, and themselves formed up a large body of men under arms on an opposite hill, from whence they, too, witnessed the execution. This added to the shame of the whole occasion.

Perhaps unsurprisingly, what little remained of the 2ⁿᵈ Btn of the 24ᵗʰ was disbanded at about this time, with the men becoming a part of the 2ⁿᵈ Btn of the 58ᵗʰ regiment, taking yet further heavy casualties at the siege of St Sebastian, and being disbanded altogether when peace arrived at last.

Once again, Jonas fell to wondering how he would have stood up to all this, had he come to serve in the 2ⁿᵈ Battalion. Once again, the casualty rate for the 2ⁿᵈ Btn had been appalling, with far more of the men ending up dead than alive. Would he have cracked? Would the mental stress have caused him to have committed some act of crass stupidity like the two men who had pillaged Lord AYLMER's tent? Surely, those two crazed fools should have been spared from a death sentence?

One of his pals, the veteran soldier 'Daddy' Dadswell, who always had strong opinions, certainly thought so too (though he was careful not to let an NCO or commissioned officer hear the words he uttered – lest he be charged with insubordination or worse.),

"Oi reckon them two swaddies were right off their rockers due to all the horrors they wos livin' through", 'Daddy' said, *"And I doan't see how Lord AYLMER could*

really have had the wind up. I mean – he knew the two swaddies well and it sounds as if they'd all been fine together before the offence was committed. Wos he implying that the two redcoats had suddenly gone so sick in the head that they terrified him? Surely, if so, the men should have been treated as if they were insane – and not responsible fer their actions! To hang 'em seems to me to have been totally wrong...No wonder all the women were in such a ferment – they've usually got a lot more commonsense than we men have...I reckon the women could clearly see the craziness of the whole situation!"

"Yes," said Jonas quietly, *"I would have thought that a flogging at the triangles – say 12 lashes – would have more than answered the need for a demonstration of discipline. To take the lives of the men seems to have been quite wrong. Hadn't there been enough bloodshed already? The casualty rate on the battlefield was appalling – there was more chance of ending up dead that of livin'."*

"Yeah – that's true enough, the 2ⁿᵈ Btn had been through hell" replied 'Daddy', *"Though our own turn may come around again soon – you mark my words!"* Jonas remembered 'Daddy's words – and, in later times, because 'Daddy' had spoken with such authority, he wondered whether 'Daddy' had been nursing a premonition to himself at this time.

In contrast to the happenings on the Iberian Peninsular, Jonas saw a quite different vision of 'hell' on 10ᵗʰ April 1813, when the celebrated Hindu religious festival of *carkh puja* took place, and he was one of the few men from his battalion who wandered along to catch a discreet sight of it. He and a small number of his colleagues stood quietly on the outskirts of a multitude of natives, clearly almost all Hindus, who were present at the event. The ceremony opened by the Hindu participants (who were all of 'low caste') sticking large sharp metal objects into parts of their bodies, including their tongues and arms, and then cavorting about like maniacs. Before doing so they appeared to have 'desensitised themselves' with opium and strong spirits. These lower caste Hindus evidently received payment and veneration from the higher caste Hindus for this extreme religious self-abuse.

The next day was even more spectacular, for the participants had two strong metal hooks passed through the muscles on their backs, under their shoulder-blades, and were spun round in the air by ropes fixed to the hooks, the other ends of the ropes being suspended from a sort of 'merry-go-round' structure. As usual with such apparently awful tortures, the stress was somewhat relieved by a supporting band passed around each man, but the performance was still quite blood-curdling to behold. It went on for about ten minutes, with the men cavorting on the hooks, kicking their legs out and throwing themselves about as they were spun round.

Subsequently they were taken down, laid flat on their stomachs, and had considerable pressure applied by a colleague standing on the sites where the hooks had been (presumably to staunch any flow of blood), before a cloth was fixed over the area, and the men regained their feet and walked away. Surprisingly, although the cloths prevented direct examination, there seemed to be no significant bleeding from the holes where the hooks had been.

"My God!" said 'Daddy' Dadswell, *"That's better than the Indian Rope Trick!"*

"What's that then?" asked Jonas. *"Aha!"*, replied 'Daddy', *"That's when a rope seems to unwind itself out of a basket like a great snake, and goes on to stand vertically*

up in the air, as an Indian plays weird and wailing music on his flute. Then another native – usually a small-boned one, or a boy – swarms up the rope. The performance is always performed on a slightly darkened stage, so one suspects a trick. Yet one feels utterly convinced at the time that the rope is self-supporting, so to speak!"

"Yeah – like these fakirs lying on their beds of nails!", interjected Corporal Jenkins, *"They have special ways of getting on and off them – so that their weight is always spread evenly over a large part of their body, and the nails don't puncture their skin – though they do have a lot of small indents almost everywhere down their backs and legs, where the pressure has come as they have been lying on the 'bed'."*

"They're a tricky lot, all right!" said 'Daddy', *"Their minds and customs are very different to ours, ain't they! But some of their performances sure are interesting to see!"*

"Yeah," said Private Dawkins, *"D'yer remember the huge reaction them acrobats got from the 16th Bengal Light Infantry wot we shared the barracks wiv during out first month at Calcutta? You know, not so much the tumblers an' that – though they were good - but more when the men came in wiv that tall 15 foot pole wiv the great metal spike in its top – an' how that native swarmed up it like a monkey an' then stretched hisself out belly-downward over the point and spun hisself rahnd and rahnd on it – like a sort of 'uman spinnin' top. 'Ow 'e didn't corkscrew hisself to death on that bleedin' great spike ah'l never know!"*

"Garn! replied 'Daddy', *"That bloke must've 'ad a steel plate wiv some sort of ruddy great dimple in it's centre, which 'e wore under his dhoti like a breast-plate – but placed lower dahn, over 'is belly - an' the metal spike just laid neatly in the dimple as he spun rahnd an' rahnd. That's why there weren't nah blood, an' why he span rahnd and rahnd so easily. It was clever, though! Heh, heh!"*

So it was clear that some of the soldiers had seen quite a lot of the varied performances by the natives – and appreciated the subtle nature of the great cleverness they often displayed.

Jonas had become a '2nd Class Soldier' on the 13th April 1813, by virtue of having served in the Army for seven years, for which he received an extra 1d a day.

Colonel Randolph MARRIOTT was raised to the rank of major-general, and Lt-Colonel Charles HICKS assumed command in June 1813, at about the same time that the rains came, marvellously cooling the hot air of April and May. Later in 1814, the command of the 1st Btn devolved upon Major WHITE.

Meantime, in October 1813, Captain Ludovic STEWART had become the commander of the Company in which Jonas was serving, but he was replaced by Captain William LANGWORTHY in February 1814. It was at about this time that a detachment from the Regiment were sent off as escorts to men being transported to New South Wales, and three soldiers were sent off to England to give evidence in a case involving High Treason. These matters caused a lot of gossip around the barracks. Perhaps unsurprisingly, once out in Australia, it was by no means unknown for the men accompanying prisoners being transported, to themselves desert and 'go native'– and it seems that a couple of the guards in this group duly became 'no exception to the rule'.

Although the Btn was regularly training on the *maidan* and undertaking frequent route-marches, the men still often had energy to burn. So, there was an accompanying need to cater for the sexual appetites of the men. As across all of 'British' India, this took the form of the 'Lal Bazaar', usually to be found within the lines of a regiment. The associated problem of sexually-transmitted diseases, which sometimes decimated the number of men available for action in times of war, was an on-going problem for the military establishment. Jonas was well aware of the risk of disease, and he preferred not to risk the services of the Lal Bazaar – though he could certainly appreciate the attractions of some of the beautiful Indian girls who worked there!

He had found that he could be both gregarious – sometimes getting uproariously drunk in carousals with his mates – but also sometimes be more in the mood to be solitary, just enjoying his own company. So, quite often Jonas used to find himself a shady seat out of the direct sun from which he could look out over the busy and colourful scene on the waterside at Calcutta. The docks there were becoming well-developed and there were all kinds of craft to be seen at different times, ranging from stately East Indiamen to the strange-looking native *panshi* or *bundarow* boats which had to be used if one wanted to voyage into the shallower waters further upstream. Jonas used to revel in the picturesque nature of the scene. However, one downside to seeing the East Indiamen was that Jonas was still having occasional mental 'flashbacks' to the horrific scene in the fighting top, when poor Corporal Jones had been so terribly mangled and the pals of Jonas had simply been wiped away from life. Seeing the stately East Indiamen tended to stimulate such sad thoughts – and also fond memories of the late Bill Hitchings.

This was exactly what happened one day in June 1813, and Jonas suddenly found that tears were running down his face again, and that he needed to wipe his eyes with his handkerchief.

"What ails thee, friend?" said a warm, friendly English voice suddenly, *"Can I be of any possible assistance to you – perhaps with the help of the Good Lord above?"*

And Jonas found that a distinguished-looking gentleman of mature years, clad in well-to-do civilian clothes, was standing beside him. The crown of the gentleman's head was quite bald, but he had a generous crop of greying hair extending around the back of his head. His eyes were dominating, but in a kindly way.

"It's all right, Sir", Jonas replied, *"Just old and unwelcome memories flooding back to me! They will soon pass."*

"Flooding seems to be exactly the right word", remarked the gentleman, *"Floods of tears in a vale of floods – for the river here can rise enormously after the Monsoon rains come. Many lives and properties are sadly often lost along the crowded banks of the Ganges and the Hoogly, in the terrible flooding which can then ensue. But I suspect that your own tears have a quite different origin to that."*

"Indeed they do", replied Jonas, *"Not that I am indifferent to the fate which often overtakes the poorer natives in the Delta hereabouts. As I have seen for myself, their lot is often desperate indeed."*

"Ah, yes – truly it is exactly so. But tell me, young man – though, of course, only if you feel so disposed – why were you so distressed? Can you talk to me about it? It might help you, were you able to relate what (I assume) befell you. Was it all a long time ago – or just recently?"

"Time drags from day to day – yet also somehow passes so quickly. It is somewhat to my surprise that I must tell you that the incidents actually took place about three years ago. We soldiers are not really allowed to talk about the details of actions in

which we have been involved. Let me just say that three comrades of mine were killed right beside me in combat against some French ships. Two fine sailors who were also by way of becoming friends of ours were also killed. In fact, of the five men, four of them were wiped away from this world in an instant – their bodies never being found – just as though they had never been here in this World at all. The other soldier was very badly dismembered and must have died beside me in a few seconds. I was knocked about and rendered unconscious for a while, so I cannot tell exactly how swiftly he left this life – though it must have been mercifully quick. As it was, I was the only one left to tell such of the tale as human memory can carry."

"I see. That whole incident must have been horrific indeed."

"Yes – but that was only a part of it. You see, a naval officer, who had become a real friend, had been terribly wounded elsewhere in the ship, in the same battle. I was later taken to his side in the sick-bay of the ship, where he talked devotedly to me, enquiring earnestly about my wounds, but himself rapidly fading away due to his own awful wounds, and taking his last breath even as he spoke to me."

"Oh, my dear boy! And were you yourself badly wounded?"

"No – knocked about all over – but without any serious wound".

"And have you perhaps been carrying guilt that your own life was spared?"

"Yes – I was carrying great guilt about that – at least, I was until Mrs Murphy talked very kindly to me."

"Ah – I imagine that she was a lady who had great understanding of life in general, and of your situation in particular. Such people are to be greatly treasured."

"Yes – She must have seen the low state into which I had fallen – and she came up to me 'out of the blue' some days after the actual event, and spoke to me most encouragingly – saying that I had been spared for a purpose, and that life was how the Good Lord disposed of it. She said that I clearly had a lot more life yet to live on this Earth...And..."(Jonas brightened a little, and spoke rather more cheerfully)...*"she also gave me a little snifter of her fantastic 'potcheen' to help me on my way!"*

"Aha! Truly the most remarkable woman then! I have heard about the powers of 'potcheen' – though I have never had the occasion to drink any of it. In fact, I am a teetotaller, and my calling leads me to preach against the potential evils of strong drink – for I am a missionary – what the Hindus sometimes call a 'baba-ji'. Yet, I must concur that there can come about twists and turns of fate whereby a sip or two of strong liqueur can become a wonderful restorative for a human being who is in deep mental or physical distress."

"Yes, true – I have seen that come about several times in my life."

"Hmm. Perhaps I may introduce myself. My name is William CAREY, and I am a Christian Missionary, trying my hardest to bring Christianity to these native people, with their varied religions. I was born in England and I have been out here in India for nearly twenty years now, and, sad to report, we still have only a very small congregation stemming from the natives – though a good many of the white and half-white people do regularly attend our services."

"Ah – Well, my name is Jonas GREEN, Sir. As you can see from my uniform and the brass plate in my shako, I am a Private in the 24th Regiment of Foot. I was born in England, in Suffolk. Well, now, a missionary Mr CAREY! And you talking to a member of the 'brutal and licentious soldiery', recruited to kill as many Frenchmen as possible,

just so long as the war lasts? And, who knows, maybe ere long to kill some of the more unruly of the native Indians as well. So, here I sit, for all I know already a murderer of my fellow-men and with every intention of killing more in conformance with any orders I may receive. Moreover, perhaps even more heinous, I was born into a family of Strict Baptist Non-Conformists! Whatever will your masters in London – or, indeed the new Bishop of Calcutta just appointed here for the first time – have to say about that!"

"Well, Jonas, perhaps I should clear a point. That is to say, I am not a member of the Established Church, but I am actually a Non-Conformist myself! I am a minister of the Reformed Baptists. So your parents and I would not be too far from seeing eye to eye on religious matters.", and he went on,

"I do not think that my sponsors back in England need to know of every person to whom I speak – especially if my approach stems from a genuine sympathy for my fellow-man. I always remember the story about the old Arab, 'Abu Ben Arnim' I think he was called – you know, the man who had the dream in which he saw a heavenly angel writing in a great book – and he asked the angel what he was writing so busily, whereupon the angel replied, "I write the names of those who love the Lord." – "Aha", said the old Arab "I am no Christian – but put me down as 'one who loves his fellow-men'". Then, the following night the Arab dreamed again, and the angel reappeared to him, showing him the pages in the great book – and, Lo and behold, the name of 'Abu Ben Arnim' headed all the rest!

"Yes, I have heard that same story," said Jonas, "and do you find that you can truly love the Hindus and other races to be found here?"

"Most certainly – I feel that I have made a number of real friends amongst them. Their cultures may be very different to ours, but in some respects they can teach us a great deal about living good lives. Mind you, there are certain aspects to their lives which I feel are terribly wrong – such as the Hindu practice of 'Suttee' – also the infanticide of unwanted children – especially girls - and the cruel selling of children of both sexes for financial advantage. Such children often become the playthings of rich and disgraceful men, and their fate can thereafter be dreadful indeed. Trying to teach the population 'true Christianity' can be very uphill work."

"Do I detect just a little bit of frustration in what you say, Mr CAREY?"

"Well ... Perhaps...You see I have translated some biblical tracts into the Hindi language and passed them about amongst the Hindus...and just today, for the fourth or fifth time now, I have heard of yet another fakir – or baba-ji, if you prefer the term – who has used the tract to set up what amounts to <u>his own version</u> of Christianity – using our normal teachings about Jesus Christ and Mary the Virgin, but weaving about them all kinds of other myths and beliefs and mysteries which he has himself totally invented – and then using them to set various weird acts going by any disciples whom the baba-ji manages to pick up from his fellow-natives – people who are often very simple and untaught peasants and easily persuaded to believe almost anything that the baba-ji tells them – no matter how outrageous it may be. Only a small number of these people are brought into our true faith, despite my best efforts. Indeed, it took me seven years after my arrival here in 1793, before I gained even one convert. Mind you, my learning of their language had a strong effect – albeit that it all took time, of course."

"Oh – yes, I think I can understand the significance of what you are saying. But, don't you sometimes feel that we are wrong to try to impose Christianity upon peoples

whose various religions must outdate Christianity by a huge number of years? Who is to say that Christianity is the only true way? And do not these poor people lose their caste, and become alienated by their own people, if they become Christians? Indeed, alienated to the point that they are not allowed to draw water from the local well, the oilman and the grocer will not trade with them, the barber will not shave them, and so on and so forth – so that their life becomes completely unbearable?"

"Oho, young man. You can clearly think for yourself."

"Well, I've seen a village 'punchayat' at work, sitting 'en masse' under a large tree with its airborne roots hanging down all around like a great cage, and terrorising simple country folk away from following even the twisted form of 'Christianity' that a baba-ji had brought amongst them. It reminded me of a heavily poisoned form of the nasty behaviour that some vicars in England exhibit, to stop people from leaving their Church of England congregations to become Non-Conformists of one kind or another!"

"Aha, mm... You say that you were born to Non-Conformist parents. Does that mean that you are, yourself, a Strict Baptist – or – since being a soldier is against their tenets - are you a non-believer... an agnostic, perhaps?"

"I have many doubts. I used to envy my parents their extreme faith in the Good Lord above. But I think that my recent bitter experiences – the very sudden deaths of my friends – the manner in which life can suddenly be snatched away from one – have all added to my doubts. The other battalion of my regiment has been suffering from very heavy casualties in Portugal and Spain. It seems that the men have a greater chance of dying than of continuing in life. One can also see how fragile life can be amongst the many different races living in India. Every day one can see half-burnt corpses rotting by the river banks, or drifting down Mother Ganges on their way to the sharks in the Bay of Bengal – and dead people – especially the so-called 'untouchables', can sometimes be seen just left to die in the streets like so much rubbish. It is very hard to know what to make of it all."

"You clearly have a fine and enquiring mind, Jonas. Dare I ask if you can read? You may like to know that I once wrote a large book entitled "An Enquiry into the Obligation of the Christians to Use Means for the Conversion of the Heathen". In that book I attempted to answer all the arguments, such as you are beginning to put forth."

William CAREY continued, *"Since coming to India, I too have suffered some grievous blows – the mind of my dear wife has been badly affected and our children have barely survived various tropical illnesses. I have often had the most terrible doubts as to whether I should have worked so hard to persuade my wife to accompany me out from England all those years ago. It was also a good many years before the Honourable East Indies Company began to tolerate me and my fellow-missionaries, so my early years were difficult ones indeed. Also, as I have just said, it has been hard uphill work to gain native converts to my faith. Yes, I have many times prayed desperately hard to the Good Lord to be merciful to me and mine, and to show me the way forward – and, in return, I have striven mightily on His behalf, learning and translating the scriptures into about forty of the native languages and setting up a college at Serampore, on the west bank of the Hoogly. The college is for people of all nationalities, and different castes and beliefs. Perhaps it is through the good work of the Lord behind the scenes that I have been able to do such things here in India. If, one day in the future, I can persuade the Hindus to abandon the cruel practice of Suttee, I will take that as another manifestation of the work of the Lord...Oh, Jonas, I cannot* prove *to you that there is a Lord who 'controls our destinies and shapes our ends', I can only tell you my earnest belief that if you lead a good Christian life, He will be forever by your side."*

"Thank you, Mr CAREY, I appreciate all that you say. Indeed, those are very much the words that my parents back in England would have said to me. I must confess that I am more of a talker than a reader, and my ability at reading is still rather poor. However, I have heard of your mission here in India, and, if I may, I will, perhaps, attend your Sunday services once in a while. For the moment, though, I must bid you 'au revoir', for I am due back on parade in the barracks in a quarter of an hour. May I just say thank you very much indeed for your great kindness in speaking to me in my moment of despair. My bitter sadness has left me – for the present, at least."

"Not at all, Jonas. It was my very great pleasure. I shall look out for you at our Sunday services, where you will always be most welcome. Please try to bring a few of your comrades along with you. We normally have tea and cakes which we pass around afterwards, to create a sociable atmosphere. May the Good Lord Above always be with you."

And the two men went off in their different directions, each reflecting deeply on what had been said between them.

In fact, Jonas did attend a few of the Sunday services held in the Chapel of the Mission, becoming very impressed by the messages which William was doing his best to convey to the congregation. Jonas also met the great man at Serampore, two or three times, and he enjoyed walking in the large botanical garden which William CAREY had organised there. However, Jonas still had major doubts about many aspects of religion and whether or not he had any real place within it.

And. in a way, the matter resolved itself, because, by mid-1814, the Battalion was on the move, heading away from Calcutta and never to return there.

Chapter Eight

The Years 1814-1817: The Wars against
(i) the *Ghurka*s and (ii) the *Pindarees*

On 15th July 1814, the Battalion was warned to ready itself for a long march. Two days later they were paraded in full kit, with their tents, cooking-vessels and other heavy equipment being carried by pack-mules – each mule having an Indian *Sepoy* in charge of it. The regimental marquees were carried on elephants, each with its *mahout*. The Battalion was under the command of Lt-Colonel CHAMBERLAIN. The men now faced the march to Dinapore, in Bihar State, proceeding at the comfortable rate of just over eight miles per day, and following the south bank of the River Ganges for all of the distance – after, that is, they had completed the initial march northwards along the banks of the Hoogly River, which was of itself a tributary of the Ganges. Their march twinned with the coming of the monsoon rain. This was regarded as something of a blessing, because, on the march, the regiment straggled over a great distance, and, in the dry season, the tramping feet of the men and of the many animals would have raised a huge amount of stifling dust. Luckily, the northward-sloping terrain of the so-called 'Gangetic Plain' was not too difficult to traverse, and on the days when there was no rain, it had often been possible to use the river alongside which they marched, for washing and cooling-off - though care was necessary when they were passing rapids or when the river was in spate. Its condition tended to vary over the various stretches, with surging rapids and waterfalls in places and calmer waters in between – often in the form of large lakes.

During its stay at Calcutta the battalion had attracted many followers, all hoping to make some kind of living off it – thus there were not only servants to officers (and to some of the soldiers), plus tent-people and camel or elephant-handlers – but also the *bazaar*people, *coolies, bangywallahs* (i.e. pedlars of cannabis), jugglers, *nautch*-girls and sundry others. In fact, including the sutlers, and the wives and children of the troops, the overall force moving through the country was large indeed, though experience showed that many of the followers would quickly melt away were substantial enemy forces to be encountered. As things stood, however, it was estimated that each officer had about twenty heterogeneous followers and some of the rankers also had one or two to themselves.

The countryside through which they passed during the opening weeks of their trek varied considerably, sometimes with overhanging cliffs, sometimes bordering vast flat expanses of water, sometimes with green woods and fields adjacent to the river. Generally, the land was intensively cultivated and the small villages consisted of buildings crammed together in what seemed to be the least space possible, and always heavily-populated with people. Donkeys, camels and other animals were used to work the primitive irrigation systems for the fields, which were sometimes bordered with thickets of banyan, mango and pipal trees. These trees were sometimes alive with green parrots and monkeys. Snipe and partridges were also plentiful. There were also constant rumours of the presence of jackals, leopards and tigers – and sometimes the officers would go off in hunting parties, often mounted on elephants, trying to seek them out. Sometimes there were herds of water-buffaloes in the river or on its muddy banks, often with herdsmen working among them or clinging to the beasts in deeper water. The coming of the Monsoon rains through which they marched was quickly changing the landscape, day by day, from a 'sere and yellow' one to a sort of luxuriant green.

The cantonments at Dinapore proved to be based on a narrow strip of ground running southwards from the River Ganges, with a deep muddy nullah at its end in which rice was being grown. Fed by the River Sone, the marshy ground extended to the west, making that area of ground impassable for cannon and wagons during the rainy season – and difficult even for infantry.

Be that as it may, having eventually arrived at the cantonments, in November they became part of a large army consisting of English soldiers of the 24th, 87th and 66th regiments, and several battalions of native troops and artillery (the latter two elements raised by the Honourable East Indies Company), all of whom were assembling there with orders to attack Nepal. This war had come about because there were long-standing disagreements between the Indian authorities and the Nepalese people over land which the Nepalese had successfully seized. The Earl of Moira (later the Marquis of Hastings) had organised this army, which consisted of some 17,000 men, with 68 guns. It was divided into four divisions, each tasked to attack one or another of the extended line of Nepalese conquests. The task of the fourth division which was made up of the 24th and the 6,000 native troops who would accompany them, all under the command of General MARLEY, would be to strike directly for Katmandu, the walled Nepalese capital city, high in the Himalayas and currently about 125 miles due north of their position as the crow flew. The four columns were to set out as soon as the rains and the consequential flooding had eased. The flooding was real enough, and seven privates were drowned in a tributary of the Ganges in two separate incidents involving accidents with boats in October, and then another man was drowned in November.

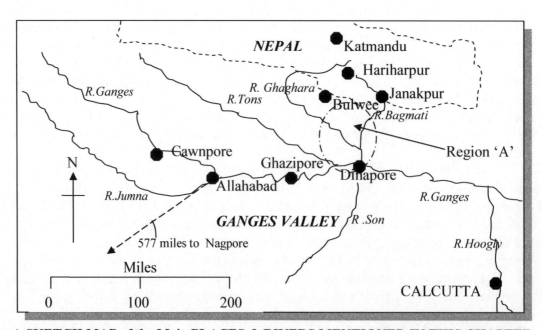

A SKETCH MAP of the Main PLACES & RIVERS MENTIONED IN THIS CHAPTER
Smaller encampments named in the text – such as Amoura, Ancoun, Barhurn, Bawburn,
Bunssaraeepokra, Guhrwar and Singramsed – are all thought to have lain lay within Region 'A'

Jonas found that he was just a tiny part of this considerable enterprise. So far as was known, no Europeans had ever set foot even in the tree-covered lower parts of the huge mountain range of the Himalayas – and here was a whole army attempting to climb much higher. It was a daunting, albeit exciting, prospect – and it seemed that a very determined enemy, who was very familiar with the territory, might well be soon doing his level best to stop their progress! Jonas found that he was checking and re-checking his weaponry, for which he now carried his own auger and pricker, a brush and other handy small tools. He also felt happy that he and his mates were now equipped with lead balls incorporated in their cartridges, so that loading their muskets had been speeded up to an extent – even if it meant having to hold each lead ball briefly in the loader's mouth as he distributed the powder into both the priming-pan and the barrel, before spitting the ball out into the muzzle of his musket. It also meant a further slight revision of the drill, bcause the emptied cartridge was now used to wad the ball *after* the ball had been inserted.

His division of the army set off for Katmandu on the 26th November 1814 – but it somehow soon seemed to be 'dithering about' unnecessarily.

So far as Jonas was concerned, it was Private 'Daddy' Dadswell who summed up the situation best. He'd become a part of the twelve-man section who shared a bell-tent with Jonas. One night in February 1815, 'Daddy' suddenly decided to vent his thoughts about what was going on. *"Oi reckon that our General is wetting his breeches about wot we is all a'doin',* said the grizzled old warrior, veteran of campaigns in Egypt and in Canada. *"It's them high mountains wot does it – they can cast vast shadows into the minds of men. If you're in command, you starts to think about having to send small scoutin' and protective picquets up into every peak which overlooks the route through the high passes which your army is a'goin' to 'av to march froo – an' then you starts ter fink, what if some of 'em little detachments gets silently swallowed up by enemy soldiers 'iding in the mass of trees, an' wot if then the enemy starts to snipe at the main column, or, wuss, cuts orf their retreat – an' calls up hidden reinforcements an' starts to butcher th'ole column. Panic could ensue – especially wiv the native troops! It just doan't do – ter fink too much – a commander MUST be resolute in his actions!"*

He went on, *"So, Oi reckon that is why we're seeing so much indecision coming dahn the line to us poor redcoats! If it comes from the top – an' I reckon it does just that – then our company commanders are buggered by the indecision, because all they can do is ter follow the orders from above. None of 'em has the balls to take his own initiative or to raise his voice in protest. The only good thing is that their heads are just as much on the line as our own are!"*

As usual, the officers' servants had their ears open, and various rumours swept through the army at that time, generally supporting what 'Daddy' Dadswell had said. The first strong rumour was that Major-General Rollo GILLESPIE, in command of the 2nd Division of the Army, after a lot of shilly-shallying, had utterly failed in his attempt to capture Kalanga, where the Ghurkas had constructed a fort out of heavy logs and large stones. This fort was situated on a small jungle-covered hill. Apparently General GILLESPIE had given out confusing orders to his men, who had then failed to support him properly, and he had himself then been killed by the *Ghurka*s in what amounted to a precipitate single-handed charge. Clearly, a lot of confusion had reigned and the *Ghurkas* had shown themselves to be foes who were both brave and well-organised. By the end of

118

the battle the British cannons had pulverised the fort into rubble, killing many of its defenders – including women and children – but, overall, the British had suffered more casualties than their resolute enemy. The second strong rumour was that their own commander, Major-General MARLEY, had apparently been reprimanded by Lord MOIRA about his indecisiveness, and the general, apparently greatly worried about the Nepalese having captured a couple of isolated outposts, was now suddenly 'missing' from camp, having nominated no deputy. Seemingly, he'd suffered from a total breakdown.

Both these rumours seemed to be true. The Major-General was temporarily succeeded by Colonel DICK, who, in turn, was succeeded by Major-General George WOOD. However, matters scarcely improved at all in regard to the procrastination and caution being demonstrated. The troops found it thoroughly demotivating – especially when a very long march beside the forest belt to Janakpur and back seemed to achieve nothing – except to show that the Nepalese had evacuated some positions there. 'Daddy' Dadswell was to be heard singing quite loudly;

> *"Oh, the Grand Old Duke of York,*
> *He had ten thousand men:*
> *He marched them up to the top of a hill;*
> *And he marched them down again!*
> *And, when they were up they were up;*
> *And when they were down they were down:*
> *And when they were only half way up –*
> *They were neither up nor down!"*

In January 1815 the 24th were in camp near Bawburn, West Bengal. The weather was cold, but this was a healthy spot, for a muster roll taken there showed that no men had died that month, whereas the regiment was normally losing men to fatal illnesses at a rate of between two and three men every month. By February the regiment had moved to Bunssaraeepokra, by March to Ancoun, by April to Barhurn and by May to Gurhwar, all in West Bengal. The death rate had climbed again, to about four men per month, and the heat by then was becoming extreme.

"By the bowels of Christ!", said 'Daddy' Dadswell, *"Talk about lions being led by donkeys! When the Hell are they goin' ter give us generals wiv the power of command – Men who are willing to lead us up into them mountain passes? An' there's every sign that the weather 'ull close in soon! Then where will we be?"*

Sure enough, the weather did deteriorate, for the Monsoon arrived early, and the 24th went into temporary cantonments at Amowa in May 1815, and there they remained. By that time Jonas had seen his company commander Captain LANGWORTHY, retire on half-pay, and he had been replaced by Captain William HEDDERWICK, who was an energetic veteran of the recent Peninsular War. Amowa was not a very healthy place to be, and the 24th would lose about forty men during the six months they were stationed there. By October 1815 their numbers had fallen to an all-time low (up till that time) of only 788 men fit to muster. To add to their woes, yet another three men were drowned in another boating accident in the Ganges.

The rest of the army was broken up. Only the wing of the army under Colonel OCTERLONY had achieved any success at all, terminating with his capture of the Nepalese stronghold of Malaun back in May. The first and more or less abortive Nepalese War was over for the time being. The Commander-in-Chief, Lord MOIRA, must have been grinding his teeth with the frustration of it all.

Matter improved at last in the 'Post-Monsoon' weather of October 1815 when Lt-Colonel KELLY (now a veteran of the recent fighting in the Spanish Peninsular) arrived from England and took command of the 24th. He brought with him about 290 men from the newly-disbanded 2nd Btn.[9] They were much-needed, for forty men were being discharged from India to become Pensioners of Chelsea Hospital, back in England. The net result was that the strength of the 24th rose to just under 1,000 effectives, bringing them back to nearly full status.

Jonas felt that this was just as well, for operations connected with the 2nd Nepalese War began in the New Year, with the 24th marching to form an encampment at Bubupee, near the hamlet of Bulwee, again as one of four separate columns, under the overall command of General OCTERLONY. For this mission the 24th had been reinforced by a whole battalion of native infantry and by detachments from two others. There was also a native labour-force with white engineer-officers, for they were having to advance up local pathways that were little better than sheep-tracks and General OCTERLONY was having roads built as they went, so that he could constantly move his heavy guns forward to cover his troop-movements. (It was also said that the general had taken measures to cut off the food-supplies from Bilaspur as a part of his attacks on the various strong-points held by the *Ghurka*s.) There were still many camp-followers to each unit - servants to officers and some even to soldiers, tent-people and camel or elephant-handlers – plus the usual *bazaar*people, *coolies, bangywallahs,* jugglers, *nautch*-girls, etc., – so that the overall force currently moving through the country was large indeed.

As a sign that thought was going into the enterprise, lightweight food supplies were now available for the 24th when its men were on the move, and every man was now expected to be carrying three days rations of rice and at least a one-day supply of ready-cooked rice.

The combined force in which Jonas was serving had marched for a couple of weeks along the banks of the River Bagmati, before starting to climb the foothills of the Himalayas, on their way to attack the fortress of Hariharpur. The marching had now become appreciably harder due to the general steepness of the terrain. By the time that they would reach their target they would be at least 6,000 feet above sea-level and overlooked by mountains soaring to well above 20,000 feet! At times they crossed bridges over deep rocky chasms down which torrents of icy cold water rushed from the high mountains towering above them. The chasms were often filled with tumbled rocks covered in ferns and flowering creepers – and sometimes dappled with beautiful orchids. Sometimes the men sang in rhythm with their marching, and sometimes they chatted idly a bit, to relieve the tedium of marching. Sometimes they were too short of breath to do either. By now, their sick had been sent to the rear and a great many of the camp-

---

[9] It is believed that some of these men were veterans of the fighting in the Peninsular.

followers had melted away – a sure sign that a formidable enemy could well be encountered soon.

"Just look at them elephants," said grey-haired 'Daddy' Dadswell as they were marching on a slightly easier stretch, one day in March, *"They make the business of pulling them 8-pounder guns and the howitzers look as easy as pie, no matter how steep the goin' gets. I loves them elephants. There's times I wish I was a 'mahout', a'ridin' on one of 'em, and saving me poor ol' legs – though I'm not too sure that I'd be wantin' the job o' washing an elephant every day – an' they need a powerful lot o'feedin'!"*

"Yeah", replied Jonas from the next file, *"I love to hear the soft slidin' noise of their huge feet. They seem to be such gentle giants – though I saw a male one once that was affected with 'must'. He was quite impossible for his mahout to control – He had a horrible liquid oozing out of his eyes and his sexual urges were simply running amok!"*

"Aha!" said 'Daddy', *"I reckon that not even an 8-pounder gun would hold back an elephant with 'must'! T'would be quite a sight to see one performin' with a heavy gun bein' thrown about as he gyrated on his ladyfriend – so to speak!"*

"Yeah, said Private Dougal Donald, *"D'you remember that one which had 'must' when we were at Madras. The mahouts managed to put chains on each of his legs and fixed the other ends of the chains to a ruddy great tree – one much too big fer him to pull out of the ground. Then they half-starved the poor old sod, an' every day they pricked him around his head and ears wiv' dam' great bamboo poles wiv metal spikes on their ends. He didn't just bleed – he had blood simply pulsing out of him. I reckon that it took them a long week to calm the poor thing down – though they darn well did it!"*

"By God," said 'Daddy', *"I sometimes gets quite a tread on – but I don't think I could stand being prodded and bled like that fer long!"*

"Nah!" exclaimed Dougal, *"Your prodding is a quite different fing – and any bleeding is more likely to be by the 'other party' in the deal!"*

"You men are sex-mad!", exclaimed Captain HEDDERWICK, the veteran recently back from the Peninsular War, who happened to be marching alongside the file, *"Besides which, camels are even worse than elephants if they get the hump! They spit – and they can be full of sexual diseases! Have you men ever heard of the poem about them, sung to the tune of the Eton Boating Song?"*

"No sir!" chimed in 'Daddy' Dadswell, *"As an old campaigner from the Egyptian wars, may I dare to ask how it goes, please Sir?"*

Captain HEDDERWICK had a good voice, and he needed no further bidding to break the monotony of the march, so he promptly started off,

"The sexual life of a camel, is stranger than anyone thinks,
For oft in his moments of leisure, he tries to bugger the Sphinx!
But the Sphinx's anal orifice, is blocked by the sands of the Nile:
Which accounts for the hump on the camel – and the Sphinx's inscrutable smile!"

"Heh, heh!" exclaimed old 'Daddy', amidst the general laughter from all the men within earshot, *"Oi loves a good Limerick, Sir! – And seeing where we've been in recent years, isn't there one which starts off,*

"There was a young man from Bengal, who had a mathematical ball...."

"Oh yes, I know," said Captain HEDDERWICK, *"It goes…"*

But just then a mounted *havildar* of the advance party came cantering up on his charger, with a spare horse on a loose rein. He was a very handsome man, with a swarthy face, a splendid black moustache, fine dark eyes and an immaculate uniform.

"Excuse me, Captain sahib," says he, *"Major HUGHES sends you his best compliments. He has told me to inform you, Captain sahib, that there's some sort of stockade up ahead, which the Ghurkas have put across the path. He is wanting you to join him at once, for a quick parley before an attack is mounted – which he will lead!"*

And in a moment, Captain HEDDERWICK, using the swiftly-cupped hands of the quick-witted 'Daddy' Dadswell as an impromptu 'mounting stirrup', had quickly stepped into the saddle of the spare horse and was galloping up the slope towards the front of the column. His parting words had been, *"Sorry men, duty calls – more Limericks later if Lady Fortune smiles on us!"*

"Well, here we go at last, I reckon, lads!" says 'Daddy'. *"And abaht bleedin' time, too! Best to double-check all yer equipment is on top line, fust chance we get!"*

"Too right, 'Daddy'", chimed in Sergeant Lucas, *"Though every man should keep his weapon and ammunition in first-class order at all times! Always best to check, though! From what I have heard these Ghurkas are doughty fighters!"*

A few minutes later, Captain HEDDERWICK returned, still on the borrowed horse, dismounted at the head of the Company, and was seen to be issuing forthright orders to his platoon sergeants, whom he had immediately called around him, using his hands expressively to emphasise the points he was making. The sergeants then headed quickly back to their platoons.

"Right men!", yelled Sergeant Lucas, *"We're goin' to attack that small hill just orf to the left of the track ahead of us, and abaht a half-mile orf from 'ere. We'll advance in column until I tells yer otherwise. Drop yer large packs 'ere, and leave 'em lie – Corporal Donahugh, take two men and stand guard over the packs until relieved. NOW MEN WE GO! The main thing is speed… By the centre, DOUBLE-MARCH!*

And off went the platoon, jogging well, despite the heat, towards the small hill. As they neared it, the crackle of musketry could be heard, and a familiar noise, as of bees buzzing around the men's ears could be heard. *"PLATOON, HALT!…* PLATOON *FORM LINE"*, shouted Sergeant Lucas at the top of his considerable voice. "PLATOON PRIME AND LOAD! Ram yer bullets well in – but DON'T FIRE UNTIL I TELLS YER…Right, *PLATOON ADVANCE*!"

Panting now, and beginning to stream with sweat, the men had formed quickly into line, a move that they had practised so often that they could almost do it in their sleep. Well-practised at the task, they were carrying their loaded muskets at the high port as they again began to advance. The other platoons were advancing on either side of them. The enemy's bullets continued to buzz around them.

Jonas wiped the sweat from his eyes. Out of the corner of his eye he could see that a few men of the 24th were already down, their bodies making small half-hidden red-uniformed humps in the rough grassland. Still distant, the peaks of the enormous snow-capped mountain range looked down on them. The hill was now near enough for the silhouettes of Nepalese defenders to be seen on its crest, and also the smoke arising from their muskets. There was the reflected flash of *tulwars* to be seen, as the *Ghurka* officers exhorted their men, who were getting off rather 'patchy' volleys. It was becoming very clear that the *Ghurka*s were brave, highly organised and well-lead.

'Daddy' Dadswell was close by Jonas, *"Well, 'ere we go again – bet we go in with the cold steel as we close wiv 'em, Jonas – Then we'll really see how them tulwars do agin' our baynits, eh?"* But, suddenly, there was a heavy thump, and 'Daddy' gave a sort of strangled sigh as he collapsed to the turf. Jonas bent over him, seeing the blood swiftly pulsing out of 'Daddy's chest, as 'Daddy' tried again to speak, *"Sorry, pal,"* he panted, *"looks like it's...down to you...to finish this 'un."* He smiled at Jonas, but with his near-toothless mouth falling slackly open as he did so, and with the eyes glazing over and rolling up into their sockets.

From that moment Jonas became a killing machine. A red mist came down over his eyes and he became impervious to pain. All he wanted was to kill the enemy – there was no longer any logic – all he wanted to do was to lay hands on an enemy and to kill him by the most violent means he could muster. He was barely any longer a soldier – more a deadly assassin – so angry that the only expiation lay in snuffing out the lives of these men who had dared to kill one of his friends. He had so much adrenalin coursing through his veins that he was near-impervious to orders. He had become just like the bloodthirsty *Berserker* Viking warrior who lurked somewhere in his distant ancestry.

He advanced with the extended line of surviving men of the 24th, but he was with them only because, like him, they were all closing fast with the Nepalese defenders. He obeyed the next order almost mechanically, but also because he so much wanted to use his 'cold steel'. The commands came from Captain HEDDERWICK, who was also well to the fore, *"COMPANY HALT. COMPANY PRESENT! AIM AT THE ENEMY'S MUZZLE-FLASHES!...COMPANY FIRE!...COMPANY FIX BAYONETS!... COMPANY CHARGE! LET'S HEAR YOUR BATTLE-CRY MEN!...St GEORGE FOR ENGLAND! HUZZAH! TALLY HO!"*

And in they went, yelling like fiends, after a well-disciplined and devastating volley, going in with the bayonet. Jonas was right up in the forefront, his bayonet brushing aside the *tulwar* of a *Ghurka* officer, the butt of his musket smashing the officer's face into bloody ruin, the recovered bayonet next thrusting hard into the back of a *Ghurka* soldier who, after a *kukri*-slash more or less in vain at Jonas, had turned to flee, having just caught sight of the fearsome, implacable and terrible face of Jonas. Jonas was not yet done – he needed more men to kill. It was as if from a great distance he heard two of his fellow-soldiers calling to him, *"Jonas – STOP, STOP! They're begging for quarter! Please Jonas, stop the carnage!"* In fact, it only gradually dawned on him that, at considerable risk to their own lives from his temporary insanity, his pals were physically restraining him. His bayonet was literally dripping with blood.

Jonas slowly emerged from his terrible berserker rage. He had found a great joy in killing men. He now found that his own body had cuts and heavy bruises which he had not felt at all. He knew that, unless his limbs had actually been cut off, he would have gone on fighting to the death. It was both scary and, at the same time, invigorating.

As he came back to sanity, he saw the terrible effects of his handiwork on the two dead *Ghurka*s *(for someone else's bayonet had finished off the officer)*, and a sort of guilt later came over him. The 24th had seized the hill, overwhelming the comparatively small but very brave *Ghurka* picquet which had been posted upon it.

The hill was only about a half-mile ahead of the main *Ghurka* fortress at Malhon, and the *Ghurka*s there, well led by General Amar Singh THAPA (the uncle of the King of Nepal), promptly decided that the hill was far too important to lose. So, they promptly counter-attacked – and in great force. They also brought up some cannon, toiling like demons to drag the guns into place and then to work them.

Jonas and the rest of his Company, well led by the experienced Captain HEDDERWICK, now formed an extended line covering the northerly aspect of the crest of the hill, with the other two companies of the 24th covering the east and west flanks – all volley-firing at the main groups of enemy troops as they advanced up the slopes. The southern side of the hill was covered by two companies of native troops, with the other three of their companies being held as a reserve, in case the enemy began to drive in on any of the four sectors. There were also two old 8-pounder guns in action, which were positioned near to Captain HEDDERWICK's Company, but a little nearer to the crest of the hill.

It was clear that the *Ghurka*s were having some success in working their way around the base of the hill, with the clear intention of cutting off the whole detachment. (Later Jonas learnt that Captain HEDDERWICK was considering leading the two companies of *sepoys* who formed the reserve, in a rather desperate counter-attack on those encircling groups of *Ghurka*s.) However, other reinforcements from the main column were quickly pushed forward by the experienced Major HUGHES, together with a couple of 6-pounders and two small howitzers transported by elephants, and, working together, the infantry and the guns stopped the *Ghurka*s in their tracks and then soon silenced the enemy cannon-fire.

Shortly after midday, the *Ghurka*s retired, and the British were able to consolidate the hill-top position. By that time Jonas had lost count of the number of volleys which he and his comrades had fired. His water-bottle was empty and his thirst was so severe that he had been reduced to taking water from the bottles of dead men. His hands and face were black with the stains of burnt powder. His shoulder was badly bruised from the recoil of his musket. Jonas and his comrades had been more than grateful to the chains of brave *sepoys* who had led mules laden with small arms ammunition (combined powder and shot) from the rear and up the hill to their position, and each soldier had filled and re-filled his ammunition pouches several times. A number of the ammo-bearing *sepoys* had been struck down by the enemy counter-fire, their shattered bodies and a couple of their dead mules now lying silent in the grass. Another badly-wounded mule was moaning, kicking about and trying desperately to regain its legs, until a soldier went up to it, put his musket to its head, and said, *"Sorry, pal, but best thing"*, as he squeezed the trigger.

Now that the fighting had eased off, Jonas and his pals could start to search over the battlefield. A swift count suggested that at least a hundred of the enemy were dead and, as Jonas saw with his own eyes, there were maybe three times that number of *Ghurka* wounded. Probably to their surprise, these men were being given the same medical aid as the fifty or so British wounded. Jonas had already seen that the *Ghurkas* tended to be of small, square stature, and, on looking at them more closely, he found that they had pleasant, round faces and almond-shaped eyes, rather like the more attractive of the Chinese coolies he had seen years ago, working at the Capetown docks. Their physical appearance was quite unlike that of the native Indians. Almost against himself, he felt that, despite their language and cultural differences, these sturdy little Nepalese men and the British soldiers shared a sort of smiling respect for each other, and might easily become friends.

A roll-call was taken after the battle, which *(as Sergeant Lucas later said)* told that the 24th had lost eight men killed and some 27 wounded in greater or lesser degree, including three officers – Major HUGHES being one of those wounded. This list of the 24th accounted for over half of the total British casualties.

Jonas was whacked. He had burnt off so much energy in his spell of madness that his body was now quite limp. He was also trying to come to terms with his weird mental state. He needed time to adjust to this new killing machine that was 'him'. When he thought about it, there was actually yet another 'him' – a soldier who took post and fired his weapon time and time again, obeying orders to the letter, ignoring the shot and shell all around him, and taking little notice of the comrades who were falling beside him. This second 'him' was actually the braver of the two, because he no longer had the 'red mist' veiling his eyes, but was scared stiff internally that he was going to be killed or dreadfully maimed at any moment – yet was closing his mind to it, and taking comfort in the professional way he was aiming and firing his weapon, and gaining a sort of exultation whenever he sensed that his own bullet had 'found a billet' in an enemy soldier – so that there was one less man coming on towards him.

Later, he tried to talk to Corporal Heyward about this matter, but without much success. The Corporal had no experience of any 'red mist' affecting himself or anybody else. He felt that most soldiers were like the second 'him' of Jonas, in greater or lesser degree. The more that men trained, and experienced war, the better they would become at it – and the less likely they would be to run if confronted with what looked like a stronger enemy force – though he did agree that every man had his own 'limit' as to how much combat he could endure.

The next day, Major ROBISON, pushing forward with an advanced guard past the hill, found the stockade across the path deserted. Pressing on to Hariharpur, he found that place also evacuated. It was promptly occupied by the British and turned into a base. However, there was no need for more fighting, for the *Ghurka*s had now had enough, and asked for terms. Understandably, it seemed that they desperately wanted to keep the British out of their capital city of Katmandu, to stop it from being sacked and ruined. On 6th March 1816 peace was concluded with the Rajah of Nepal, and the 24th could return to their cantonments in Amowa, even as the rainy season began again. It would be fair to say that there was bitter disappointment in those of the troops who had been hoping to gain by plunder from the sacking of Katmandu. On the other hand, in general there was great respect for the *Ghurkas*, and General Amar Sing THAPA had been permitted to march out proudly leading his surviving men, still equipped with his arms and accoutrements, with his colours flying and his personal property still intact.

Whilst at Amowa the number of men of the 24th fit to report for duty again became very low, aggravated by the loss of men killed or wounded in the fighting against the *Ghurka*s, and by the rather unhealthy climate. At the June muster there were only 829 effectives.

In July the 24th marched for two weeks to reach Dinapore. Soon after they arrived there, the grenadier and light companies, under Brevet-Major HUGHES, who was by then recovered from his wounds, marched off to the imposing fortress of Allahabad, at the confluence of the Ganges and Jumna rivers – a place where grapes and melons grew in profusion. As usual, the British soldiers had their own colloquial name for the place, namely the *'Isle o' Bats'*. Once there, they formed part of a flank battalion in the army commanded by Lord MOIRA (who had by then achieved the title of Marquis of Hastings). He would lead them in the war against the troublesome *Pindarees*, a confederation of men of different races and religions who lived by brutally raiding peaceful towns and villages. The *Pindarees* were being aided and abetted by the *Marattas*.

According to what Jonas heard later, the flank battalion then became engaged in a long march going southwards down the Ganges Valley in the hope of trapping the Pindarees against the Bombay and Madras armies, which were advancing northwards up the same valley. In the event, various delays occurred due to an outbreak of cholera and other events, but Lord MOIRA later drove his men into a whole series of marches and counter-marches against the elusive Pindarees.

We will revert to those matters later. Before they came to pass, however, in November 1816, about eighty time-expired men were returned to England, but the 24th had been augmented in the previous month by reinforcements from England and the net effect was that they remained almost up to strength. Indeed, although two of his men had died of sickness, Captain HEDDERWICK had the unusually high number of 110 men in his company at this time, before he was replaced by Captain Daniel BABY, who had last been in command of Jonas and the company back in 1810.

Jonas had always fought against 'going sick'. If he went down with constipation or with a stomach-bug, he might ask the surgeon for a 'bolus' (or a 'No.9' pill – the Army's bowel-opener and 'cure-all') – but he had always eschewed trying to find a bed in sick quarters. Hence he had appeared in every muster until that time as 'fit for duty'. However, in the cool weather of February 1817 he felt really bad, with a raging temperature, violent and blinding headache, heavy sweating and the inability to see properly. His pals also told him that he had been mentally rambling and shouting in his sleep the previous night.

So, reluctantly, he reported sick. The medical staff took one look at him and said *"Malaria"*. He was immediately admitted to the Regimental Hospital and told to undress, to put of a nightshirt and to get into a cot. His condition rapidly worsened, his temperature rose alarmingly and he became delirious – soon becoming unconscious. The surgeons had seen men in his very severe condition all-too-often, and expected that he would quickly die of inflammation of the brain. They therefore just made him as comfortable as they could and then more or less abandoned him to his fate.

However, very luckily for Jonas, there were a couple of the *Ghurka*s who had been wounded in the Battle of July 1816, who were now well recovered from their wounds, and who were working cheerfully at the hospital. They had been retained as general orderlies at the hospital, performing various of the menial tasks to do with general hygiene, especially in sluicing out bedpans, in helping very sick patients to wash, and in suchlike matters.

These two men had virtually no comprehension of English, but they quickly realised that the surgeons had pretty well given up on Jonas as a hopeless case. For reasons which became apparent later, they had taken a shine to Jonas, and they resolved to try to save him. They therefore set about undressing him and sponging him down with lukewarm water whenever his temperature soared. They wrapped him up warmly whenever his temperature dropped and he started to shiver uncontrollably. They constantly applied cold compresses to his head. They somehow managed to gets sips of water into him. They cleaned him up when, all unknowing to him, he passed urine in his cot, or his bowels opened. They changed his bedding, and washed the soiled clothes. One or other of them saw that he had their care for 24 hours a day and seven days a week.

His fever broke after a week, but it was not until the eighth day that Jonas began to return to consciousness. The first thing he heard was Corporal Jenkins quietly singing a Welsh lullaby as he made his way across the tent, just happening to pass close by the cot of Jonas.

"Oy, Jenks," he muttered through dry lips, *"Gi'us a drop of water."*

"By God, Jonas bach! We all thought you was a gonner!", cried out the Corporal, *"Here you are, man – sip this – welcome back!"*, and, slipping his arm under the head of Jonas he gently raised it enough for Jonas to be able to drink some water, which was marvellously refreshing for him.

However, Jonas managed only a couple of sips before his head started to spin, and he was glad that Corporal Jenkins was alert enough to see that his eyes were starting to go out of focus, whereupon the Corporal carefully laid Jonas down again.

"Rest easy, mon," said the Corporal quietly, in his sing-song Welsh voice, *"You've had a very close call, our Jonas, and it'll take time before you begin to get any strength back, isn't it? Mind you, I don't think you'd be here at all if it hadn't been for those two wonderful Ghurkas!"*

"Wot Ghurkas?" said Jonas weakly, *"I don't know any Ghurkas…"*

"Well – You may not know them – but they certainly know you! They've been looking after your every need day and night for the last week. They're the most devoted nurses we've ever seen…Undoubtedly you owe your life to them!"

"I doan't understand. Surely I've only been here for a day or two?"

"Oh no, Jonas! This must be at least your eighth day here…"

"Good Lord! I had no idea…Oh dear….I'll have to think about that later..", and Jonas drifted off to sleep again, to wake again a day later, once more with a great thirst…

This time, however, one of the *Ghurka*s who happened to be working nearby saw that Jonas had opened his eyes, and he was quick to give Jonas a drink, using his eyes to the full to carefully appraise the physical state of the patient as he did so.

In the meantime the other *Ghurka* had entered the tent, and the two men then exchanged a few words in a language which Jonas found utterly incomprehensible, the second one nodding in obvious agreement and heading out of the tent, only to reappear after a short while, bearing a small mug of what proved to be hot beef-tea. This the *Ghurka*s then aided Jonas to sip, mouthful by mouthful until it was all gone. *"Ayo Jonas Sahib!"* said one, smiling broadly in an encouraging and congratulatory way. *"Yes – but I don't know your names!"* said Jonas, receiving only puzzled but smiling looks in return.

"The shorter one's called 'Prakash", chimed in Corporal Jenkins, *"and we think that the other one is called 'Diprasad' – or something like that. We're having quite a job to understand their lingo…"*

"Yeah – it's even harder than your bleedin' Welsh!" said Private Tomkins (who was never a respecter of persons), speaking from the bed opposite. *"But if the Ghurkas don't understand me I just shout louder and louder until they do!"*

"Why do you think they've been so good to me?" asked Jonas, *"Have they taken care of other patients too?"*

"Not so'as you'd notice", replied Corporal Jenkins, *"I wouldn't say as to 'ow they've never lifted a finger, like, to help various soldiers in bother – but to nothing like the degree they've looked after you! I've tried asking them why, but I can't get any real sense out'v'em."*

However, Havildar Sing of the 26th Native Infantry, who'd had a leg amputated after the battle of July 1816, had recently been admitted for further treatment on his stump. He was sitting on a bed in the other side of Jonas. *"May I please to make a comment?"* he asked in his own sing-song way.

"Yeah, sure – off you go Gunga Din", said Private Tomkins.

"My name is 'Sing'", said the Havildar reprovingly…

"Yeah…Sorry…Sing, why don't you sing!" replied Tomkins, with a cheeky grin on his face.

"Well…All I wanted to say was that I do not know their language well – but I believe that the two Ghurkas saw Jonas in his madness and – what do you call it – yes, his bloodthirstiness. You know, when Jonas went in with the bayonet, leading the charge up the hill…When Jonas was full of battle-rage…It seems that the Ghurka officer that Jonas struck down was the son of a rajah, and previously regarded by the Ghurkas as near-immortal. So Jonas has gained great credit and respect amongst the Ghurkas – and these two men did not want to see him just die of a horrible sickness…"

"Gor blimey, Jonas – looks like you're famous! But Sergeant Lucas has heard about you an' yer leadin' the charge, an' he plans to cut yer down to size agin', cos he don't like soldiers runnin' amok, as he calls it!", said Corporal Jenkins to Jonas, with a bit of a twinkle in his eye.

"Oh No!", uttered Jonas, *"I just hope he will remember that all my courage had gone by the afternoon – so I was bleedin' terrified as per usual! It was only the sheer ritual of havin' to fire my musket hundreds of times over – an' the fact that I had good, steady soldiers on each side of me – that stopped me from runnin' away in sheer terror. Those Ghurka foes just seemed to keep coming on at us no matter how many we shot down. The field was covered in their bodies – it was God awful!"*

"Yeah – You're right, bach. They sure were brave fighters!" replied Corporal Jenkins, *"They kept attacking us all through the morning and it wasn't until the afternoon that they desisted. I'd got through all my water long before that, and boy-oh-boy, wasn't I parched!…Talking of which, where's that bleeding chawallah?"*…and (shouting across the large hospital tent to the Indian charwallah), *"HEY MAHOMMET, CHAR IF YOU PLEASE!"*

Jonas had indeed been seriously ill, and he remained in the hospital from February to June 1817, suffering from frequent flare-ups of his fever and delirium as his malaria gradually began to wear itself out. He was extremely lucky that the illness did not seriously affect his brain. He was far from being alone in the hospital. For example, in the stiflingly hot weather of June there were 14 men from his company reporting sick, with seven others from the regiment being invalided home to England. The number of deaths from sickness was also considerable, averaging about seven per month for the battalion as a whole.

Jonas had returned to duty in the Monsoon weather of July, but a route march in a deluge of rain proved to be too much for him, and he collapsed. He was therefore returned to the hospital, where he spent a further month, frustrated almost out of his wits, before returning to duty in September.

It was at about this time that the number of effectives in the 24th began to plummet, falling to 870 by December 1817, and to 824 six months later. By December 1818, it would be down to 770. It was not helped by being at Untari for four months, because the death rate there averaged some 14 men per month.

In had been in the Post-Monsoon period of October 1817 that the regiment had marched to Untari, via Hossambar, to 'take post' on the extreme left of Lord MOIRA's Grand Army in the on-going war against the *Pindarees*. This motley but highly mobile tribe consisted, in total, of perhaps 20,000 well-mounted and armed brigands, 5,000 infantry and over 60 guns. Their depredations had been vicious and widespread, even including a raid on Madras. Lord MOIRA had been manoeuvring to trap them in a pincer movement of which one jaw consisted of a force of the Bombay and Madras Armies, advancing up the valley of the Ganges from the south – whilst the other jaw consisted of the forces under Lord MOIRA himself, moving down the Ganges valley from the north. To prevent the *Pindarees* from 'melting away' from the trap, the battalion companies of the 24th were now being sent to seal off the eastern flank (i.e. the borders of Bengal), as a part of this huge movement. In all, it is probable that some 120.000 troops were involved.

Jonas (who had completed his 14 years in the Army in October 1817) and the other men stayed at Untari for four months, fulfilling their 'deterrent' role, but never seeing any action. Effectively, however, the *Pindarees* were wiped out, principally by mounted forces. There was only one pitched battle, which took place at Mehidipur on 21st December 1817, involving 6,000 troops (nearly all *sepoys*) under General Hislop, against 5,000 *Pindarees*, with the heavy loss of 778 men killed and wounded on the British side, but defeating the *Pindarees* and capturing virtually all of their 60 guns. Mopping-up operations continued for a long time, however, and it was not until February 1819 that the last fugitive gang had been exterminated.

Prior to that period, with the bulk of the job done, the 24th returned to Dinapore in March 1818, there being rejoined by their flank companies, who had been based at Allahabad, and from whence they had played a slightly more active role in the war.

Chapter Nine

The Years 1818-1823: Quitting Dinapore:
the Great Route Marches, ending at Bombay:
Home to England

On 15th December 1818, the Regiment marched westwards to Ghazipore, in Uttar Pradesh, arriving there on the 24th. It was there that they over-wintered, finding that a very cold wind sometimes swept down on the area from the Himalayas. Their cantonment was located near to the impressive tomb which the British had built some years earlier to Charles the 1st Marquis Cornwallis, a governor-general of India, who had been involved (with General David BAIRD) in the defeat of Tipoo Sultan in 1792. There was also a Shiva Temple nearby. The people for miles around were involved in handloom weaving and the production of perfumes, all the local fields being planted with rose-bushes and with the smell of 'attar of roses' being particularly pervasive all around Ghazipore.

It may have been these attractive scents which led to Jonas having what amounted to his only love-affair in India. Once again, he had managed to find a Hindu family, the Kapoors, who were willing to let him use some of their materials and tools to make copper pots and pans – a skill at which he was becoming increasingly proficient. The Kapoors also introduced him to the process of tinning the inside of the objects which were destined for culinary use, to eliminate the risk of metal-poisoning from the untreated copper.

One day, a very elegant young Hindu woman of high caste, accompanied by two female attendants entered the Kapoor's shop and, at her request, was shown into the workshop at the back. She was clearly taken aback at seeing a British soldier happily working away there, with his jacket and cap off, and with his shirt-sleeves rolled up. In fact, in a *lingua franca* of a hotch-potch of Hindi and English, but mostly by gestures, Jonas and Ranji Kapoor had just managed to share a bit of a joke and the two men, laughing uproariously, quite failed for a few seconds to see the dignified entry which the lady was making. Whereupon, seeing her presence, Ranji immediately leapt to his feet and made a deep *nastase*, momentarily leaving Jonas rather bewildered as he tried to comprehend and assimilate what was going on.

"Oh dear!" he exclaimed in English, *"I'm so sorry Your Ladyship!"*, and he too, scrambled to his feet, and made a deep bow, murmuring, *"Delighted to be of service…"*.

The young Hindu lady smiled broadly and gave a tinkling laugh, *"Oh my goodness me! I had not expected to be called upon to speak my schoolgirl English today! Why on Earth are you, an English soldier, working in an Indian bazaar?"*

Jonas dared to raise his eyes, finding the most lovely pair of brown eyes gazing at him. He gulped a little, *"Er, well – As a matter of fact I'm just learning a bit of a trade. I thought it might come in handy to help me to earn a livin' if I ever manage to survive long enough to be demobbed back home in dear Old England…"*

"Oh – and are those objects on that little table over there the ones that you have made yourself?"

"Er, yes, they are of my work...But Ranji's pieces – the ones on the adjacent table – are of much better workmanship than mine, Your Ladyship. Ranji is my teacher – my 'guru'..."

"I will buy some of Ranji's in a moment, perhaps...But it is your work which fascinates me at the moment." Then, giving Jonas her flashing smile, she added, *"For an Indian lady to have pans made by an English soldier must have a certain special kudos, I feel. How much do they cost?"*

Jonas thought for a moment. He was tempted to say, 'Please take whatever you like, ma'am – with my compliments!' – but then he thought, no, because that might force Ranji to do likewise – and the Kapoor family desperately need every rupee that they could earn....and, who knows, this lady might conceivably bring them in a lot of trade today and maybe in the future too...Oh, heck! What should I say? Then, inspired, he said. *"Would it be acceptable if I asked my Guru, Ranji, to set the price, my lady – He is far more skilled than I at judging what little my work as an apprentice is worth on the open market – and he knows all the ins and outs of the marketplace far, far better than I will ever do. He will also be able to aid you or your servants to whichever of all the items in this fine shop will best meet the needs and be of the greatest service in the culinary activities at your splendid home."*

"Please, may I ask your name, soldier?" she asked by way of an indirect response.

"Private Jonas Green of the 24th Regiment of Foot, Your Ladyship. "My friends call me 'Jonas'."

"Well, Jonas, my name is Princess Rhani Khan." She smiled beguilingly and added, *"Your skilful answer to my question as to the price of your products means that I shall now be completely fleeced by Ranji here! However, I can well understand what you were doing...So* (she added teasingly) *I will not hold you in the bad odour for what you were doing."*

She saw that Ranji was looking mesmerised by what was virtually an unknown language to him, so the princess turned to him and explained that she wanted to buy a pot or two, but that the English soldier had said that he, Ranji, was his guru and that the Englishman had passed the matter of business over to him to deal with. Ranji demurred a little that he would ever aspire to be a guru, but replied that he would be highly honoured to deal with the matter of business.

And so it came to pass that Jonas saw one of his pans sold for the first time ever, together with three of the excellent hand-beaten family-made products – and, after the usual hard bargaining which was the normal practice in India, Ranji cleverly clinched the deal by adding as a little gift (though only after an enquiring glance at Jonas) a pretty little copper 'Ali Baba' lamp which Jonas had just completed. Princess Rani was delighted with it, and left with a pretty *nastase* to all and sundry in the shop, taking her attendants with her and leaving behind an ambiance of her jasmine perfume and a memory of her delightful smile.

This was the beginning of several visits which she made to the shop over the following weeks. The Kapoor family made clear to Jonas that the princess had clearly been disappointed on the occasions when he had not been present. When he was present, she made it very evident to him that she welcomed the opportunity to talk a little English with him. *"I had a lovely English 'ayah', but she was taken by the last outbreak of cholera which we had here, and I miss her terribly. She taught me much about the history of your wonderful country. My brother has been sent to your world-renowned university of Oxford – but, being a mere girl, the family will not let me follow him. Do you think that's fair?"*

"Well," said Jonas, *"With a girl every family wants to keep her not only virtuous and unblemished, but clear for all to see that she is so. A girl is like a precious jewel to be protected at all costs, come what may…I must confess that I look forward very much to your visits…But, at the same time, even though you are always well chaperoned from having servants accompanying you, I am very concerned that you should not risk any slur from any quarter at all from conversing with a common English soldier. Maybe, if I was of officer rank, it would be rather more acceptable for a lady of your high class – but even then there might be certain problems…I mean, you do understand that I am just a humble chap – what some people call a member of the 'brutal and licentious soldiery'!"*

"Oh my dear Jonas," she responded, *"I am only too aware of all that – and I am being careful. I much appreciate the care which your comments show you have for me. I think you should know that you are not just a 'common soldier'. There is far, far more to you than that. I saw that clearly from the first moment that I laid my eyes on you. You have a fine brain and very high morals. I love to converse with you. Yet I am also aware that, although my father's kitmagar made the customary deep nastase to me today as I left the house, he also gave me a strange look out of the corner of his eye, and I fear that he may yet make trouble for me with my father."*

"There you are, then, My Lady," said Jonas, *"You would be as well to stay away – at least for a while…",* then adding gently as he saw how her face was falling, *"It really would be the best course."*

And the Princess did take heed of his words, and she did stay away for some weeks, during which Jonas regularly attended the Kapoor's workshop and toiled away at improving his metal-working skills. He was pleased to note that the Kapoor family had indeed found that the princess's earlier visits had attracted other custom, and they had been able to expand their premises to some extent.

For his part, Jonas found that he missed her far more than he had expected, and he found that she had begun to 'visit' him in his dreams, usually fantastically and most erotically.

It was therefore with something of a shock that Jonas looked up one day from a complex piece that he was finishing, to see the lovely face of the princess looking down on him. *"Oh my goodness me!"* she cried, *"That is the best thing that I have seen you do yet, Jonas – Very well done!"*

"Oh, thank you very much, My Lady!", he exclaimed, rising quickly to his feet and all-too-conscious of the blush that was rushing over his cheeks at the sight of her beauty and as the thoughts of the fantastic dreams he had been having about her came rushing back into his mind. He had to very swiftly sort out fact from dreams within the recesses of his brain…

"And may I ask, what is that strange piece you are making called?", she asked.

"In England it would be called a kettle, My Lady – It would be used to boil water over a fire… and the boiling water would often be used to infuse tea…probably using leaves imported from China – or maybe from the hills of Kashmir."

"Ah, yes...I see that you have put special pieces in the handle to stop the heat from rushing through the metal to it – so that one's hands do not get burnt. I love the way you have shaped the...what do you call it... the long thin piece in the front...Ah, yes, the 'spout' is it not? And you have made this beautifully-fitting lid for it, too. I think it is really splendid...May I buy it?" And, with a brilliant and slightly wicked smile, sufficient to make Jonas nurse wild hopes that she might even have dreamed a little about him in return, she enquired, *"Should I speak to Ranji again?"*

"Yes, please, My Lady. Ranji is still my 'guru'..."

And so the deal was done, and the princess left the shop, with smiles all round and accompanied by both of her servants, one of whom was carrying the kettle.

However, almost immediately, Jonas became aware of a hullabaloo outside the shop, and, peering out into the bright sunshine he saw that two murderous-looking tribesmen had grappled with the servants and that a couple of other tribesmen armed with vicious-looking tulwars were threatening the princess. They were urging her at sword-point into a palanquin borne by two other burly tribesmen.

The princess had gone deathly white, though she had kept her self-control. Her eyes, casting wildly about, encountered those of Jonas. *"Help, Jonas!"* she cried out wildly, *"These men are bandits and they want to ransom me! Please help!"* She had no time for more, because one of the bandits picked her up and threw her bodily into the palanquin, promptly tying the curtains into place to prevent her escape.

Jonas glanced quickly around the bazaar. How on earth could he immediately stop the kidnap – and without causing a native riot? As usual, there were men of his battalion scattered here and there around the various shops, and he was suddenly inspired. *"BUNDALOO!!"* he yelled as loudly as he possibly could, and *"BUNDALOO!!"* again. This was the recognised call for his regiment whenever a street brawl threatened – usually of the drunken men of one British regiment against the men from another. The call would be repeated loudly by every man who heard it, and bring more and more men to the spot, all 'looking to help out and ready for trouble'.

In what seemed like seconds the narrow street was filling with his fellow-soldiers. "STOP THAT PALANQUIN!" yelled Jonas, and the red uniforms were all round it in an instant, though not in time to prevent the quick-witted bandits from dropping it and swiftly melting away into the native crowd.

Jonas dashed to the palanquin, untied the curtain and helped out the shaken princess. *"Oh, Jonas, you are magnificent! Thank you my dear, dear soldier!"*

The other soldiers were gathering around, all full of questions and getting just half-answers. The princess drew herself up, and spoke out as loudly as she could. *"My grateful thanks to all you dear soldiers of the 24th Foot! You have saved me from a terrible fate!"* - and, having delivered herself of that pretty little speech, she fainted dead away, collapsing full into the welcoming arms of Jonas to the accompaniment of friendly but rather raucous cheers from his fellow-soldiers.

Jonas carried her into the shop, and laid her on a divan, where Ranji's wife and the princess' servants, who had also been very frightened from being so savagely handled, gently ministered to the princess. She soon recovered her wits, and a cup of tea revived her well.

"Oh, Jonas," she said at last, *"I shall have to tell my father, the Rajah, of what has befallen me today. If I do not, word will certainly reach his ears from my servants. I*

do not think he will welcome the idea of my having to have been rescued by British soldiers, and by one British soldier in particular. I think he will stop me from coming out again unless accompanied by some of his own well-armed guards. This will make my visits here much more difficult. Oh, I am so sorry...I will never, ever, forget you."

"Nor I you, My Dear Lady!" responded Jonas, "Have a great life and perhaps, who knows, at some time in the distant future we may meet happily and unrestrainedly in a very different time and place." He badly needed to add more, for his heart was bursting, and he decided to risk also saying, "Farewell, you who have brought great light into my darkness." She promptly hid her face, but he always fancied that his words brought tears to her eyes. And so they parted...forever.

In April 1819, Captain Ponsonby KELLY took over the command of the Company in which Jonas was serving. By that time the warm spring weather had begun to return to Ghazipore, and the enervating heat of summer followed. It was in June of 1819 that several earthquakes were felt throughout India, the worst occurring in the Kutch, well over to the west of India, where some 2,000 persons were buried in an enormous land-displacement. Luckily, Jonas, still based in Uttar Pradesh, felt only the more minor shocks, disturbing though they were. Summer was followed by the Monsoon, which continued until October.

Just over a year later, with the cooler weather of November 1820, the 24th moved into temporary camp at Singramsed, leaving there on 12th November for Cawnpore, still in Uttar Pradesh, which they reached on 12th December. This populous town, with its cantonment built in 1766, was constructed along the banks of the Ganges, with *ghats*, or landing-places, crowding all along the tree-lined riverside and with mosques and temples scattered alongside them. The *ghats* always seemed to have bathers on their steps and girls, many very graceful in their movements, always passing along the way, often smoothly carrying earthen water-pots balanced on their heads. Cawnpore had an entrenched fort covering perhaps three or four acres, and a general hospital. Lt Colonel ROBISON took command of the 24th at Cawnpore in April. He was relieved by Major Thomas CRAIG in August 1821.

Setting out on the 15th November 1821, in the Post-Monsoon period, the Regiment moved again, via Camp Banda, to Nagpore, reaching there in late January 1822, with Lt Colonel ROBISON once more in command. This march of 577 miles to Nagpore, in the state of Maharashta, was achieved at the rate of 8½ miles per day, allowing for halts. Nagpore was said to lie at the dead-centre of India. Its name could be interpreted as meaning the 'City of Snakes', though it was more famous for the oranges which were cultivated there. It may well be that the 24th were ordered to Nagpore as a 'military deterrent' against a suspected flare-up of trouble following the annexation of the territories of the Peshwa by the Honourable East Indies Company in 1818. The annexation had followed a failed attempt by the Peshwa to throw off ever-increasing British interference with domestic *Maratha* policy. This British annexation, coupled with HEIC acquisitions in Gujarat, had converted the Western Presidency into a huge province of some 70,000 square miles with a coastline of some 400 miles. Bombay now had the huge hinterland it so badly needed if it were to thrive.

In March 1822, orders were received from Calcutta for the 24th regiment to be held in readiness to embark for home. If they so wished, men were allowed to volunteer to join other corps and stay in India: 483 of the 770 or so men did so. The 13th and 44th Regiments seemed to be popular choices, but some men joined the Honourable East India Company's forces.

Captain Ponsonby KELLY fell seriously ill in September 1822, and was taken into hospital. Captain William GILL then took over command of Jonas' company. Well after the Monsoon period, on the 23rd November 1822, the regiment started from Nagpore to Bombay – a distance over the hills of 533 miles at 8½ miles per day, with one or two short stops, and arriving at the city of Bombay on 29th January 1823. (In December 1822 they had been in camp at Beroart.)

Once in Bombay the 24th moved into brick-built cantonments on the Colabar peninsular, with the old Portugese-built fort of Bombay standing just to the north of them, together with three attractive and quite well tree-shaded *maidans*, where their parades took place. As at Madras and Calcutta, there were impressive white colonial houses at Bombay for the white residents and officials in this vicinity, into some of which houses the more senior officers installed themselves. The busy and well-stocked *bazaar* which lay to the north of the fort was always teeming with native people, whose multitude of shacks sprawled across the rest of the city. On the waterfront Jonas encountered a pervading smell which was new to his experience. This was the powerful aroma from the drying in the sun of *bombil* fish, which was widely practised for the production of so-called 'Bombay Duck'. As another local industry, cotton, which was grown extensively in neighbouring Gujarat, was made into finished goods in Bombay and, through the port, raw cotton was also exported in bales to China and other parts of the globe.

Bombay was the largest Indian city which Jonas had ever seen. It was a very large and fine port, and shipbuilding and sail-making (using the locally-produced cotton) were actively carried out there, sometimes under contract to the British Navy. The Parsees of the city were prominent at both those manufacturing occupations. They were sometimes called the Jews of India, and some of them had become very wealthy merchant bankers, serving every race and caste, and wielding huge influence in Bombay. And this despite the fact that the Parsees existed as only a comparatively small population in Bombay, and seldom married outside their faith. Indeed, they were a close community and much inter-breeding had been going on amongst them down the centuries, ever since their arrival in India as refugees from Persia in the 8th Century.[10]

Jonas found that the Parsees had well-built 'Fire Temples' in the city, where their priests carried out elegant ceremonies based on the worship of fire. Jonas also walked around the 'Towers of Silence' in which the Parsees disposed of their dead, finding the towers to be rather eerie places, usually with vultures perched around the tops of the high perimeter walls, just waiting to strip the flesh from the bones of the next batch of cadavers to be laid out naked on the roof-platform, the dreadful sight of which was mercifully hidden from the view of any people on the ground. Once the bones had been picked clean, the attendant priests would place them in an ossuary in the tower. On the

---

[10] The author's English-born wife has some Parsi blood, from ancestors once based at Bombay. There is a proud family legend that they were involved in making high-quality sails for the schooner HMS *Pickle*, which achieved fame in 1805 by racing at high speed in near gale-force winds from Trafalgar to Falmouth, England, bearing the glad news of the British defeat of the combined French and Spanish fleets – but also the tragic news that the celebrated British Admiral, Lord Nelson, had been mortally wounded in the battle.

whole, although the procedure seemed more than a little macabre, Jonas felt that this means of disposal was more effective than the Hindu process of cremation. Such cremations were carried out on the waterside steps of the so-called 'burning ghats' at Benares and at other religious sites. Unfortunately, the cremation process often left bodies only partly-consumed – with the remains then having to be thrown into 'Mother Ganges' or some other nearby river, to carry them away from the sight of the mourners – though all-too-often to become rotting 'flotsam and jetsam' lower down the river.

However, Jonas did not have long to familiarise himself with the features of the city of Bombay, because, on the 14th March 1823, he was one man of a detachment of 262 privates, 67 drummers and non-commissioned officers, and nine commissioned officers, under the command of Major CRAIG, who embarked in the East Indiaman *Charlotte* and the Free Trader *George IV.* Jonas actually embarked in the *Charlotte,* and, standing on board her, he had a superb view of the natural harbour and could see its potential for enormous expansion in the future.

A few weeks after Colonel ROBISON had been succeeded in command, he had headed back to England, taking ship ahead of the above detachment of the 24th. Sadly, however, he died just two days from home on the return voyage. (2nd May 1823).

For the main detachment of the 24th the journey home was uneventful. However, in the minds of the men it seemed to go on for ever, even though it scarcely lasted for more than the expected four months. For Jonas, one of the most memorable features was a chance conversation he had with James Gubbins, a man who had been the Orderly Room Clerk towards the end of their foreign service. James, who had an enquiring mind with a mathematical bent, had said,

"A few weeks ago, with the end of our service in India coming up, and having a bit of time on my hands, I decided that I would go through the muster books and make a count of the number of men who had died since the 24th left England's shores, back in 1806. I had a bit of a job, because the loss of some records during the sea-battle of the 3rd July messed me up a bit – and, unsurprisingly, there seemed to be some 'double-entries' at around that time and also instances of men who had gone missing but whose deaths never seem to have actually been recorded. Old Colonel MARRIOTT had done his best to compile lists of the casualties at that time, but I reckon there were still flaws and uncertainties in the material he was trying to work from."

"Anyway, allowing for all that, Jonas, I reckon we lost well over 600 men dead over the 16 and a bit years – mainly due to tropical illnesses – quite small numbers of 'em due to combat, and with a further number being drowned in ol' Father Ganges! That's a terrible river when its in spate, ain't it?"

"Gawd alone knows about the many others who were sent 'ome early as invalids – I reckon it might have been as high as 100 men and more in some years, but it is difficult to tell. I do know that it was quite usual for (say) a couple of men to die on each ship making the return passage, but as to how many died shortly after their discharge from the Army once they got back to Old England, I suppose nobody has the least idea! In a way, Jonas, the invalids seem to be in the saddest position of all."

"Yes," said Jonas, *"I once tried to keep a mental tab on about fifteen of the young men who were with me at the start, and who had completed their first seven years at the same time I did. I know for a fact that five of 'em died in various places in India – the fifth one – that was Maurice NICHOLLS – only last year – and I reckon that another five*

of 'em were discharged sick over the years. That only leaves three or four of us who may have survived in the Army long enough to qualify for our pensions. If I do get home in one piece and survive for a few years happily drawing my pension, I shall feel myself to be a very lucky man indeed!"

"Uh, huh!" replied the other, "I estimate, in crude terms, that, in addition to the 1,000 and more men we started off with, we must have absorbed a battalion of reinforcements (say a little over 1,000 men) sent out to us, mainly from England, whilst we were abroad. Of that number we must have lost about 680 men dead from the total of something over 2,000 – that is, about a third of them – with a further large number being sent home early, as invalids. That leaves only about 500 men – say 25%, who might qualify for a pension."

He went on, "What you are saying from yer own personal observations – call it 3 or 4 surviving from 15 – would support that, my ol' Jonas. That is, somewhere about a 25% chance of drawing a pension. Not good the odds, are they? You and I must indeed be lucky men! Stay fit, Jonas, me ol' pal – and live long once yer leaves the Army, to make as much of yer pension as possible!"

The majority of the men were disembarked at Gosport on the 3rd July, but it would not be until the 11th July that Jonas and the others (once again under the command of Captain BABY) disembarked at Gravesend, and from whence they marched to Chatham. As if to emphasize what James Gubbins and Jonas had been discussing, two privates had died during the voyage. And Jonas was one of eleven men invalided at Chatham on 19th August. His sixteen years of 'East Indies' service each counted as more that a year of 'Home Service', thus bringing him up to the qualifying period to become an Army Pensioner, and he was discharged to Out-Pension on 30th September 1823.

Jonas later learnt that the average rate of deaths from sickness in the British Army in India ran at 69 per 1,000 men, per annum, in the period 1825-1836. It seems that the rate in the 24th Btn had averaged 'only' about 50 per 1,000 per year in the preceding decade – strangely enough, considerably better than what seems likely to have been the dreadful 'norm'. (For Indian 'Sepoy' troops, due to their greater natural immunity, the rate was only about 18 per 1,000.)[11]

And so ended a massive chapter in the life of Jonas. He had endured a number of 'close shaves with death' but, somehow or other, he had come through everything that had been thrown at him. But the thirty-six year-old who came ashore at Chatham in 1823 was a vastly different person to the stripling who had set forth from England for foreign climes back in 1808. Not only was he far more mature and experienced, but he was also in a poor state of health and very nearly 'broken down'.

---

[11] Ref 'The Oxford History of the British Army', ISBN 0-19-285333-3.

Chapter Ten

The Years 1823 to 1845: Back in 'Civvy Street', Married Life, the Final Years

For Jonas, leaving the protection of the Army was utterly devastating. For all his adult life he had been instructed what to do. So long as he obeyed orders and 'kept his nose clean' all had been relatively well for him. Now, suddenly, there was nobody to tell him what to do – and nobody to think for him. He greatly missed having his comrades all around him, men with whom he could identify and share his troubles. Moreover, he did not feel well. Basically, he felt like a boat without a rudder at the dubious mercy of wind and tide. Jonas well knew that a good many soldiers never survived the stress of re-entering civilian life – and he, too, came very close to roaming the streets like a lost vagrant.

True, he had his papers of admission as an out-pensioner sewn securely in his pocket and he also had some coins in his pocket – actually in worth about 60/-, and thus the equivalent of about sixty days at his pension rate of 1/- a day. And, although still aged only 36, he should be able to start to draw his pension within the month, and thereafter until the day he died. He knew that the pension was a fantastic benefit, which few men managed to achieve. Jonas had told the authorities that he would be living in Aldham, Suffolk, but would he truly head for that place? Were his parents and his brothers still alive and living in that area? He had no idea.

Jonas decided that he would initially head back for Gravesend. It was on a whim, but it was also on the start of his northwards route from Chatham to Suffolk – and he had heard a coachman shouting out that it was back to Gravesend that his coach was bound. So, Jonas took a stage-coach for the second time in his life, but riding 'inside' this time.

Once at Gravesend he headed for the docks, reckoning that he would probably find somewhere there where a reasonably cheap meal and overnight lodgings could be had. In this he was successful.

The following morning he was quickly up and about, and he saw that a couple of outbound East Indiamen were at the dockside embarking troops. Exactly as had happened on his departure for South Africa seventeen years before, there were highly distressed women and children being left on the dockside for whom no place existed on the ships. It was an extremely sad sight, and Jonas felt very sorry for all of those involved.

He had suddenly begun to feel not too good in himself, and he sensed that he had one of his flare-ups of high temperature coming on. So he found himself a reasonably comfortable hidy-hole in a pile of net-like trawls and other fishing-gear, climbed in and drifted off to sleep.

It was late afternoon when Jonas was awakened by a quiet sobbing noise. Peering out from his shelter, Jonas saw that a good-looking young woman was standing nearby, crying gently and muttering to herself, *"I'll be damned if I will – he can go to hell* (sniff, sniff), *but how am I ever goin' to get meself back to Norfolk"*.

"Excuse me," said Jonas, emerging from his hidey-hole, *"Can I possibly be of any help to you, Miss?"*

"Oh, Lordie me!", said the girl, *"Another soddin' redcoat! Why doan't you just take a runnin' jump into the river over there!?"*

"I'm sorry," said Jonas, *"I was only asking if I could help you!"*

"Well", said the girl, *"It's a redcoat who has got me into this mess – and now he's abandoned me far from my home! He's gone off with the other soldiers in that damn great ship, but I've been told that there's no room for me to go with him! I'll swear that the devil went orf wiv' a smile on his face, an' left me all on my Tod Sloan! The rotten swine!"*

She went on, *"Then there's this really horrible civilian who's come up to the women like myself who've been left stranded on the dockside, and he's offered us his 'protection'! He's all smiles and charm, but I know what that means – he'll have us all in prostitution, the blackguard! I doan't want to be no prostitute! - But then, I ain't got no money either!"*

The girl looked at Jonas and said, *"Now what's your game – you're not another bleedin' pimp are you?"*

"By no means!" replied Jonas, *"I'm a soldier just returned from many years of service in India – and, having seen women in your sad case before now, I was just wondering if I could help in any way. I have no nasty motive, I can positively assure you ma'am..."*

"Then why do you look so worked up? You're as red as a beetroot and you have sweat pouring out of your face..."

"Oh....That's just a tropical fever...malaria...I suffer from it now and again...it should pass in a day or two...I'm sorry if I frightened you..."

"Are you telling me that you have a fever? Am I liable to catch it from you?"

"No, it's not infectious. It is supposed to be spread by mosquitoes – and there aren't any in this country, really. I caught malaria when I was out in India."

"You don't look at all good to me. I think you should be in a warm bed somewhere...Do you have a place to go to?"

"No – not really – I am just discharged by the Army and I am supposed to be heading north – to Suffolk..."

"Me too – except that my home parish is still further north, in Norfolk...Down here I'll be treated like a soddin' vagrant – and told to get my carcase out of Gravesend right away!"

"Look", says Jonas, *"I don't know your exact circumstances – but I do like the cut of your jib, as the sailors say. I suspect that you need a bit of help – and so do I, because I fear that this bug is going to make me really ill soon – it sometimes does that. It means that I may pass out completely before long – this heavy sweating can be an early sign of it."*

He went on, *"How would it be if we took a room in a decent-looking pub, and kipped down there together. I promise you that I'll be far too ill to start any hanky-panky nonsense. I'll give you a little money so that you can get yourself a meal – and perhaps you'll be so kind as to try to get a little beef-tea or the like down my lips, for I'll likely be too far gone to really know about it! I'll doss down on the floor and you can have the bed – just so long as you keep a blanket or two over me when I get the shakes. Then, tomorrow, we'll see what to do next towards heading for our respective homes. Dare I trust you with my precious little bit o' spare change, ma'am – and dare you trust me with your rather lovely body – if I might make so bold? Incidentally, my name is Jonas – Jonas GREEN."*

"Oh – I'm Liz...Well, normally, I wouldn't even consider taking a room with a man. My family would be horrified...But they bit their lips when, like a really silly stubborn-head I ran off with my soldier – the one who's now let me down completely – so I suppose – being in desperate straights, I may now have to trust yet another soldier."

"Right!" replied Jonas, *"Well, the pub I stayed in last night wasn't bad. Shall we try our luck there? Do you mind if I call you my wife? – It'll save a lot of explanations, if I say we've just managed to meet up again. You can also say that you're concerned about me, and want to pack me off to bed because I am unwell and not yet used to being back to the coldness in England after my service in the tropical East Indies. Er, look...Here in my haversack I have three metal rings which I made when I was in India."* He quickly rummaged in his haversack and pulled out a cloth, which he opened to reveal the rings. *"They look a bit like gold, though – in truth - they're just a cheap alloy and will soon tarnish. They vary a bit in size. Take the one which fits you best. If you wear a ring, it will make our story about being married seem just that bit more convincing."*

The girl agreed, and they took a room for the night - whereupon Jonas, having given the girl a shilling for her meal, passed out like a light being switched off. All unknowing to him, the girl managed to get him into the bed, once she had removed his shoes and jacket, taken off his leather stock from his neck and loosened his collar. She was feeling weak and chilled, and she was also starving hungry, and so she went and got herself a hot meal – the first she had enjoyed for two days – and returned with a mug of hot beef tea for him. However, he was too deeply unconscious for her to get anything at all into him.

Overnight, his temperature mounted and he became delirious. The girl became seriously worried about him and consulted the publican about what best to do. That worthy told her the address of a nearby doctor, and she went round and asked the doctor to have a look at Jonas. Once she had indicated that she would be able to pay him, the doctor quickly came around to their lodgings and checked the patient.

"He certainly has a very high fever, Mrs Green," said the doctor, *"You did right to call me in. I am going to give him some quinine, which should help. I will leave you a further quantity, and I want you to get a large dessert spoonful of the medicine into him every four hours. I hope and expect that the fever will break and leave him in a day or two. If not, come back and see me again. Now, that will be one and sixpence please, Madam!* And, Elizabeth (for that was her name), having no money of her own, dug into the jacket-pocket of Jonas to pay the fee.

Jonas was still delirious, and he out-fought her when she tried to get the next dose of medicine into him. In the end she was compelled to enlist the help of the publican to hold Jonas whilst she prised his mouth open and emptied the filled spoon between his lips. The publican also helped her to remove the patient's trousers, to make him more comfortable.

"By God! – He's a strong-un, is yer husband, Mrs Green!" Said the landlord, his chest heaving with the effort he had put in to restrain Jonas. *"Oi reckon he's been in a few battles in his time – ranting on like he does about the Ghurkas coming over the hill – and him wanting to bayonet 'em all. A nightmare, I would call it. Has he ever told you*

about the wars, Mrs G? I reckon that's one hell of a man you've got yerself there. What was he like afore he went orf to foreign parts?"

And Elizabeth strove to make appropriate noises in answer, to keep up the pretence of the marriage. *"Oh, my dear Jonas,"* she said to the sweating and raving figure when they were on their own once more, *"Please come out of it soon, it's all getting just too difficult for me to cope with!"*

But it was not until the third day that his fever broke. He returned to consciousness to find himself lying in the sweat-soaked bed. *"You were the one supposed to be in the bed!"* he said.

"Well – I have shared it with you on some of the nights," she said with a smile, *"Though you have not exactly been sociable with me!"*

"What do you mean – on some nights?" said Jonas, *"Are you telling me that I've been out of things for more than just the one night?"*

"You certainly have, Jonas – and I've been begging you to come back to sanity because I've had to use some more of your money...And I had to pay the doctor, too."

"What doctor? Have I been totally out of it? How on earth have you managed? How many nights? Oh, I'm so sorry!"

"Well – three nights actually – Oh Jonas – you've been really ill and I was seriously worried as to whether you would survive! Have you been ill like this before?"

"Yes, I did have a couple of bad bouts of it when I was in India – and the medicos did warn me that I might have further outbreaks at times – though the illness should gradually burn itself out. Tell me – how have you managed to keep me so relatively clean? Did you get the landlord to deal with my waterworks – I'm sure I must have passed urine at times?"

"No. I dealt with that – you had wet the bed a couple of times, and washing the bedclothes was becoming heavy work – a laundry job really. I already thought I was dipping too much into your funds! So I got the landlord to find me a couple of wide-necked bottles that would do the trick. Then I kept one bottle permanently between your legs, changing it for a clean one as necessary. There was still the odd bit of a spill – but much less often...and less badly..."

"You mean – you dealt with it all – including pointing of things in the right direction, so to speak?"

"Yes – well, my father was fatally ill a couple of years ago, and Mother and I took it in turns to nurse him until he died. He was in a very bad way for several weeks, and totally unable to help himself – especially towards the end." (Elizabeth deliberately chose not to mention that the bowels of Jonas had opened spectacularly on the second morning, and that the landlady had been an absolute jewel in helping her to lift and turn the deeply unconscious Jonas to clean him up and to get him into a fresh shirt. Elizabeth suspected that the landlady had quietly burnt the badly soiled sheets and the wet rags they had used to do the cleaning, with the landlady actually washing and returning only the shirt.)

"Oh, Elizabeth – you are a fantastic woman," said Jonas. *"I am exceedingly obliged to you. Are you all right for money? Do you need more?"*

"As I have said, I've dipped into your money, though only when I've really needed it. I'm up to date with the landlord – and I paid the doctor's fee. We shall need some more money to pay for a hot meal tonight – you must be starving now – and we'll

have to settle with the landlord tomorrow for tonight's hire of the room. Oh, and while we're at it, please call me Liz or Lizzie – Elizabeth sounds so formal!"

"Well done, Elizabeth – er, sorry, Liz. I'm not sure that I could manage a full meal at present – but some beef tea or soup would go down a treat...But you must certainly eat a proper meal..."

And so the two of them began to put their whole trust each other, and to form a mutually caring and progressive relationship. They stayed at the pub for another two nights, by which time Jonas had started to eat again and his strength was creeping back. It turned out that the landlady hailed from Newcastle, and, with her help, they made contact with one of her relatives, the skipper of a collier which was moored for a couple of days at Gravesend, but bound up the East Coast the next day. The collier was travelling half-empty for its return voyage to Newcastle, and the skipper, who normally would never have considered doing so, was pleased to have a couple of 'paying passengers' aboard. All the more so because they told him they were not too fussed about the basic and coal-stained nature of his boat. Furthermore, on learning that the ship's cook had jumped ship at Gravesend, Elizabeth boldly offered to be the ship's cook as far up the coast as Lowestoft. The skipper jumped at the chance, so Elizabeth worked her passage – and that meant that she had no fare at all to pay.

Jonas was able to convalesce from his fever as the collier forged its way north, spending much of his time with Lizzie in the cosy warmth of the galley, and helping her to an extent, in preparing the meals for the small crew, who worked 'watch and watch about'. This meant that Lizzie had two sets of meals to prepare every day as breakfast, dinner and supper for the two watches – so she appreciated all the help she could muster. She had never performed such a role before, and she became very anxious when she cooked and served up the first meal, especially as, by then, the collier was beating its way through an increasingly lively sea, and was running with its lee side deep into the 'oggin'. Luckily, Jonas knew about 'fidding' the cooking-vessels and taking measures to prevent the dishes on the mess-table from sliding off and crashing down on to the deck. So all passed off well, and the skipper and his crew expressed great satisfaction with Lizzie's cooking.

Jonas and his 'wife' shared a tiny cabin, still completely innocently. Jonas longed to know if Lizzie was still a virgin – or whether her former soldier had made passionate love to her – but he did not quite have the courage to ask her outright. He felt that their relationship was still too tender and fragile to risk asking such a question – but the unspoken question kept burning into his very soul. Sooner or later it would surely have to come bursting out.

They reached Lowestoft safely, and disembarked there. The skipper shook hands heartily with each of them and said he was quite distressed to see Lizzie go, *"Weyho, Mrs Green, you've done a grand job o' cooking for me an' the lads! We haven't eaten so well in years, and we're all very sad to see you go!"*, he remarked in his broad Geordie accents. *"We all bid you and yer husband a very safe journey home."*

The collier was berthed well out along the mole, and there was a mass of trawlers and other fishing boats crammed into the harbour. The masts and rigging of the ships made it look as though the waterfront was a forest, and the clutter of stores of all sorts on the jetties, and the need to negotiate the swinging lock-gates controlling the river running inland, made progress to the landward side quite difficult. However, Jonas and Lizzie eventually succeeded.

By mutual consent, they then sought a green space off the High Street where they could sit and discuss things for a little while.

"We need to talk," said Jonas, *"Do you want to head for your home in Norfolk – or would you consider continuing with me?"*

"Is that what you want?" asked Lizzie.

"Um, well...that is ...I'm not really sure...it depends...I don't know...er...Look I like you a lot..."

"Only 'like'....I had hoped that you might be getting to love me...a little... at least.."

"Well...I do...I think you're a very fine person...."

"But you don't love me..."

"Um...yes...I do, but..."

"Oh Jonas...what is that little 'but' about?

"Oh, Lizzie! It's just my silly brain!"

"Is it about my earlier relationships, Jonas?"

"Yes...Thoughts keep buzzing around in my head...I can't get rid of them!"

"Oh, Jonas! Isn't what I did before in this life my business. You have never owned me...at least...not until recent days...and, in a way, not even then..."

"I know...Yes, I do know that..."

"I've never asked you if <u>you've</u> had other women...In the delirium arising from your illness you have often raved madly about somebody called Rani and you have cried your eyes out over a certain Mrs Murphy's breasts... "

"Have I really?! Oh, goodness! No...I know you haven't quizzed me about my past...

"If I were able to tell you that I am a virgin...that I have kissed and been kissed by another man...but that it has never gone further than that...would you be inviting me to travel with you...and perhaps to be assuming that our relationship will go deeper..?"

"That would be fantastic..."

"But, if I do not feel able to give you that assurance...would you throw our future lives together away? You must have seen many soldiers marry widows or women of easy virtue...Have they not often had very happy marriages together?"

"Yes...certainly...some of them at least..."

"Well...Why don't we continue together, at least for the present? We can stay friends...and...who knows, we may find ourselves drifting closer together as time goes on. I have no particular desire to go home...certainly not at present."

"All right. Let's go and see if we can find a stage-coach heading southwards for Ipswich."

"Fair enough. However, there is one other matter I think we should clarify. I come from Strict Baptist stock, and that's how I was raised. True, I kicked over the traces...but I do not want to abandon that faith altogether. Now, from some of your wild talk when you were delirious, I understand that your parents were also Strict Baptists. It seems to me that you more or less denied their teaching, in order to go off and be a soldier. From your ramblings when you were delirious, I also believe that William

Carey, the famous missionary, had a big effect on you, when you were out in India. Do you wish to revert to being a Strict Baptist – eventually...if not right now?"

"That's a difficult question, Liz. In some ways I feel unworthy to do so. You see, I've killed men during the wars in which I've fought – and I sometimes feel bad about that...especially when I think of the guilty exultation I've sometimes felt at the moment of killing somebody..."

"Oh my Jonas! You are a bit of a scrambled egg – but I love you for it. And I'd love to be able to spend some more of my life with you. Shall we go and see if we can find that stage-coach?"

And so they made their way to Ipswich. From there, a carrier's cart conveyed them westwards to Somersham, where, nigh seventeen years earlier, Joseph Green, the father of Jonas had used the money gained by his sons Sam and Jonas to buy some land and build his house. Jonas immediately saw that a second house had been built on the land since he had last seen it. However, he got something of a shock when he knocked on the door of the first house – and it was answered by a woman of mature years whom he totally failed to recognise at first.

"I'm sorry," she said, *"But soldiers and their women beggin' for scraps are not welcome around here – We get far too many on 'em! Be off with you!"*

"Excuse me", replied Jonas, *"But may I just ask if this is still the house of Mr Joseph Green?"*

"Of course it is," said the woman, *"But who are you ter be askin'?"*

"Well," declared Jonas, *"I am his second son, and I am here to claim my birth-right, for, years ago, I put a lot of money in trust here!"*

"Oh, Lordie me!" cried the woman, *"You must be our long-lost Jonas, back from the dead!"*

"Well, as you can see, I ain't quite dead yet! May I ask who you may be?"

"I'm the second Mrs GREEN – the second wife of Joseph. Don't you recognise me Jonas? Oh dear! About four year arter your true mother passed away – yer father married me. I were a widder woman. I were born in Offton at about the same time as yer Dad was born in Great Bricett...You didn't really take to me, as I remember it..."

"Oh My God! Yes – o' course I remember – Oh, I'm so sorry! May I ask, is Dad around?"

"Oh dear me, yes. He'll be home soon. But what I am doing a'blethering 'ere...Come in at once an' sit yerselves down ...an' I'll make the three of us a nice cup o' tea...and you can tell me all about yer adventures. Oh, an' 'oo be this 'ere young lady – is she yer wife, Jonas?"

"Not yet – but maybe soon, perhaps. Tell me – where's our Sam? Did he marry his beloved Sarah...Have they had any littl'uns? Do they live in the house next door? What has happened with Joshua, my younger brother?"

"Oh, dear! What can I say? It was ever so sad, but Joshua died whilst he wor still small, I'm very sorry ter hev ter say – and Sam died after Sarah had just the one child – a sweet little daughter they called Maria. He's been dead and gone for years now. Sarah was broken-hearted when he went. However, as you know she is a lovely girl and several of the men in the village had soon set their caps at her. She resisted them for several years – but in the end she married again, to that there Thomas FARROW. She

lives in Great Bricett now, with little Maria – and she has a couple of children by Tom…So we doan't really see much of Sarah nor Maria no more, I'm sorry ter say…'"

"Oh my goodness – I shall miss Sam a lot. He was a very fine brother, and I was hoping to introduce Lizzie to him and Sarah…"

"Yes – we miss him very much still…I got along wiv him extremely well. Oh. Look, I can hear yer Dad coming into the house (and, raising her voice), *"Oh JOSEPH – JUST LOOK WHO'S HERE!"*

There then followed a joyous reunion of father with son, a swift appraisal by each of the physical state of the other (both had aged to quite a degree since their parting sixteen years previously), an introduction of Lizzie to the father – and then a quick look around the second dwelling.

"Um – this house did belong to Sam and Sarah o'course", said Joseph, *"But she has moved away to live with Tom FARROW. So, the house could be yourn now, Jonas. I've bin rentin' it out to make a bit o' money, but I could soon get rid of the tenants."*

"Doan't be too hasty about that, Dad." said Jonas, *"I have a different idea."*

"What be that our Jonas?"

"Well, I've done a lot o' livin' under the stars during my army career – and we've made some prodigious marches…Five hundred miles has not really been exceptional. Also, as Lizzie can tell you, I have quite a turmoil in my head at times – especially when I think about the men I've killed – and also when I think about the friends who've been killed beside me. The upshot is that I think I would do better to buy myself a pony or a donkey and a well-equipped cart, and to go on the road, as a dealer and jobber. I learnt a bit about metal working when I was out in India. I could make a regular route and keep goin' around in a big circuit, gradually getting' meself well known as a good tradesman. That way of living will give me a sort of freedom, and God's canopy of stars over my head at night. I just doan't feel right when confined in a house, somehow…"

"If that's how you want to live – then why not? I always said that you had inherited yer mother's Romany looks and ways…A roamin' Romany, eh! Good luck ter yer! Well, now, there's a damn good wheelwright in Elmsett – he's a distant relation of our's and his name's Bob FIRMIN – an' I'm sure he'll agree to set yer up well if I take yer round there tomorrow."

The father then looked at Lizzie, who was looking a little set-faced,

"Well now…How about you, Lizzie? You and Jonas seem very close – almost like a married couple…Are you two married? Dare I ask what your background may be? Are you a Baptist like the others in this family? Would you be prepared to go on the road with our Jonas? It ain't the life for everyone!"

"Well, Mr Green", responded Lizzie, *"There's a deal of questions you have asked me. What can I reply? Um, well, Jonas and I are certainly very close. He plucked me out of a very difficult situation indeed, and I nursed him when he was dangerously ill with malarial fever. We have probably saved each other's lives – and we are indeed close – though we are not married – not even engaged, in fact. At the moment we are just 'good friends' as the saying goes. As a matter of interest, like Jonas, I was raised as a Strict Baptist. Whether either or both of us will continue in that faith seems to me to be currently uncertain. As to whether I could stand the wandering life of the wife of a dealer and jobber – I simply do not know – and Jonas hasn't even asked me if I want to try. There is much to be resolved between us, before things get that far – if they ever do".*

145

"And what do you want to happen in such aspects?" the father asked of Jonas.

"I really cannot say", replied Jonas, a little stiffly.

The older man studied the faces of the two of them for a moment or two, then quietly and gently he smilingly said, *"Well...How would it be if you both lived here for the time being? You can pay me a small rent, and we'll all board together. Perhaps Lizzie can do some of the household chores at times, for Mary is now of an age where she has to be careful not to overdo things. Then, if and when Jonas goes off on the road, Lizzie can either stay here – or accompany you, Jonas – as the two of you decide."*

So that was agreed. A few days later Jonas got his cart. It was cleverly designed to carry all the tools of his trade ready to hand and a certain amount of merchandise for sale, but yet also provided him with adequate sleeping quarters and the ability to stretch a roof-like tarpaulin over his eating area, should the weather come on to rain. He bought some good tools, and he quickly began to build a reputation as an honest trader and worker all along the route he developed in the rural area to the east of Ipswich.

Once every quarter he had to present himself to a local Justice of the Peace and make affidavit that he was not drawing on any other local funds. The main intention of this procedure was to prevent fraudulent claims being made on his pension when he eventually died, and the documentation which he had to permanently keep about him contained dire warnings to anybody who might contemplate doing such a reprehensible act. The documentation had its own value, and he made up a copper tube to contain it safely. The tube was permanently sealed at one end, and had a removable cap at the other.[12] A copy of every quarterly affidavit had to be sent to Chelsea Hospital, where its receipt was noted in a very large register. In the event of the death of a pensioner, the hospital was supposed to be informed immediately. The absence of an affidavit would cause an obvious gap in the records – and official enquiries would promptly be put in hand at the pensioner's home-address, to make sure that the pensioner's documentation was not being used fraudulently.

Lizzie found that she pined for Jonas when he was away from Somersham and off on his route. Once he was sure that the business was going to work, he invited her to join him on a trial basis. They set off on a day in midsummer, and slept under the brilliant canopy of the stars. Jonas warned Lizzie that the weather was not always so good, but Lizzie found it enchanting. She also liked the way in which Jonas was welcomed at the various stops along his route, and the professional way in which he set about repairing all kinds of items – especially cooking-pots and pans.

On the third night on the road, he kissed her tenderly and it was if a valve had been released in both of them. They were miles from anywhere and he stripped her naked in the bright moonlight, with her active aid – slipping out of his own clothes at the same time. They then made passionate love. It was only when he saw the dark streak of blood running down the inside of her thigh that he realised,

"Hey – You're a virgin!"

"I was – until just now!" she replied,

"Oh, my dearest darling!", and he was immediately suffused with the most tender of loving feelings mingled with the great passion he already felt towards her. *"Did I hurt you?"* He asked. *"Only a little – it's already forgotten."* She replied quite calmly, though she hardly recognised the sound of her own voice, and went on, rather more shakily, for

---

[12] The author still holds the tube and the now rather tattered documentation, as a family heirloom..

she'd never talked of such things with a man before, *"I knew that men's things grew quite big – but I didn't know they became so very hard and hot and…well, powerful, too. I wasn't sure that I'd be able to take you!"*

"And I didn't know that women were so intricately formed", he said, as he examined her intimately. *"Nor was I sure that they enjoyed sex and could truly achieve a climax, though, if I may make so bold, that certainly seems to have happened with you. Whoopee! Indian customs seem strange on such matters, and there was always a dispute when my Army mates talked of such things – though I suspect that some of them only had sex as a commercial transaction, which must be something quite different. I suppose it's all about love, really."* And he continued to make a very close exploration of her body, fondling her breasts and then kissing the inside of her thighs most intimately. *"Well,"* she replied, *"It's certainly love with me, and I'm very glad that you seem to know exactly what you're doing. I love the feel of your gentle hands and your strong arms around me."* And so matters continued until they fell into a blissful and exhausted sleep.

They were married, at Elmsett, on the 5th April 1825, by banns. Their witnesses were his cousin George GREEN and George's wife, Elizabeth GREEN, with whom they had already begun to develop a close friendship.

They set out on their married life in the dealer's cart. Their first child was a son, William, who was born at Needham Market on 19th January 1826. It had been their intention to gain the shelter of the house at Somersham, but the babe came earlier than expected. It was a bitterly cold day, but Jonas built up a goodly fire, and he kept a kettle on the boil. They had plenty of warm blankets and the cart was remarkably snug. Aided by a farmer's wife from a nearby house, Jonas acted as the impromptu 'midwife'. Happily, all went well.

Their next child, David, was also born on the road, again in January, but this time in 1828. A daughter, Emma, followed, in the more propitious month of May 1831, and they finished with a son, Joseph, born in October 1835. By that time Elizabeth was in her forty-third year, and they considered it wise to have the confinement in the house of the father of Jonas, at Somersham. They also called in the aid of Joseph's wife, Mary, and she called in the local midwife. Once again, all went well.

There then followed the most settled and contented part of the life of Jonas, now a lot easier in his mind, and generally based in the house at Somersham – with his lovely wife at his side, and bringing up their children together. He limited his rounds as a Dealer and Jobber, but sufficiently to bring him in a living and it was well-supplemented by the one shilling that his pension paid him every day – drawn quarterly.

Like his father before him, Jonas strove to develop the minds of his children, leading them to question and analyse what was going on around them. He did, however, introduce quite a leavening of humour and whimsy in their upbringing, much of it based on his experiences during his Army career. One of his biggest triumphs was to get his eldest son, William, into nearby Claydon Grammar School – where the boy thrived. Rightly, as it turned out, Jonas considered that William, who readily picked up practical as well as theoretical skills, would prosper in life. However, Jonas secretly worried that it might be the case that the boy's huge personality would lead him to develop into a grown man whose success and power would be almost too daunting to those around him – and perhaps especially to William's own sons when they eventually came on the scene.

David, the second son of Jonas, was of a different personality. He looked as if he was going to 'follow in his father's footsteps' as a Dealer and Jobber. Physically, the boy was well-built and he had a strange sort of personal magnetism and charisma about him which would surely be of huge benefit to him in the rapidly-changing world of industrialisation which was clearly racing towards the whole nation.

Joseph, the youngest boy, was probably still too immature to make any judgements about, though his eyes were fascinating, for they somehow had the visionary look of an Old Testament prophet about them. Indeed, both of the two younger boys seemed to have much more of the romantic about them than did their highly prosaic and businesslike elder brother.

As for the daughter, young Emma – well she was the light of her parents' eyes. Her personality simply sparkled and she brought a wide variety of friends into the household. The greatest sadness of the married life of Jonas and Lizzie came in 1839, when Emma, who was then eight years old, contracted scarletina. She had a raging fever and a terribly sore throat – her heart could not withstand the strain, and she died.

The lives of Jonas and Elizabeth would never be the same again. They were utterly grief-stricken and vowed that they would be buried beside their lost child when their time came.

The death of Emma was the final straw that drove Jonas to re-embrace the Strict Baptist Faith – and he became a vigorous lay preacher. He found that this was the best way to 'keep his ghosts quiet'. Even so, his dead friend Bill Hitchings, the late Corporal Jones, others of his dead comrades and the dead Ghurkas still occasionally 'visited' him in his dreams – usually when he had slight flare-ups of his latent malaria.

It was almost by accident that he actually became a preacher. It just happened that he and Lizzie regularly attended a Sunday bible meeting - and, one day, the scheduled preacher failed to turn up. (It was later learned that he'd collapsed with an epileptic fit.) Due to his travelling work Jonas was well-known to many of the people amongst the congregation - and he suddenly found that he was on his feet and talking quite easily to them all, his spontaneous preaching clearly going down well with the people. They asked him to continue in the succeeding weeks, since the regular preacher remained quite unfit to resume his duties, and Jonas quickly became attuned to the themes that the congregation liked to hear. He began to revel in the heady feel of being on his feet in front of a crowd, and in drawing emotional reactions out of them. He worked extremely hard at interpreting the gospels and applying them to the stresses and strains of daily life as known to the country people. His own widely ranging experiences in India and South Africa, in times of peace and in times of war, were of enormous help to him. He found that his growing audiences liked 'fire and brimstone' in the sermons he delivered, and, being a passionate man, he gave them more and more of that kind of preaching. However, the more he gave, the more they wanted!

People in distress began to seek him out for help and advice during the weekdays, and he began to work so hard and obsessively for the community that Lizzie became concerned about his health, and begged him to ease off. However, this was much easier said than done.

When Jonas was out in India, and in despair at the loss of his friends, the missionary, William CAREY, had been kind to him. Jonas had heard of the death of William CAREY which had taken place in India on the 9th June 1834, and he had told

Lizzie some more of the details of how the great man had befriended him when he was at a low ebb. Lizzie hugged this treasured memory to herself, and, when Jonas died suddenly, in his bed, on 16th May 1845, aged 57, a deeply-mourning Lizzie wrote a quotation which had been a favourite of William CAREY's (*taken from a hymn by Isaac WATTS*)[13] against the entry of Jonas' death in the family bible,

> *"A weary, poor and helpless worm,*
> *On Thy kind arms I fall…"*

By that time William the eldest son was aged 19, David was 17 and Joseph was 10, so Jonas had been able to see how the quite different natures of the three boys were shaping. All three sons attended the funeral of their father, which took place in the grounds of the Strict Baptist Chapel in Somersham. Young Emma's body was later re-buried beside her father, and a massive joint headstone was placed there – looking rather like a pair of separate stones, but actually joined. (*See photograph just below.*)[14]

Jonas was only briefly outlived by his 'ag lab' father Joseph, who died of Typhus fever on 11th Dec 1846, aged 77, Elizabeth being the informant of his death. (Mary, the widow of Joseph, went on to live to the considerable age of 84, dying on 24th May 1851.)

All three sons of Jonas subsequently did their level best to look after their mother, who would die at Ipswich in 1855, at the age of 63. Her body would be interred in her husband's grave.

Photograph taken by the Author in 1994.

The Headstone to the Graves of Jonas, Elizabeth and their daughter Emma, in the grounds of the Strict Baptist Chapel at Somersham, Suffolk. By 1994, when this photo was taken, the headstone was very nearly 150 years old.

---

[13] This then well-known quotation had been inscribed on the headstone to William CAREY's grave in India.

[14] The headstone to Jonas was still standing in the first decade of the 21st Century. The author has occasionally tended the grassed-over grave and planted bulbs upon it, talking the while in a one-sided conversation with the long-time inhabitants, so that their spirits might know who he is.

The origins of Elizabeth still remain something of a mystery. It is likely that her parents were Non-Conformists. At the time of the 1851 Census her words were interpreted by the compiler to state that she had been born at 'Bassen, Norfolk', but that place appears never to have existed, and researches at Norfolk places with similar-sounding names – such as the Barshams - have led nowhere.

Almost a century-and-a-half later, the actual bible-page on which Elizabeth had written the details of the death of Jonas, and quoted the lines of William CAREY, would be passed into the author's keeping. He is a great-grandson of Joseph, who was the *youngest* son of Jonas GREEN. June GREEN, the relative who passed the document on to him, was the widow of Peter GREEN, a great-grandson of William, who was the *eldest* son of Jonas. The author has also maintained contact with a descendant of the 'middle son of Jonas', namely, David Green – so all three sons 'kept the Green line going forward' towards the present day. *(See the Green Family Tree on Page 152 and the notes in the Appendix on Page 153.)*

THE END

Post Scriptum

It is clear that there was an efficient clerk keeping an eye on the records at the Chelsea Hospital, for at the end of September 1845, three months after the sudden death of Jonas had been recorded by the Coroner, a Military Provost arrived at the village of Somersham, demanding to know why the Pensioner Jonas GREEN had failed to send in his regular 'quarterly affidavit'. Had he died and was somebody committing the heinous and treasonable crime of continuing to draw on his pension?

The Provost's enquiries quickly revealed that no such crime was being committed – although the authorities should have been informed that Jonas had passed away on 16th May 1845 – so that the relevant entry in the great pension book maintained at Chelsea Hospital could have been closed down. To tidy up matters, on 1st October 1845, Mary GREEN (the step-mother of the deceased) and a neighbour, Catherine BLOMFIELD, were led before George KERRIDGE the local registrar, where a note was added to the Death Certificate of the 'Jobber' Jonas GREEN, to the effect that Jonas he had <u>also</u> been an 'Out-Pensioner from the 24th Regiment', and both women 'made their marks' as witnesses thereto. The author still holds a copy of this unusually modified document.

[NOTE: It seems surprising that Elizabeth, as the widow and 'next of kin' of the deceased, was not the key person to be called upon to 'give witness' to the Provost. We know that Elizabeth was living in Ipswich by 1851, and it may be the case that she had already moved there by September 1845, following the death of her husband, having perhaps sold off the house, and evidently taking her three sons with her – so that she was not readily available in the village of Somersham. However, in her absence, one would have thought that the next of kin to call upon would have been Joseph, the father of Jonas. Was it perhaps the case that, at age 76, he was already showing signs of dementia, making him ineligible to witness any document, so that his wife and carer, Mary, the step-mother of the late Jonas, came to the fore?

Another possible explanation is that Mary may still have been recorded (with her husband) as the next-of-kin of the deceased, had the relevant record never been up-dated from the time of Jonas joining the Army, back in 1807 and having been still valid up until 1823, when he was discharged from it. It will be recalled that he did not marry until 1826. Perhaps he had failed to notify Chelsea Hospital of his change in status?]

BACKGROUND

As we have seen, the central figure of this book was definitely a 'real-life' great-great grandfather of the author and his siblings. As shown in this story, the adventurous life of Jonas GREEN took him to various far-flung places around the globe. Against all the odds, he somehow survived his military service long enough to qualify as an Out-Pensioner of Chelsea Hospital, of which matter the records are preserved in the National Archives at Kew. He later married and raised a family. He left behind paperwork relating to his pension, and, in 1946, much-aided by one of his grand-daughters, one of his grandsons once recorded for posterity the very little that direct <u>human memory</u> then still retained of him.

This book is based on archival searches of the family history of the line down which Jonas was descended, the places where he lived and the family that he raised, and mainly works from various military documents, such as the 'muster rolls' and other records of the infantry regiment in which he served as a private soldier from 1807 to 1823, and also the appropriate regimental histories. In that context, the actions of the more senior Army commanders and other real-life figures in the backdrop to the story are authentic, having been based closely on historical record.

However, so far as individual private soldiers like Jonas are concerned, only very limited facts exist, and considerable liberties have been taken in attributing various characteristics to him, to 'put flesh on the bones'. The over-all aim has been to bring the central figure of Jonas 'back to life', and to find out 'what made him tick', insofar as such a thing is ever possible. In doing so, the author has used quite a lot of imagination (and transmogrified personal experience), for which he prays he may be forgiven – especially by his long-deceased forbears! He hopes that the end result has been a 'good yarn', and that he has not 'over-gilded the lily' – for just the basic records alone which bear on the life of Jonas would comprise a fascinating even if disjointed and rather 'bare-bones' true-life story.

N.B. The next page shows a family tree for Jonas, with some of his forebears and descendants. The Appendix which follows contains references to the many historical facts on which the skeleton of the story is based, and makes acknowledgements to the various national and county repositories involved. It also names the fellow family-history researchers and other family members who kindly shared data with the author when he was investigating the roots of the Green Family.

<u>Postscript</u>. Only 78 Privates of the 2,000 and more men who had served in the 1st Btn of the 24th Regiment were actually awarded the 'Army of India' medal which was issued in 1851. By then Jonas had been dead for five years – and he was thus just one of the thousands who 'failed to qualify'.

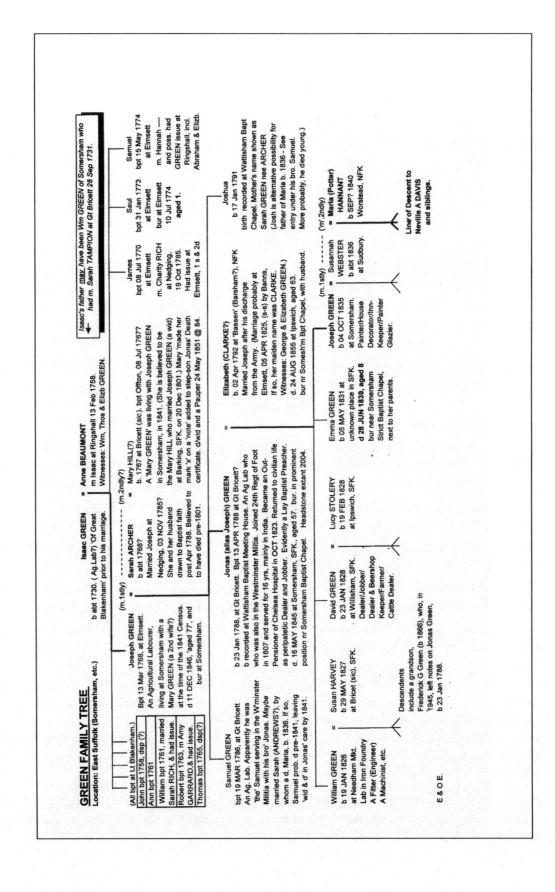

GREEN FAMILY TREE
Location: East Suffolk (Somersham, etc.)

Isaac GREEN = Anne BEAUMONT

Isaac GREEN b abt 1730. (Ag.Lab?) 'Of Great Blakenham' prior to his marriage.

Anne BEAUMONT m Isaac at Ringshall 13 Feb 1758. Witnesses: Wm, Thos & Elizb GREEN.

Isaac's father may have been Wm GREEN of Somersham who had m. Sarah TAMPION at Gt Bricett 28 Sep 1731.

(All bpt at Lt Blakenham.)
John bpt 1758, dsp (?)
Ann bpt 1761
William bpt 1761, married Sarah RICH, & had issue.
Robert bpt 1763, m Amy GARRARD, & had issue.
Thomas bpt 1765, dsp(?)

Joseph GREEN — Bpt 13 Mar 1768, at Elmsett. An Agricultural Labourer, living at Somersham with a Mary GREEN (a 2nd wife?) at the time of the 1841 Census. d 11 DEC 1846, 'aged 77', and bur at Somersham.

(m.1sty) Sarah ARCHER b abt 1768? Married Joseph at Nedging, 03 NOV 1785? She and her husband drawn to Baptist faith post Apr 1788. Believed to have died pre-1801.

(m.2ndly) Mary HILL(?) b. 1767 at Bricett (sic). bpt Offton, 08 Jul 1767? A 'Mary GREEN' was living in Somersham, in 1841. (She is believed to be the Mary HILL who married Joseph GREEN (a wid) at Barking, SFK, on 20 Dec 1801.) Mary 'made her mark 'x' on a 'note' added to step-son Jonas' Death certificate. d/wid and a Pauper 24 May 1851 @ 84.

James bpt 08 Jul 1770 at Elmsett m. Charity RICH at Nedging, 19 Oct 1785. Had issue at Elmsett, 1 s & 2d

Saul bpt 31 Jan 1773 at Elmsett bur at Elmsett 10 Jul 1774 aged 1.

Samuel bpt 15 May 1774 at Elmsett — m. Hannah — and poss. had GREEN issue at Ringshall, incl. Abraham & Elizb.

Joshua b 17 Jan 1791 birth recorded at Wattisham Bapt Chapel. Mother's name shown as Sarah GREEN nee ARCHER (Josh is alternative possibility for father of Maria b. 1836 - See entry under his bro. Samuel. More probably, he died young.)

Samuel GREEN bpt 19 MAR 1786, at Gt Bricett An Ag. Lab. Apparently he was 'the' Samuel serving in the W'minster Militia with his bro' Jonas. Maybe married Sarah (ANDREWS?), by whom a d, Maria, b. 1836. If so, Samuel prob. d pre-1841, leaving 'wid & d' in Jonas' care by 1841.

Jonas (alias Joseph) GREEN b 23 Jan 1788, at Gt Bricett. Bpt 13 APR 1788 at Gt Bricett. b recorded at Wattisham Baptist Meeting House. An Ag Lab who was also in the Westminster Militia. Joined 24th Regt of Foot in 1807 and served for 16 yrs, mainly in India. Became an Out-Pensioner of Chelsea Hospital in OCT 1823. Returned to civilian life as peripatetic Dealer and Jobber. Evidently a Lay Baptist Preacher. d. 16 MAY 1845 at Somersham, SFK., aged 57. bur. in prominent position nr Somersham Baptist Chapel. Headstone extant 2004.

Elizabeth (CLARKE?) b. 02 Apr 1792 at 'Bassen' (Barsham?), NFK Married Joseph after his discharge from the Army. (Marriage probably at Elmsett, 05 APR 1825, (s-s) by Banns. If so, her maiden name was CLARKE. Witnesses: George & Elizabeth GREEN.) d. 24 AUG 1855 at Ipswich, aged 63. bur nr Somesh'm Bpt Chapel, with husband.

Joseph GREEN b 04 OCT 1835 at Somersham. Painter/House Decorator/Im-Keeper/Painter Glazier.

(m.1sty) Susannah WEBSTER b abt 1836 at Sudbury.

(m'2ndly) Maria (Potter) HANNANT b SEP? 1840 Worstead, NFK

Line of Descent to Neville A DAVIS and siblings.

Emma GREEN b 05 MAY 1831 at unknown place in SFK. d 28 JUN 1839, aged 8 bur near Somersham Strict Baptist Chapel, next to her parents.

William GREEN = Susan HARVEY

William GREEN b 19 JAN 1826 at Needham Mkt. Lab in Iron Foundry A Fitter (Engineer) A Machinist, etc.

Susan HARVEY b 29 MAY 1827 at Bricet (sic), SFK.

David GREEN = Lucy STOLERY

David GREEN b 23 JAN 1828 at Willisham, SFK. Dealer/Jobber/Dealer & Beershop Keeper/Farmer/Cattle Dealer.

Lucy STOLERY b 19 FEB 1828 at Ipswich, SFK.

Descendents include a grandson, Frederick G Green (b 1866), who, in 1945, left notes on Jonas Green, b 23 Jan 1788.

E & O E.

APPENDIX

The following records have been consulted from time to time over the last twenty years, to form the skeleton of true facts upon which the story-line has been constructed. A lot of these records have since been computerised, and are probably now only available 'on line'. However, the author had the good fortune to see many of the documents at first hand. (NOTE: Sadly, no evidence of any appropriate family Wills were found in any repository.)

<u>*Records held by the National Archives*</u>

The <u>primary sources</u> used by the author were the <u>sixteen</u> bound and weighty MSS volumes in copperplate writing, covering the period 1806 to 1823, namely:-
WO12/4066 Monthly Pay List and Muster Roll (24th Foot Regt.) to
WO12/4082 Monthly Pay List and Muster Roll (24th Foot Regt.), inclusive.
(These key reference books give the name and show the rank, location and state of health of each man in the 24th Regiment, together with the pay awarded to him, month by month. There are sometimes also invaluable little notes of associated matters enclosed in the books.)

In regard to the earlier career of Jonas, in the Militia, the author used the volumes:-

WO13/1471 R/Westminster Militia 1805 to
WO13/1479 R/Westminster Militia 1807, inclusive, and
WO13/2532 Supplementary Militia (Westminster 1803-16)
(Generally, the above volumes are less complete than the WO12 series, but they fulfilled the same basic function as the WO12/4066-82 volumes for the author.)

Some reference was also made by the author to:-

WO12/4067 Names of Dead and details of Place, and
WO12/4068 Names of Dead and details of Place
WO12/4134 Monthly Pay List and Muster Roll (24th Foot Regt.)
WO12/4135 Men transferring to 1st Btn, Dec 1806-Mar 1808
WO22/38 Trades
WO25/1250 Casualties
WO25/1653 Casualties
WO25/1654 Casualties
WO25/1655 Casualties
WO25/2816 Regimental losses of the 24th Foot (Materials)
WO25/2526 Casualties
WO25/2527 Casualties
WO25/1654 Muster Book 1821
WO25/1655 Muster Book for 1822
WO97 Soldiers Discharged
WO117/1 Pensions *(A physically impressive, very large book.)*
WO120/24 Service Records (on Microfilm) *[Jonas Green et alia.]*
WO120/57 Pensions Paid on Admission, 1823 *(As an Out-Patient to Chelsea Hospital.)*

Records held by the British Library (India Office Records)

The author is very grateful to the India Office for permission to quote from the Log Books of various East Indiamen, especially the 'Astell', and also the 'William Pitt' & the 'Euphrates' for the years around 1810. (Also the Log Book of the 'Ceylon', which only exists in part.) The Log Book of the 'Windham' has not survived for the period in question. However, by associated research of the Muster Rolls of the regiment it has been possible to reconstruct the lists of officers and men carried in the 'Windham' in June/July 1810. The following India Office references apply, IOR/L/MAR/B/12A (For the 'Astell'), IOR/MAR/B/291E (For the 'Ceylon'), IOR/L/MAR/B/262D (For the 'Euphrates'), and IOR/L/MAR/B/184L (For the 'William Pitt').

Records held by The National Army Museum (used for background data only)

Orderly Book of a Detachment at Secunderabad 1816/17 Accession No 6807/320

Records held by the National Maritime Museum

The author has built up generalised background data and 'feel' (i.e. rather than using actual quotations) by studying exhibits and drawings in the museum and by reading such items as 'Le Combat du Grand Port, 1810', from a newspaper article in Le Figaro (Supplement) dated 1st October 1910, including the testimony of Mr and Mrs Welland, who had been passengers in the 'Ceylon'. He has also drawn basic data from Reference Works concerning the ships the 'Abraham Newland', the 'Ocean' and the 'Kingston'. Also further background data from Reference Works concerning the construction of 'East Indiamen', the routes which they followed, their length of service, the business arrangements of their commanders, etc.

Persons who have Contributed to the Life Story of Jonas

Mrs June GREEN: who held various old documents of her late husband's branch of the Green Family, including the family Bible entries of the 19th Century mentioned in this book. June had herself conducted some previous research into the general history of the Green Family, the results of which she kindly shared with the author.

Mrs Constance GREEN: whose late husband had inherited the copper cylinder containing the tattered papers relating to Jonas becoming an Out-Pensioner of Chelsea Hospital in 1823. This filled copper tube was passed to the author, and is now held in trust by him.

Mr Frederick GREEN: whose letter of 1946, (later passed to the author by June Green) told the little that was remembered as 'family lore' of the life of his grandfather Jonas, as had been compiled by Frederick himself, verbally aided by the thoughts of his 1st cousin, Mrs Annie Barham née Green (a half-sister to Joseph Walter Green – see next item.)

Mr Joseph Walter GREEN: for telling the author (in 1940) his dim recollection that his own grandfather Jonas (who had died well before Joseph Walter or any of the other grandchildren were born) was an old soldier who had fought the French and 'might even have served at the Battle of Waterloo'. Also for himself being a wonderful grandfather to *the author, and for telling him a little of his own war of 1914-18 as a member of the Royal Garrison Artillery in France and Flanders.*

<u>Mr George William ENGLISH</u>: For being a wonderfully unflappable great-uncle, friend, and fellow-beachcomber in the author's boyhood at Felixstowe, and for phlegmatically telling him tales of the Boer War of 1899-1901 and the Great War of 1914-18, in both of which he was an infantryman on active service in the East Surrey Regiment.

<u>Mr Alfred William DAVIS</u> (Commissioned Gunner R.N.): for being a charismatic father and for leaving a verbal & photographic legacy of his naval service 1911-1941, including three long periods in South Africa. He was killed in action in 1941, gaining a posthumous Mention in Dispatches. (It was at Capetown that the author's elder sister had been born.)

<u>Various older Colleagues at Kodak Ltd.</u>, who had fought in WW1 and/or WW2, especially those who had spent a part of their military service out in India and Burma, and who used to chat with the author from time to time about their experiences in and out of battle.

The Author is also indebted to the many other people who also taught him about WW1, gave him his own basic Army cadet training as an infantryman during the dark days of 1942-1945, awarded him his War Office Certificates Parts 1 and 2, inculcated his love of a Lee-Enfield rifle, and contributed to his understanding of the military mind and discipline.

<u>*Parish Records*</u>

The microfiche of the Parish Registers for Somersham, Great Bricett, Elmsett, Flowton and neighbouring parishes in Suffolk, as maintained by Ipswich CRO and Bury St Edmunds CRO, have been invaluable. The tithe map for Somersham has also been of service.

<u>*Civil Records (Commencing in mid-1837)*</u>

Copies of relevant birth, marriage and death certificates relating to the Green Family, the earliest dating back to 1845, were purchased from the (former) Family Records Centre at Islington and used in the research.

Census Records were also consulted. The ones which were found to yield positive results were as follows:

<u>*1841 Census of Somersham:*</u>
HO107/1019/8 7 9 (Family Head: Jonas GREEN, aged 50.)
HO107/1019/8 7 8 (Family Head: Joseph GREEN, aged 70.)
<u>*1851 Census of Somersham:*</u>
HO107/1797 554 12 (Family Head: Mary GREEN, (widow) aged 83).
HO107/1797 556 16 (Relevant Lodger: David GREEN, aged 22.)
<u>*1851 Census of Ipswich:*</u>
HO107/1799 201 12 (Family Head: Elizabeth GREEN, (widow) aged 59.)

<u>*It is from various parts of the above data that the author has constructed the Green Family Tree on Page 152. Any errors in it are entirely of his own making.*</u>

A Limited BIBLIOGRAPHY

It is rare to find books which deal with the history of South Africa and India during the early years of the 19th Century. Despite this, the author has managed to find and read a variety of published books which have some relevance to the story he has produced. Books which have been of exceptional factual relevance are as follows:-

'Historical records of the 24th Regiment', by Colonels Paton, Glennie
and Penn Symons, 1894
'A History of the 24th Regiment (1689-1937), by C T Atkinson
'A Picturesque Tour along the Rivers Ganges and Jumna in India', by
Lt Col Forrest, printed in 1824
'The Naval History of Great Britain', by William James, 1808
'Her Majesty's Navy', by C R Low, J S Virtue & Co Ltd., 1893
'Her Majesty's Army', by Walter Richards, J S Virtue & Co Ltd., 1893
'The Empire and the Army', by John Fortescue, Cassell & Co., 1928.

SKETCHES

The Sketches 'made by Bill Hitchings' appear on Pages 61 and 63.
There is a Sketch-Map of a part of the Ganges Delta on Page 116.

An INDEX

NOTE: Surnames given with capitals throughout are those of actual people, mostly of officer rank, who are officially recorded as having lived at the time and place shown: surnames given in mixed case are pure invention. Names of Ships and Foreign words are all given in italics.